HAMMOND'S
FAMILY REFERENCE
WORLD ATLAS

New Revised Edition

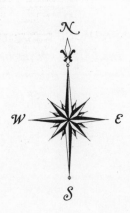

HANOVER HOUSE
GARDEN CITY   NEW YORK

Contents

GAZETTEER-INDEX OF THE WORLD

This alphabetical list of grand divisions, countries, states, colonial possessions, etc., gives area, population and index references and numbers of plates on which they are shown on the largest scale. The mother country of colonial possessions is indicated by abbreviations enclosed in parentheses. The index reference shows the square on the respective map in which the name of the country, state or colonial possession is located.

ABBREVIATIONS

Aust. —Australian	Indon. —Indonesia	pen. —peninsula	U.A.R. —United Arab Republic
Belg. —Belgian or Belgium	I. —Island	Port. —Portugal or Portuguese	U.S.A. —United States of America
Br. —British Commonwealth of Nations	Is. —Islands	Rep. —Republic	U.S.Adm.—U.S. Administration
	It. —Italian or Italy	S. —South	U.S.S.R. —Union of Soviet Socialist Republics
Dan. —Danish or Denmark	N. —North	Sp. —Spain or Spanish	
E. —East	Neth. —Netherlands	sq. mi. —Square miles	U. of So. Africa —Union of South Africa
Fr. —France or French	N.Z. —New Zealand	S.S.R. —Soviet Socialist Republic	
Gr. —Greece or Greek	Pak. —Pakistan	Trust. —Trust Territory	W. —West

Country	Area (Square Miles)	Population	Index Ref.	Plate No.
Aden (incl. Protectorate)				
(Br.)	112,000	650,000	E 7	56
Aden Colony	75	80,516	E 7	56
Admiralty Is. (Aust. Tr.)	820	13,000	E 6	68
Afghanistan	250,000	12,000,000	H 3	57
Africa	11,850,000	190,000,000	......	62,65
Alabama, U.S.A.	51,078	3,061,743	......	82
Alaska, U.S.A.	571,065	128,643	......	80
Albania	11,096	1,112,355	E 5	50
Alberta, Canada	248,800	1,123,116	......	186
Aleutian Islands (U.S.A.)	6,800	5,600	D 4	80
Algeria (Fr.)	851,284	8,681,785	G 5	62
Andaman Is. (India)	2,508	21,316	E 3	59
Andorra	191	5,265	G 1	46
Angola (Port.)	481,351	4,111,796	K14	64
Antarctica	5,500,000	......	......	35
Antigua (Br.) (incl. Barbuda and Redonda)	171	41,757	G 3	75
Antilles, Greater and Lesser	......	......	D 3	75
Arabia	1,000,000	10,700,000	D 5	56
Arctic Ocean	......	......	......	36
Argentina	1,078,266	21,000,000	......	70,72
Arizona, U.S.A.	113,580	759,587	......	84
Arkansas, U.S.A.	52,725	1,909,511	......	86
Armenian S.S.R. (U.S.S.R.)	11,500	1,345,000	F 6	53
Ascension Island (Br.)	34	159	D13	64
Asia	16,500,000	1,301,000,000	......	54
Australia, Commonwealth of (Br.)	2,974,581	7,579,358	......	66
Australian Capital Territory	939	16,905	J 7	67
Austria	32,369	6,918,959	B 3	48
Azerbaidzhan S.S.R. (U.S.S.R.)	33,100	3,100,000	G 6	53
Azores Islands (Port.)	890	318,558	H 4	34
Bahama Islands (Br.)	4,404	79,000	C 1	75
Bahrein Islands (Br.)	213	109,650	F 4	57
Balearic Islands (Sp.)	1,936	422,127	H 3	46
Barbados	166	192,800	G 4	75
Barbuda and Redonda Is. (Br.)	63	979	G 3	75
Basutoland (Br.)	11,716	563,854	M17	65
Bechuanaland Prot. (Br.)	275,000	294,232	L16	65
Belgian Congo	902,274	11,121,463	L12	65
Belgium	11,775	8,512,195	C 6	44
Bermuda (Br.)	21	37,000	G 2	75
Bhutan	18,000	300,000	E 2	59
Bismarck Archipelago (Aust. Trust.)	19,660	145,000	E 6	68
Bolivia	412,777	3,019,031	G 7	70
Bonin Is. (U.S. Adm.)	76	......	E 3	68
Borneo	208,286	......	E 5	61
Brazil	3,286,170	52,645,479	......	71,73
British Columbia, Canada	359,279	1,398,464	......	188
British Honduras	8,867	59,220	B 1	76
Brunei	2,226	40,657	E 5	61
Bulgaria	42,796	7,022,206	G 4	50
Burma	261,610	18,489,000	E 2	59
Byelorussian S.S.R. (White Russian S.S.R.) (U.S.S.R.)	80,100	7,220,000	C 4	53
California, U.S.A.	156,803	10,586,223	......	88
Cambodia	69,884	3.748.000	C 3	61
Cameroons (Br. Trust.)	34,081	1,027,100	J10	62
Cameroun (Fr. Trust.)	161,787	3,065,800	J10	62
Canada	3,621,616	16,081,791	......	174
Canal Zone (U.S.A.)	362	52,822	E 3	76
Canary Islands (Sp.)	2,894	776,912	B 4	46
Cape of Good Hope, U. of So. Africa	277,169	4,053,848	L18	65
Cape Verde Islands (Port.)	1,557	147,328	H 5	34
Caroline Islands (U.S. Trust.)	525	36,980	E 5	68
Cayman Is., Jamaica (Br.)	104	6,670	B 3	75
Celebes	72,986	5,500,000	G 6	61
Central America	217,813	8,918,547	......	76
Ceylon	25,332	6,657,339	D 4	59
Chad (Fr.)	455,598	2,052,469	K 8	63
Channel Islands (Br.)	75	102,776	B 3	40
Chatham Islands (N.Z.)	372	505	J10	68
Chile	286,396	5,809,000	G 8	70,72
China	3,724,273	464,743,549	E 1	59,60
Christmas Island	60	866	O11	55
Colombia	439,828	11,260,000	F 3	70
Colorado, U.S.A.	103,967	1,325,089	......	90
Comoro Is. (Is. Comores) (Fr.)	849	156,150	P14	65
Connecticut, U.S.A.	4,899	2,007,280	......	92
Cook Islands (N.Z.)	99	14,088	K 7	69
Corsica (Corse) (Fr.)	3,367	267,873	G 6	41
Costa Rica	19,238	800,875	C 3	76
Cuba	42,857	5,31t,.000	B 2	75
Curaçao (Neth. Antilles).	173	95,195	E 4	75
Cyprus	3,572	450,114	B 2	56
Czechoslovakia	49,356	12,090,164	D 2	48
Dahomey (Fr.)	42,471	1,476,000	G10	62
Daito Is. (U.S. Adm.)	18	2,691	M 6	60
Damão (Port.)	213	63,521	C 2	59
Delaware, U.S.A.	1,978	318,085	......	115
Denmark	16,556	4,279,151	B 3	43
District of Columbia, U.S.A.	61	802,178	B 5	114
Diu (Port.)	12	19,731	C 2	59
Dominica (Br.)	305	53,900	G 4	75
Dominican Republic	19,129	2,121,083	D 3	75
Ecuador ...... approx.	115,000	3,076,933	E 4	70
Egypt, U.A.R.	386,000	19,087,304	M 6	63
England and Wales	58,340	43,744,924	......	39
Eritrea	15,754	1,086,000	O 8	63
Estonia (Estonian S.S.R.) (U.S.S.R.)	17,400	1,000,000	C 3	52
Ethiopia (excl. Eritrea)	350,000	10,000,000	O 9	63
Europe	4,129,908	551,000,000	......	37
Faeröe Islands (Dan.)	540	29,178	D 2	37
Falkland Islands (Br.) (incl. S. Georgia)	5,618	2,239	J14	73
Federation of Malaya	50,690	4,908,086	C 4	61
Fernando Póo (island) (Sp. Guinea)	800	17,249	H11	62
Fiji (Br.)	7,036	259,638	H 8	68
Finland	130,500	4,029,803	E 2	43
Florida, U.S.A.	54,262	2,771,305	......	94
Formosa (Taiwan) (China)	13,885	9,863,264	K 7	60
France	212,736	40,502,513	......	40
Franz Josef Land (Zemlya Frantsa Iosifa)	......	......	A 7	36

Country	Area (Square Miles)	Population	Index Ref.	Plate No.
French Equatorial Africa.	961,392	4,168,910	K10 & J12	63 64
French Sudan	584,942	3,137,000	F 8	62
French West Africa	1,814,852	16,377,000	F 8	62
Gabon (Fr.)	90,733	423,904	J12	64
Galápagos Islands, Ecuador	3,042	1,346	F 6	34
Gambia (Br.)	4,033	278,858	C 9	62
Georgia, U.S.A.	58,518	3,444,578		96
Georgian S.S.R. (U.S.S.R.)	29,400	3,555,000	F 6	53
Germany, East (German Democratic Rep.)	41,535	18,488,316		42
Germany, West (Federal Republic of).	95,914	50,579,878		42
Ghana	99,536	4,118,450	F10	62
Gibraltar (Br.)	2	23,232	D 4	46
Gilbert, Ellice and Phoenix Islands	196	32,311	J 6	69
Gôa (Port.)	1,313	540,925	C 3	59
Great Britain and Northern Ireland	94,279	50,210,472		38
Greece	51,182	7,856,000		51
Greenland (Dan.)	839,999	21,412	B12	36
Grenada (Br.)	133	72,387	F 4	75
Guadeloupe and Dependencies (Fr.)	688	278,864	F 3	75
Guam (U.S.A.)	203	59,498	E 4	68
Guatemala	45,452	2,787,030	B 2	76
Guiana, British	89,480	375,701	J 2	70
Guiana, French	35,135	25,499	K 3	71
Guiana, Netherlands (Surinam)	54,300	219,000	J 3	71
Guinea	96,525	2,130,000	D 9	62
Guinea, Portuguese	13,948	510,736	C 9	62
Guinea, Spanish	10,830	161,032	H11	64
Haiti	10,714	3,111,973	D 3	75
Hawaii (U.S.A.)	6,420	499,794		81
Holland (Netherlands).land	12,883	9,625,499	E 4	44
Honduras	45,000	1,505,465	C 2	76
Honduras, British	8,867	59,220	B 1	76
Hong Kong (Br.)	391	1,857,000	J 7	60
Hungary	35,875	9,204,799	E 3	48
Iceland	39,709	144,263	C 2	37
Idaho, U.S.A.	82,808	588,637		98
Ifni (Sp.)	676	45,852	D 5	62
Illinois, U.S.A.	55,947	8,712,176		100
India	1,059,342	356,755,978	C 2	59
Indiana, U.S.A.	36,205	3,934,224		102
Indochina	285,927	26,876,510	C 2	61
Indonesia	735,286	79,260,000	C 6	61
Iowa, U.S.A.	55,986	2,621,073		104
Iran (Persia)	628,000	19,000,000	F 3	57
Iraq	116,600	4,799,500	D 3	56
Ireland	26,601	2,898,264	B 4	39
Ireland, Northern	5,238	1,369,579	C 3	38
Isle of Man (Br.)	221	55,213	D 3	39
Israel	7,978	1,813,000	B 3	58
Italy	116,000	47,020,536		47
Ivory Coast (Fr.)	183,397	2,066,000	E10	62
Jamaica (Br.)	4,411	1,237,391	C 3	75
Japan	142,272	83,199,637	N 4	60
Java and Madura	51,032	52,000,000	K 2	61
Jordan	34,750	1,329,174	D 4	58
Kansas, U.S.A.	82,113	1,905,299		106
Kentucky, U.S.A.	40,109	2,944,806		108
Kenya (Br.)	219,730	5,377,393	O11	65
Kerguelen Arch. (Fr.)			M 8	34
Korea, North	49,096	6,474,000	L 4	60
Korea, South	36,152	21,526,374	L 4	60
Krētē (Crete), Greece	3,232	441,687	E 6	51
Kuria Muria Is. (Br.)		70	G 6	57
Kuril Is. (Chishima), (U.S.S.R.)	5,700	15,000	T 5	54
Kuwait	8,000	170,000	E 4	56
Laccadive Islands (India)	746	21,035	C 3	59
Laos	89,343	1,200,000	C 2	61
Latvia (Latvian S.S.R.) (U.S.S.R.)	24,600	1,800,000	B 3	52
Lebanon	3,475	1,165,208	C 3	56
Leeward Islands	423	108,838	F 3	75
Liberia	43,000	1,600,000	E10	62
Libya	679,358	1,100,000	J 6	62
Liechtenstein	65	13,757	E 1	45
Lithuania (Lithuanian S.S.R.) (U.S.S.R.)	31,200	2,700,000	B 3	52
Louisiana, U.S.A.	45,177	2,683,516		110
Loyalty Islands (Fr.)	800	11,854	G 8	68

Country	Area (Square Miles)	Population	Index Ref.	Plate No.
Luxembourg	999	290,992	H 8	44
Macao (Port.)	6	389,000	P 7	55
Madagascar (Fr.)	241,094	4,294,985	R16	65
Madeira Islands (Port.)	308	269,179	A 2	46
Madura I.	1,752	2,444,000	K 2	61
Maine, U.S.A.	31,040	913,777		112
Malaya, Fed. of.	50,690	4,908,086	C 4	61
Maldive Islands	115	82,068	L 9	55
Malta (Br.)	122	305,991	E 7	47
Manchuria (China)	412,801	36,903,000	K 2	60
Manitoba, Canada	219,723	850,040		182
Mariana Islands (U.S. Trust.)	142	6,286	E 4	68
Marquesas Is. (Fr.)	480	2,976	N 6	69
Marshall Islands (U.S. Trust.)	61	11,033	G 4	68
Martinique (Fr.)	425	261,595	G 4	75
Maryland, U.S.A.	9,887	2,343,001		114
Massachusetts, U.S.A.	7,907	4,690,514		116
Mauritania (Fr.)	328,185	523,900	D 8	62
Mauritius (Br.)	720	432,468	S19	65
Mexico	760,373	25,581,250		77
Michigan, U.S.A.	57,022	6,371,766		118
Middle Congo (Fr.)	175,676	675,400	J 2	64
Midway Islands (U.S.A.).	2	437	J 3	69
Minnesota, U.S.A.	80,009	2,982,483		120
Mississippi, U.S.A.	47,420	2,178,914		122
Missouri, U.S.A.	69,270	3,954,653		124
Moldavian S.S.R. (U.S.S.R.)	13,100	2,660,000	C 5	53
Molucca Islands	30,168	544,302	C 5	68
Monaco	370 Acres	19,242	G 6	41
Mongolian Republic	625,946	2,000,000	O 5	54
Montana, U.S.A.	146,316	591,024		126
Montserrat	32	14,333	G 3	75
Morocco	171,583	9,809,387	E 5	62
Mozambique (Port.)	297,731	5,730,930	N16	65
Natal, U. of So. Africa..	35,284	2,202,392	N17	65
Nauru (Aust.-N.Z.—Br. Tr. Terr.)	8	2,855	G 6	68
Nebraska, U.S.A.	76,653	1,325,510		128
Nepal	54,000	6,910,000	D 2	59
Netherlands (Holland).land	12,883	9,625,499	E 4	44
Netherlands Antilles	383	154,914	E 4	75
Nevada, U.S.A.	109,802	160,083		130
New Britain (island) (Aust. Trust.)	14,600	105,000	F 6	68
New Brunswick, Canada..	27,473	554,616	C 3	176
New Caledonia (Fr.)	7,201	61,250	G 8	68
Newfoundland, Canada...	42,734	415,074	J 4	177
New Guinea, Netherlands.	161,514	1,000,000	K 6	61
New Guinea, Territory of (Aust. Trust.)	93,000	1,100,023	B 7	61
New Hampshire, U.S.A.	9,024	533,242		132
New Hebrides Islands (Br. and Fr.)	5,700	48,538	G 7	68
New Ireland (island) (Aust. Trust.)	3,800	33,960	F 6	68
New Jersey, U.S.A.	7,522	4,835,329		134
New Mexico, U.S.A.	121,511	681,187		136
New South Wales, Australia	309,432	2,984,838	H 6	67
New York, U.S.A.	47,929	14,830,192		138
New Zealand, Dominion of (Br.)	103,934	1,702,298	K 6	67
Nicaragua	57,143	1,053,189	C 2	76
Nicobar Islands (India)...	635	12,452	E 4	59
Nigeria (Br.)	338,593	24,300,000	H10	62
Niger Colony (Fr.)	501,930	2,168,000	H 8	62
Niue I. (Br.)	100	4,253	K 7	69
North America	9,124,000	216,400,000		74
North Borneo (Br.)	29,387	331,361	F 4	61
North Carolina, U.S.A.	49,142	4,061,929		140
North Dakota, U.S.A.	70,054	619,636		142
Northern Ireland (Br.)	5,238	1,369,579	C 3	38
Northern Rhodesia (Br.*)	290,320	1,849,000	L15	65
Northern Territory, Algeria	80,117	7,864,792	G 4	62
Northern Territory, Aust.	523,620	10,868	E 3	66
Northwest Territories, Canada	1,258,217	19,313		191
Norway	124,560	3,278,546	B 2	43
Nova Scotia, Canada	20,743	694,717	D 5	176
Nyasaland Prot. (Br.*)...	36,829	2,178,013	N14	65
Ohio, U.S.A.	41,122	7,946,627		144
Oklahoma, U.S.A.	69,283	2,233,351		146
Oman, Sultanate of	82,000	830,000	G 6	57
Ontario, Canada	363,282	5,404,933		180
Orange Free State, U. of South Africa	49,647	879,071	M17	65

* Member of Federation of Rhodesia and Nyasaland.

Country	Area (Square Miles)	Population	Index Ref.	Plate No.
Oregon, U.S.A.	96,350	1,521,341	......	148
Orkney Islands, Scotland.	376	21,258	E 1	38
Oubangui-Chari (Fr.)	239,382	1,068,400	K10	63
Pacific Islands (excl. Australia)	262,718	4,313,654	......	68,69
Pakistan	364,218	75,843,000	B2,D2	59
Palau Islands (U.S. Trust)	189	6,596	D 5	68
Panamá (excl. Canal Zone)	28,575	801,290	D 3	76
Papua Territory (Aust.)..	90,540	282,072	B 7	61
Paraguay	150,518	1,251,517	H 8	70
Pennsylvania, U.S.A.	45,045	10,498,012	......	150
Persia (Iran)	628,000	19,000,000	F 3	57
Peru ... approx.	513,000	9,651,000	E 5	70
Philippines, Republic of the	115,600	19,234,182	H 3	61
Phoenix Is. (U.S. and Br.)	16	984	J 6	69
Pitcairn Island (Br.)	2	138	O 8	69
Poland	119,734	24,976,926	......	49
Portugal	35,413	8,490,455	B 3	46
Prince Edward Island, Canada	2,184	99,285	F 3	177
Principe and S. Tomé (Port.)	372	62,000	H11	64
Puerto Rico (U.S.A.)	3,423	2,210,703	G 2	75
Qatar	5,000	31,000	F 4	57
Québec, Canada	523,860	4,628,378	......	178
Queensland, Australia	670,500	1,106,269	G 4	67
Réunion (Fr.)	970	242,067	R20	65
Rhode Island, U.S.A.	1,058	791,896	H 5	117
Rio de Oro (Sp.)	71,583	24,000	D 7	62
Rio Muni (continental Sp. Guinea)	10,040	142,237	H11	64
Ruanda-Urundi (Belg. Tr.)	20,309	3,889,051	N12	65
Rumania	91,671	15,872,624	G 3	50
Russian S.F.S.R.(U.S.S.R.)	6,501,500	113,200,000	F 3	52
Ryukyu Islands (U.S. Adm.)	921	914,462	L 6	60
Saguia el Hamra (Sp.)	31,660	14,298	D 6	62
St. Croix, Virgin Is. (U.S.A.)	80	12,103	H 2	75
St. Helena I. (Br.)	47	4,748	E15	64
St. John, Virgin Is. (U.S.A.)	20	749	H 1	75
St. Lucia	233	70,113	G 4	75
St. Pierre and Miquelon Is. (Fr.)	93	4,354	H 6	177
St. Thomas, Virgin Is. (U.S.A.)	32	13,813	G 1	75
St. Vincent	150	61,647	G 4	75
Sakhalin (U.S.S.R.)	35,400	300,000	T 4	54
Salvador, El	13,176	1,858,656	B 2	76
Samoa, Western (N.Z. Tr.)	1,133	78,155	J 7	69
Samoa (U.S.A.)	76	18,937	J 7	69
San Marino	38	12,100	D 3	47
Sarawak (Br.)	47,071	546,385	E 5	61
Sardinia (Sardegna)(It.)	9,301	1,273,714	B 4	47
Saskatchewan, Canada	237,975	880,665	......	184
Saudi Arabia, Kingdom of	350,000	5,500,000	D 4	56
Scotland	30,405	5,095,969	......	38
Senegal	77,401	1,720,000	D 9	62
Seychelles	157	34,637	M 6	34
Shetland Islands, Scotland	550	19,343	G 1	38
Siam (Thailand)	200,148	17,324,581	C 2	61
Sicily (It.)	9,926	4,452,773	D 6	47
Sierra Leone (Br.)	27,925	1,858,275	D10	62
Sikkim	2,745	129,000	D 2	59
Singapore	220	940,824	C 5	61
Sinkiang, China	660,977	4,012,330	D 1	59
Society Islands (Fr.)	650	41,798	L 7	69
Socotra	1,400	12,000	J 8	55
Solomon Islands (Aust. Tr.)	4,070	49,067	F 6	68
Solomon Islands Prot. (Br.)	14,600	94,965	G 6	68
Somaliland, French	8,492	44,800	P 9	63
Somaliland, (Italian Tr.)	194,000	916,300	P11	63,65
Somaliland Prot. (Br.)	68,000	700,000	P11	63,65
South America	6,894,000	109,500,000	......	70,73
South Australia, Australia	280,070	646,073	E 5	66
South Carolina, U.S.A.	30,594	2,117,027	......	152
South Dakota, U.S.A.	76,536	652,740	......	154
Southern Rhodesia (Br.*)	150,333	1,794,000	M15	65
Southern Territories, Algeria	767,435	816,993	G 6	62
South West Africa (U. of South Africa Mand.)	317,725	350,037	K16	64
Spain	195,258	27,909,009	......	46
Spanish Sahara	103,243	38,298	C 7	62
Spanish West Africa	113,958	96,150	D 7	62
Sudan	967,500	8,309,663	M 9	63
Sumatra	164,148	12,000,000	C 6	61
Surinam (Netherlands Guiana)	54,300	219,000	J 3	71
Svalbard, Norway (Spitsbergen)	24,294	1,539	A 1	43
Swaziland (Br.)	6,704	185,215	N17	65
Sweden	173,394	7,046,920	C 2	43
Switzerland	15,944	4,714,992	......	45
Syria, U.A.R.	72,587	3,135,000	C 2	56
Tahiti (island), (Fr.)	600	29,684	L 7	69
Tanganyika Territory (Br. Trust.)	342,706	7,408,096	N13	65
Tasmania, Australia	26,215	257,078	H 8	67
Tchad (Chad) (Fr.)	455,598	2,052,469	K 8	63
Tennessee, U.S.A.	41,961	3,291,718	......	156
Texas, U.S.A.	263,644	7,711,194	......	158
Thailand (Siam)	200,148	17,324,581	C 2	61
Tibet, China	469,413	2,000,000	D 1	59
Timor (Port.)	7,332	424,132	H 7	61
Timor Archipelago (Indon.)	24,450	1,657,376	H 7	61
Togo (Fr. Trust.)	20,733	923,000	G10	62
Tokelau (Union Group) (N.Z. and U.S.)	4	1,388	J 6	69
Tonga (Friendly) Is. (Br.)	269	46,870	J 8	69
Transvaal, Union of South Africa	110,450	4,283,038	M17	65
Trinidad and Tobago	1,980	557,970	G 5	75
Tristan da Cunha (Br.)	38	230	J 7	34
Trucial Oman	12,000	95,000	F 5	57
Tuamotu (Low) Arch. (Fr.)	332	5,127	M 7	69
Tunisia	48,300	2,230,952	H 5	62
Turkey	296,185	24,121,778	B 2	56
Turks and Caicos Is., Jamaica	202	6,138	D 2	75
Ubangi-Shari (Fr.)	239,382	1,068,400	K10	63
Uganda Protectorate (Br.)	80,301	4,959,196	N11	65
Ukrainian S.S.R.(U.S.S.R.)	220,600	40,500,000	C 5	53
Union of South Africa	472,494	11,418,349	L18	65
Union of Soviet Socialist Republics	8,570,600	191,595,000	......	52
United Arab Republic	458,587	22,222,304	B 4 & C 2	56 56
United Kingdom	94,279	50,210,472	......	38,39
United States of America (incl. Alaska).......land	3,548,193	150,826,004	......	78
land and water	3,608,787			
Upper (Haute) Volta (Fr.)		3,070,000	F 9	62
Uruguay	72,172	2,353,000	J10	73
Utah, U.S.A.	82,346	688,862	......	160
Vatican City	109 Acres	1,010	C 4	47
Venezuela	352,143	4,985,716	G 2	70
Vermont, U.S.A.	9,278	377,747	......	162
Victoria, Australia	87,884	2,054,701	G 7	67
Vietnam, North	63,370	12,000,000	D 2	61
Vietnam, South	65,726	12,963,900	D 2	61
Virgin Islands (Br.)	58	6,508	H 1	75
Virgin Islands (U.S.A.)	132	26,665	H 1	75
Virginia, U.S.A.	39,899	3,318,680	......	164
Volcano Is. (U.S. Adm.)..	29	....	E 3	68
Wake Island (U.S.A.)	3	....	G 4	68
Wales (excluding Monmouthshire)	7,466	2,172,339	E 4	39
Walvis Bay (Br.)	430	2,263	J16	64
Washington, U.S.A.	66,977	2,378,963	......	166
Western Australia, Australia	975,920	502,480	C 4	66
West Indies (Br. Fed.)	8,000	3,000,000	......	75
West Indies (Islands)	90,000	17,000,000	......	75
West Virginia, U.S.A.	24,090	2,005,552	......	168
White Russian S.S.R. (Byelorussian S.S.R.) (U.S.S.R.)	80,100	7,220,000	C 4	53
Windward Islands	821	251,771	G 4	75
Wisconsin, U.S.A.	54,715	3,434,575	......	170
World ... land area	57,500,000	2,200,000,000	......	34
Wyoming, U.S.A.	97,506	290,529	......	172
Yap (U.S. Trust.)	87	2,560	D 5	68
Yemen	75,000	3,500,000	D 7	56
Yugoslavia	99,079	15,751,935	C 3	50
Yukon Territory, Canada.	205,346	12,190	......	190
Zanzibar Prot. (Br.)	1,020	264,162	P13	65

* Member of Federation of Rhodesia and Nyasaland.

TABLES OF
SOCIAL AND ECONOMIC DATA
OF THE WORLD

T HE HEADLINE EVENTS of the last half-century have made the average person acutely curious of the vast world beyond his country's borders. This new national concern for the external world and its problems is one of the hopeful signs pointing to a better future for mankind. However, no matter how well-intentioned our concern for international relations may be, it is of no value unless it is grounded on an intelligent appreciation of the great diversity of social, economic and political forms extant throughout the globe.

On the following pages the editors have presented information on the world's nations, products, peoples and governments arranged in easily-found tabular form. This arrangement by tables makes comparison between political units a simpler task. These data, used with the maps in this atlas, complete the story of the nations of the world.

POLITICAL DIVISION	GOVERNMENT	MONETARY UNIT	LANGUAGE	MAJOR PRODUCTS
ADEN	British colony administered by a governor and an executive and legislative council.	East African shilling	Arabic Hindu	Salt, cigarettes, dhow building, fish, cloth, dyeing, sesame oil, soap, sorghum, ship-bunkering.
ADEN PROTECTORATE	Ruled by native sultans and sheiks advised by a British agent responsible to the governor of Aden.	East African shilling	Arabic	Dates, gums, tobacco, fish oil, butter, wheat, barley, sesame, millet, sorghum, aloes, ghee; goats, sheep, camels, cattle.
AFGHANISTAN	A constitutional monarchy ruled by a king, a cabinet and a bicameral legislative assembly.	Afghani rupee	Afghan (Pushtu) Persian	Wheat, barley, millet, corn, sorghum, lentils, vegetables, fruits, nuts, castor beans, madder, asafetida, cotton, tobacco, fat-tailed sheep (karakul), camels, zebus; wool, skins; sheepskin, textiles, leather, carpets, rugs; gold, iron, lapis lazuli, coal, copper. lead. silver.
ALBANIA	A Soviet-type republic with president, cabinet and one-house legislature. Actually ruled by the communist party politburo.	lek	Albanian	Corn, tobacco, wheat, flax, oats, barley, rye, rice, olives, fruit; cattle, sheep; fish; wool, hides; dairy products, furs; bitumen, salt, lignite, aluminum, petroleum, copper, chromite; flour, olive oil, cheese, cement, leather.
ALGERIA	Consists of overseas territories of France headed by a resident minister assisted by a federative elective assembly and council.	franc	Arabic French Berber	Wheat, barley, oats, corn, grapes, olives, tobacco, dates, figs, flax, pomegranates, prunes, apricots, legumes, potatoes; sheep, goats, cattle, mules, horses, pigs, camels; sardines, anchovies, tuna; forestry products; iron phosphates, zinc, petroleum; wine, olive oil, distilling, flour, carpet weaving, alcohol, cotton weaving, tobacco products, wool, cork.
ANDORRA	A republic under the joint suzerainty of the French State and the Bishop of Urgel, with a council general of 24 elective members. Executive authority is vested in the First Syndic.	franc and peseta	Catalan	Tobacco, potatoes, barley; sheep, cattle; lumber.
ANGOLA	Portuguese overseas province with a governor general.	angolar	Bantu languages Portuguese	Coffee, corn, sugar, palm oil and kernels, cotton, sisal, wax, tobacco; diamonds; whale oil, fish oil, sugar, palm oil,
ARGENTINA	A republic with a president, vice-president, appointive cabinet, elective senate and house of deputies.	peso	Spanish	Wheat, corn, oats, barley, linseed, rye, grapes and other fruit, tobacco, vegetables; yerba maté; cattle, sheep; quebracho, lumber; petroleum, natural gas, gold, lead, silver, tungsten; vegetable oils, wines, hides, wool, meats, textiles, metal products, vehicles and machinery, chemicals, wood and paper products, leather, clothing and shoes.
ASCENSION ISLAND	Possession of Gr. Britain, administered through the government of St. Helena by a resident magistrate and a Justice of the Peace.	pound	English	
AUSTRALIA	Member of the British Commonwealth of Nations with a governor-general, prime minister and cabinet. Parliament consists of a senate and house of commons.	Australian pound	English,	Wheat, oats, rice and other grains, fruits, vegetables, honey; sheep, cattle; gold, coal, copper, iron, lead, silver, tin, zinc; iron and steel, wool, textiles, electrical and radio equipment and appliances, drugs and chemicals, paints, optical instruments, agricultural implements and machinery, metal work and machinery, clothing, leather, furniture, airplanes, engines, ships, processed fruit and vegetables, building materials, confectionery, automobiles.
AUSTRIA	Republic with a president, chancellor and vice-chancellor, cabinet of ministers, and two-house assembly.	schilling	German	Rye, wheat, oats, barley, corn, potatoes, sugar beets, hops, grapes, rapeseed, flax, hemp, tobacco; iron, copper, lead, magnesite, graphite, coal, aluminum, petroleum, lignite, salt; timber, pulp, poultry and livestock; steel, machinery, machine tools, chemicals, textiles, paper, building materials, processed foods, leather.
BAHAMAS	British colony with governor, executive and legislative council and house of assembly.	pound	English	Tomatoes, pineapples, okra, vegetables, citrus fruits, bananas, sisal; crawfish, shells; lumber; salt; handcraft products.
BAHREIN	Arab Sheikhdom protected by Great Britain and advised by British political agent.	rupee	Arabic	Pearl fishing, petroleum, boat building, fishing; reed mats, dates, lucerne; donkeys; textiles.
BARBADOS *	British colony with governor, executive and legislative council and house of assembly.	B.W.I dollar	English	Sugar cane, cotton; flying fish; manjak (asphalt); sugar, molasses, rum, edible oil, margarine.

* Member of The West Indies (British Caribbean Federation)

POLITICAL DIVISION	GOVERNMENT	MONETARY UNIT	LANGUAGE	MAJOR PRODUCTS
BASUTOLAND	British colony. Governed by a resident commissioner under High Commissioner for Basutoland, Bechuanaland and Swaziland.	pound	Bantu languages Afrikaans English	Corn, wheat, sorghum, barley, oats, beans, peas; cattle. sheep, goats, horses, donkeys, pigs, mules; wool, mohair.
BECHUANALAND	British protectorate. Governed by a resident commissioner under High Commissioner for Basutoland, Bechuanaland and Swaziland.	pound	Bantu languages Bushman English	Kaffir, wheat and wheatmeal; cattle, sheep, goats, pigs; hides, gold.
BELGIAN CONGO	Belgian colony administered by a governor-general.	franc	Bantu languages French Flemish	Palm oil and kernels, cotton, coffee, oil cakes, copal, rice, groundnuts; rubber, manioc, fibers; copper, cement, coal, silver, cassiterite (tin), diamonds, gold, cobalt, radium, uranium, tantulum, zinc.
BELGIUM	Constitutional, hereditary monarchy. King appoints a cabinet of ministers. Parliament consists of a senate and chamber of deputies.	franc	French and Flemish	Wheat, rye, oats, barley, potatoes, sugar beets, flax, tobacco, vegetables, fruit, hops, hemp, bulbs, livestock; fish; coal, iron, zinc, lead, copper, tin, silver; coke, steel, machinery, textiles, lace, glass, chemicals, uranium refining, sugar, margarine, cheese, vinegar, alcohol, beer, matches, paper, foods, beverages, wool, cut diamonds, dairy products.
BERMUDA	British colony with governor, executive and legislative council and house of assembly.	pound	English	Lily bulbs, onions, bananas, cabbage, tomatoes, beans; coral; fish; perfume.
BHUTAN	Ruled by a Maharaja and advised by India in foreign relations.	rupee	Bhutanese (Tibetan dialect)	Rice, corn, millet, lac, wax, musk; elephants, ponies, chowries; cloth, baskets, mats, metalwork, guns, swords.
BISMARCK ARCHIPELAGO	A part of the territory of New Guinea administered by Australia as a U.N. trust territory.	Australian pound	Papuan English Chinese	Coconuts, cocoa, coffee, kapok, rubber, grains; cattle, goats, pigs; fish.
BOLIVIA	A republic with a president, vice-president, appointive ministers of state, and an elective senate and chamber of deputies.	boliviano	Spanish, Indian	Potatoes, corn, barley, quinoa, nuts, coca, vanilla, rubber, quinine; tin, zinc, lead, copper, silver, antimony, tungsten, sulphur, petroleum; cattle; textiles, flour, cement, tobacco products, hides, beer, earthenware.
BONIN ISLANDS	Administered by the United States.	dollar yen	Japanese	Vegetables, sugar, coca; poultry, pigs, cattle; fish.
BRAZIL	Federal republic with a president, vice-president, appointive secretaries of state and a bicameral legislature.	cruzeiro	Portuguese	Coffee, corn, rice, cotton, cacao; sugar cane, cassava, beans, carnauba wax, medicinal plants, oranges, balata, tobacco, fibers, castor oil; livestock; timbo, brazil nuts; iron, manganese, gold, rutile, zirconium, diamonds, mica, bauxite, quartz, beryllium, chrome, tungsten, silver; foods, textiles, chemicals, pharmaceuticals, metallurgical products, paper and wood products, hides, vegetable oils, machinery.
BRITISH HONDURAS	British colony with governor, executive council, legislative assembly.	Br. Honduras dollar	English and Spanish	Rice, maize, beans, bananas, coconuts, citrus fruits, sugar cane; mahogany, chicle, pine, cedar; fish; rum, food products.
BRUNEI	A sultanate under British protection administered by a British resident.	Malayan dollar	Malay English	Rice, sago, rubber, jelutong, cutch, sugar cane, tapioca, bananas, pineapples; timber; domestic birds, buffalo, pigs, cattle; petroleum, natural gas; boat building, cloth, brass and silverware.
BULGARIA	Soviet-type republic with a one-house legislature, which elects a presidium whose president is the nominal chief of state. Actual power is communist politburo.	lev	Bulgarian	Wheat, corn, barley, oats, rye, tobacco, fruit, cotton, sugar beets, potatoes; livestock, silkworm cocoons; fish; coal, salt, bauxite, copper, iron, lead, manganese, silver, kaolin; tobacco products, attar of roses, sugar, flour, textiles, leather goods, shoes, lead concentrates, wines and spirits.
BURMA, UNION OF	A republic with a president elected by a bicameral legislature.	kyat	Burmese Karen Shan Kachin	Rice, sesame, peanuts, corn, cotton, millet, tobacco, sugar, beans, fruit, vegetables, pulses, rubber; teak wood, lumber; cattle, buffalo, pigs, goats, sheep; petroleum, silver, lead, zinc, tin, copper, tungsten, rubies, sapphires, amber, jade, nickel, gold, antimony, cobalt, salt; textiles, hides, matches, lacquer ware.
CAMBODIA	Constitutional monarchy with a national assembly.	riel	Khmer Tao	Rice, tobacco, kapok, cotton, pepper, coin, sugar, rubber; timber; cattle; fish; silk, cotton, textiles, pottery, rush mats, precious stones, phosphates.
CAMEROONS	Under United Nations trusteeship, administered by Great Britain.	pound	Bantu and Sudanese languages	Cocoa, coffee, rubber, bananas, palm oil and kernels; cattle, goats, sheep, horses.
CAMEROUN	Under United Nations trusteeship, administered by France.	franc	Sudanese and Bantu languages Arabic French	Cocoa, palm kernels, bananas, caoutchouc, coffee, cacao, palm oil; timber; cattle, sheep, pigs, horses, asses; rubber, tobacco.
CANADA	Member of the British Commonwealth with a governor-general, prime minister and cabinet. Parliament consists of a senate and house of commons.	dollar	English French	Wheat, oats, barley, flax, rye, potatoes, turnips, vegetables, sugar beets, tobacco, fruits, dairy products; livestock; fish; forestry products; furs; gold, copper, nickel, zinc, lead, silver, platinum, iron ore, titanium, cobalt, radium, uranium, petroleum, natural gas, coal, asbestos, salt, gypsum, quartz, sulphur, cement, clay; hydro-electric power; foods, beverages, transportation equipment, iron and steel products, aluminum, metal products, pulp, paper and wood products, textiles, electrical apparatus, chemicals.
CANARY ISLANDS	Islands forming two provinces of Spain, governed by a Cabildo Insular.	peseta	Spanish	Bananas, cochineal, potatoes, sugar cane, onions, fruits; fish; wine, sugar.
CAPE VERDE ISLANDS	Portuguese overseas province, ruled by a governor.	escudo	Portuguese	Coffee, castor beans, corn, fruit, grains, tobacco; goats, oxen, pigs, asses; hides, skins; preserved fish, salt, lime, sugar.
CAROLINE ISLANDS	A group in the United States trust territory of the Pacific Islands and administered by a high commissioner.	dollar	Micronesian dialects Malayo-Polynesian languages	Copra, breadfruit, cassava, taro, sweet potatoes; pigs, cattle, poultry, fish; phosphates.
CEYLON	Dominion of the British Commonwealth ruled by a governor-general, a prime minister, a cabinet and a bicameral legislature.	rupee	Singhalese Tamil	Tea, coconuts, rubber, rice, millet, tobacco, cacao, cinnamon, citronella, cloves, fruits, palmyra, fish; cattle, buffalo, goats, swine, sheep; graphite, plumbago, mica, ilmenite, monazite, iron ore; salt, pearls, zircon, glass sands, copra, plywood, leather, shoes, glass, steel, acetic acid, ceramics, quinine, strychine, shark-liver oil, coconut oil, textiles.
CHILE	A republic with a president, vice-president, appointive cabinet of ministers of state, elective senate and chamber of deputies.	peso	Spanish	Wheat, potatoes, oats, rice, barley, corn, kidney beans, lentils, fruits; fish; livestock; copper, silver, nitrates, iodine, iron, sulphur, gold, manganese, coal; foods, textiles, leather, wood products, cement, chemicals and pharmaceuticals, wines and beer, wool.
CHINA: MAINLAND (COMMUNIST)	In theory, government power resides in the National People's Congress and the State Council. In practice, power resides in the Communist Party's Central Committee.	Chinese dollar	Chinese Mongol Turki	Rice, wheat, sweet potatoes, corn, barley, millet, kaoliang, soybeans, cotton, tea, sugar cane, tobacco, peanuts, peas, beans, opium, tung, silk; pigs, oxen, sheep, goats, buffalo, donkeys, horses, mules, poultry; timber; fish; iron, coal, tungsten, tin, antimony, mercury, copper, lead, zinc, silver, salt, soda, gold, petroleum, bismuth, molybdenum; foodstuffs, textiles, chemicals, machinery, metal work, metallurgical products, bristles, cement, clothing, embroideries, ceramics.

POLITICAL DIVISION	GOVERNMENT	MONETARY UNIT	LANGUAGE	MAJOR PRODUCTS
CHINA: FORMOSA (NATIONALIST)	A republic whose supreme organ of government is the popularly elected National Assembly. The Assembly elects the president and vice-president. Legislative powers reside with the Legislative Yuan.	dollar	Chinese (Amoy dialect) Formosan	Rice, tea, sugar, sweet potatoes, ramie, jute, tumeric, pineapples, bananas, camphor; pigs, buffalo, cattle, goats, horses.
CHRISTMAS ISLAND	A part of Australia.	Malayan dollar	Chinese Malay English	Phosphate of lime.
COLOMBIA	A centralized federal republic with a president, vice-president, appointive cabinet, elective senate and house of representatives.	peso	Spanish	Coffee, sugar cane, corn, rice, root crops, cotton, bananas, cacao, wheat, tobacco, cinchona; cattle; rubber, fibers; petroleum, gold, silver, platinum, emeralds, salt; textiles, beer, sugar, cement, flour, tobacco products.
COMORO ISLANDS	An overseas territory of France with an administrator, privy council and an elective general council.	franc	Arabic French	Sugar cane, vanilla, rice, sweet potatoes, yams, copra, sisal, cacao, perfume plants; rum distilling.
COOK ISLANDS	Territory of New Zealand administered by a resident commissioner.	New Zealand pound	Polynesian dialects English	Citrus fruits, coconuts, copra, tomatoes, arrowroot, pineapples, breadfruit, taro, kumaras, plantains, yams; mother-of-pearl.
COSTA RICA	Republic with president, cabinet and one-house legislature.	colon	Spanish	Coffee, bananas, cocoa, abaca, sugar cane, maize, rice, tobacco; cattle; tuna; gold, silver; cigars and cigarettes, textiles, furniture and woodwork, sugar.
CUBA	Republic with president, vice-president, cabinet and a two-house legislature.	peso	Spanish	Sugar cane, tobacco, coffee, pineapples, citrus fruits, bananas, henequen; cattle; cedar, mahogany and other woods; fish; chromite, iron, manganese, copper, nickel, asphalt; sugar, textiles, alcohol, molasses, chemicals, tobacco products, electrical goods, clothing.
CURACAO (NETH. ANTILLES)	Self-governing part of Netherlands Union with governor, executive council and one-house legislature.	guilder	Dutch and Papiamento	Fish; dividivi (tannin), crude salt, phosphates; refined petroleum.
CYPRUS	British colony ruled by a governor with the assistance of an executive council.	pound	Greek Turkish	Wheat, barley, oats, grapes, raisins, olives, fodder crops, potatoes, carobs, cotton, tobacco, linseed, hemp, flax, citrus fruits, bread beans, corn, sesame, melons; sponges; fish; sheep, goats, donkeys, cattle, pigs, horses, mules; copper pyrites, asbestos, chromite, gypsum, amber, copper concentrates; tobacco products, buttons, wines, spirits, false teeth, lace, gum, boots and shoes, dried fruits, cheese.
CZECHOSLOVAKIA	Soviet-type republic with a president and a one-house elective parliament. Actual power resides in politburo, highest body of communist party.	koruna	Czech and Slovak	Wheat, rye, barley, oats, corn, hops, sugar beets, grapes, potatoes; poultry, livestock; timber; coal, lignite, iron, graphite, garnets, silver, copper, lead, salt, manganese, zinc; beer, spirits, malt, metals, munitions, machinery, iron and steel, porcelain, shoes, textiles, wood products, pulp and paper, sugar, leather, foods, chemicals, rubber products.
DAHOMEY	Territory of Fr. West Africa with a governor and an elective representative assembly.	franc	Sudanese languages French	Palm oil, shea nuts, groundnuts, cotton fiber, copra, castor oil, kapok, millet; gold, diamonds, bauxite, iron ore.
DAMÃO	Portuguese overseas province subject to government at Gôa and ruled by lieutenant-governor.	rupia	Portuguese Marathi	Salt, fish, rice, wheat, tobacco; palm-mat weaving.
DENMARK	Constitutional, hereditary monarchy with a two-house, elective legislature and an appointive council of ministers.	krone	Danish	Barley, mixed grains, oats, rye, wheat, potatoes, sugar beets, livestock, fish; clay; ships and transportation equipment, butter, bacon, eggs, cheese, milk, footwear, clothing, machines, chemicals, tobacco products, metal goods, leather goods, beverages; stone, earthenware and glassware, electrical goods.
DIU	Portuguese overseas province subject to government at Gôa and ruled by lieutenant-governor.	rupia	Portuguese Marathi	Salt; fish.
DOMINICAN REPUBLIC	Republic with president, cabinet and two house legislature.	peso	Spanish	Sugar cane, cacao, coffee, tobacco, bananas, rice, corn; cattle; lumber; gold; starch, alcohol, molasses, sugar, chocolate, meats, cigars, cigarettes, leather.
EASTER ISLAND (RAPA NUI)	Administered as part of Valparaíso province in Chile.	peso	Polynesian dialect Spanish	Plantains, sweet potatoes; fish; cattle, sheep; wool.
ECUADOR	A centralized republic with a president, a cabinet and an elective bicameral legislature, the senate including representatives of various social, economic and governmental groups.	sucré	Spanish, Indian	Rice, cacao, coffee, bananas, rubber, kapok, cotton, tagua (ivory) nuts, cinchona; livestock; gold, petroleum, salt, balsa wood; textiles, toquilla (panama) hats, buttons, sugar, flour, shoes, beer and liquors, chemicals, pharmaceuticals, cement, soap, candles.
EGYPT (See United Arab Republic)	Province of United Arab Republic.	Egyptian pound	Arabic	Cotton, barley, wheat, rice, sugar cane, onions, corn, millet, fruits, vegetables; sheep, goats, cattle, buffalo, donkeys, pigs, horses, mules; fish; petroleum, cement, phosphates, asbestos, chromite, cotton ginning, milling, pottery, perfume, soap.
ENGLAND AND WALES	England is governed directly by the government of Great Britain and Northern Ireland. Executive power resides nominally in the Crown but actually in the prime minister and cabinet. Parliament consists of two houses.	pound	English and Welsh (Celtic)	Potatoes, turnips, beets, oats, wheat, barley, rye, hay, beans, peas, cabbage, vetches, hops, fruits; sheep, cattle, pigs, horses, poultry; fish; coal, coke, gas, iron, copper, lead, nickel, tin, clay; dairy products, wool, cotton and linen textiles; electrical goods, vehicles, steel, scientific instruments, cutlery, foods and beverages, tobacco products, clothing and shoes, chemicals, pottery, china, machinery, locomotives, carpets, knitwear, lace, pharmaceuticals.
ERITREA	Autonomous state federated with Ethiopia. Administered locally by a representative legislature.	Ethiopian dollar	Hamitic languages Arabic	Coffee, barley, sisal, bananas, legumes, gum arabic, wheat, tobacco, dates, dom nuts, senna; goats, sheep, camels, horses, mules, donkeys, cattle; hides, skins; fish-meal; pearls, mother-of-pearl; gold, salt, potassium salts, matting.
ETHIOPIA	Constitutional monarchy with an emperor assisted by a council of ministers and a bicameral legislature. (See Eritrea).	Ethiopian dollar	Amharic Hamitic languages Arabic	Coffee, teff, barley, durra, wheat, cotton, sugar cane; cattle, sheep, goats, horses, mules; hides, skins; wax, gold, rocksalt.
FALKLAND ISLANDS	British colony with a governor and an executive and a legislative council.	pound	English	Forage crops, sheep; wool, skins, tallow, whale oil, whale-meat meal.
FIJI	British colony ruled by a governor with an executive and legislative council.	Fiji pound	English Fijian Hindustani Chinese	Sugar cane, coconuts, bananas, pineapples, rice, root vegetables, citrus fruits, cotton, rubber, castor oil seeds, taro, yams, cassava, sweet potatoes, groundnuts, pulses, corn, fodder crops, tobacco; cattle, pigs; tuna, bêche-de-mer, trochus shell; gold, silver; sugar, copra, coconut oil, soap, biscuits, molasses, paint, butter, ghee, candlenut oil.

POLITICAL DIVISION	GOVERNMENT	MONETARY UNIT	LANGUAGE	MAJOR PRODUCTS
FINLAND	A republic with a president, a one-house elective diet and appointive council of state.	markka	Finnish and Swedish	Hay, potatoes, wheat, oats, barley, rye, sugar beets, flax, hemp, vegetables; cattle, horses, sheep, pigs, poultry, reindeer; wood and timber; fish; copper; lumber, plywood, furniture, pulp and paper, cardboard, textiles, butter, eggs, cheese, flour, leather, chemicals, china and glass, foodstuffs.
FRANCE	A republic with a president, a two-house elective parliament and an appointive council of ministers.	franc	French	Sugar beets, potatoes, wheat, oats, barley, rye; corn, turnips, fruits, nuts, wine grapes, buckwheat; cattle, sheep, pigs, horses; fish; coal, iron ore, lignite, salt, bauxite, pyrites, potash salts, leeks, kaolin, natural gas, iron and steel, chemicals; silk, cotton, rayon, wool and linen, textiles; clothing, lace, perfumes and cosmetics, automobiles, machinery, dairy products, beet sugar, wines, porcelain, aluminum, foods, leather, spirits.
FRENCH EQUATORIAL AFRICA	Federated overseas territory of France with a governor-general and an elective grand assembly representing the 4 constituent territories.	franc	Bantu and Sudanese languages Arabic French	Palm oil and kernels, coconuts, cotton, coffee, cocoa, groundnuts, kapok, butter; hides; timber, rubber, copal gum, wax; ivory, gold, copper, lead, zinc, diamonds.
FRENCH SUDAN	Territory of Fr. West Africa with a governor and an elective representative assembly.	franc	Sudanese languages Hamitic languages Arabic French	Millet, rice, groundnuts, corn, sweet potatoes, cotton, manioc, tobacco, karite, shea nuts, yams, kapok, sisal; cattle, goats, sheep, horses, asses, camels; hides and skins; pottery, bricks, jewelry, weaving, leather, rice mills, soap.
FRENCH WEST AFRICA	Overseas territory of France with a governor-general and an elective grand assembly representing the 8 constituent territories.	franc	Sudanese and Hamitic languages Arabic French	Millet, rice, corn, cotton and fibers, nuts, oilseeds and oil, manioc, coffee, bananas, cocoa; cattle; gold, diamonds, iron ore, bauxite.
GAMBIA	Crown colony and protectorate of Great Britain administered by a governor, executive and legislative councils.	pound	Sudanese languages English	Groundnuts, palm kernels; hides and skins; beeswax.
GAMBIER ISLANDS	A group of islands in French Polynesia governed from Tahiti.	franc	Polynesian dialects	Coconuts, copra, oranges, breadfruit; pearls, pearl shell, fish.
GERMANY	Country is divided between two governments—a democratic Federal Republic of Germany in the west and a Soviet-dominated German "Democratic" Republic in the east. Federal Republic has an elected federal diet and council who jointly elect the president. German "Democratic" Republic has a communist-controlled legislative branch which selects the president, cabinet and prime minister.	East German and West German Deutsche Mark	German	Wheat, rye, barley, oats, potatoes, sugar beets, fruits, hops; pigs, cattle, poultry, horses; fish; forest products; coal, lignite, iron, copper, potash, sulphur, salt, uranium, lead, zinc, fluor spar, gypsum, vanadium, aluminum; automobiles, steel, cement, diesel oil, gasoline, cotton yarn, woolen yarn, rayon fiber, beet sugar, beer, wines, optical instruments, sulphuric acid, sodium bicarbonate, chemicals.
GHANA	Member of the British Commonwealth with an appointed governor-general and an elective parliament.	pound	Sudanese languages English	Cocoa, palm oil and kernels, sorghum, millet, corn, yams, cassava, groundnuts, cotton.
GIBRALTAR	British Crown Colony administered by a governor, executive council, and a legislative council.	pound	English and Spanish	Fish for export and processing of commodities for local consumption.
GILBERT AND ELLICE ISLS.	British colony administered by a resident commissioner.	Australian pound	English Gilbertese Samoan	Coconuts, copra, phosphate of lime; pearl shell, fish; hats, mats.
GÔA	Portuguese overseas province ruled by a governor assisted by executive and legislative councils.	rupia	Portuguese Marathi	Rice, cashew nuts, betel nuts, grains, vegetables, coconuts, mangoes; teak, bamboo, blackwood; fish; salt, manganese, asbestos, asphalt, guano, silica, coal, petroleum; sugar, textiles, distilling, dessicated coconut, tobacco products, rice milling, cocoa, coconut oil, embroideries.
GREAT BRITAIN: (see England, N. Ireland and Scotland).				
GREECE	A constitutional hereditary monarchy with a prime minister, cabinet of ministers and an elective assembly.	drachma	Greek	Wheat, barley, corn, oats, rye, tobacco, currants, sultana raisins, olives, figs, grapes, cottonseed, sesame seed; sheep, goats, cattle, pigs, horses, mules; fish; iron ore, sulphur, emery, magnesite, zinc, lead, lignite, marble, bauxite; textiles, olive oil, foods, wines, chemicals, leather, wood and paper, metal products, machinery.
GREENLAND	An integral part of the Danish kingdom, with representation in Parliament.	krone	Danish and Greenlandic	Grass for fodder; cod and other fish; sheep, furs; cryolite; processed fish, hides.
GUADELOUPE	Overseas department of France with a prefect and elective general council.	franc	French, French Patois	Sugar cane, bananas, coffee, cocoa, vanilla, cassava; fish; alcohol, rum.
GUAM	Territory of the United States administered by a governor and advisory and legislative bodies.	dollar	English Chamorro Spanish	Copra, coconut oil, corn, taro, bananas, citrus fruits, mangoes, papayas, breadfruit, sweet potatoes, cocoa, cassava, sugar cane, pineapples; cattle, pigs, poultry, buffalo.
GUATEMALA	Republic with a president, cabinet and one-house legislature.	quetzal	Spanish	Coffee, bananas, sugar cane, rubber, chicle, cacao, abaca, cattle; mahogany and dye woods; essential oils; gold; textiles.
GUIANA, BRITISH	A British colony with a governor and partly nominated, partly elected legislative and executive councils.	B.W.I. dollar	English	Sugar cane, rice, coconuts, coffee, citrus fruits, cacao; balata, rubber, green heart and other timber; livestock; bauxite, diamonds, gold; textiles, milled rice, beer and rum, lime rum and oil, sugar, woods, molasses, charcoal, matches.
GUIANA	Independent republic.	franc	French	Rice, cacao, bananas, sugar cane, corn, cassava, woods; gold; hides, rosewood essence, shoes, rum, fish glue.
GUIANA, NETH. (SURINAM)	Self-governing part of the Netherlands Union with an appointed governor, an appointive council of ministers, an advisory council and an elective legislative body.	guilder	Dutch	Rice, citrus fruits, coconuts, coffee, bananas, sugar cane, cacao, balata, corn, tobacco; lumber; gold, bauxite; sugar, rum, plywood, molasses.
GUINEA	Independent republic.	franc	Sudanese languages French	Rice, groundnuts, palm oil and nuts, wax, honey, bananas, indigo, kola, orange products, coffee; cattle, sheep, goats, pigs; hides and skins; bauxite, iron ore, gold.
GUINEA, PORTUGUESE	Portuguese overseas province ruled by a governor.	escudo	Sudanese languages Portuguese	Rice, palm kernels and oil, wax, groundnuts; hides.

POLITICAL DIVISION	GOVERNMENT	MONETARY UNIT	LANGUAGE	MAJOR PRODUCTS
GUINEA, SPANISH	Spanish colony ruled by a governor.	peseta	Bantu languages Spanish	Cocoa, coffee, vegetables and fruit; wood.
HAITI	Republic with a president, cabinet and a two-house legislature.	gourde	Creole, French	Coffee, sugar, fig bananas, sisal, cotton, rice, cocoa; logwood; molasses, sisal products.
HAWAII	Territory of the United States administered by a governor, a senate and a house of representatives.	dollar	English Japanese Hawaiian	Sugar, pineapples, coffee, molasses, bananas, rice, flowers, cotton, tobacco; beef cattle, swine, sheep, poultry; hides, wood, stone, fish, printing, foodstuffs, ironworks, fertilizers, chemicals, clothing, fiber insulating board, handicrafts.
HONDURAS	Republic with a president, council of ministers and a one-house legislature.	lempira	Spanish	Bananas, coffee, coconuts, tobacco, grapefruit, rice, henequen; mahogany; cattle; gold, silver.
HONG KONG	A British colony ruled by governor assisted by executive and legislative council.	Hong Kong dollar	Chinese English	Rice, sugar cane, peanuts, sweet potatoes; fish; poultry, pigs; kaolin, lead, iron, wolfram, silver, cement; shipbuilding and repair; rape, rubber shoes, enameled hollow-ware, textiles, electric flashlights and batteries, preserved ginger.
HUNGARY	Soviet-type republic with a president and a presidential council selected by the national assembly. Actual power in hands of politburo, highest organ of communist party.	forint	Hungarian	Wheat, corn, rye, barley, oats, potatoes, sugar beets, tobacco, grapes and other fruits, peppers, hemp, flax; pigs, cattle, sheep, horses, poultry; fish; coal, lignite, petroleum, natural gas, iron ore, bauxite, manganese; flour, sugar, distilling, brewing, iron and steel, wines, textiles, paprika, chemicals, leather, metal products, wood and paper products.
ICELAND	A republic with a president, an elective, two-house legislature and an appointive cabinet of ministers.	krona	Icelandic	Hay, potatoes, turnips, hothouse fruits and vegetables; sheep, poultry, horses, cattle; fish; dairy products, meats, animal and vegetable oils, hides, skins, leather, clothing, textiles, frozen fish, herring oil, herring meal.
IFNI	Spanish territory ruled by a sub-governor.	peseta	Berber Arabic Spanish	Barley, alfalfa, corn, tomatoes, argan oil, wheat; fish.
INDIA	An independent republic within the British Commonwealth with a president, cabinet and a bicameral legislature.	rupee	Indo-Aryan (Hindi, Bengali, Gujarati, Punjabi, Urdu) and Dravidian (Tamil, Kanarese, Telugan) English	Rice, wheat, legumes, groundnuts, oilseeds, tea, tobacco, jute, cotton, rubber, coffee, sugar cane, barley, millet, corn; cattle, goats, buffalo, sheep, pigs; fish; coal, manganese, gold, petroleum, salt, mica, iron, copper, chromite, ilmenite, diamonds, silver, bauxite; textiles, shawls, carpets, jute manufacturers, wood-carving and metal work, leather, chemicals, shipbuilding, petroleum refining, sugar refining, cotton ginning, iron and steel mills, glass, soap, matches.
INDONESIA	Republic with president, cabinet and unicameral legislature.	rupiah	Indonesian (Malay, Javanese, etc.)	Rice, sugar cane, rubber, palm oil, tobacco, corn, coconuts, copra, cassava, sweet potatoes, groundnuts, soya beans, cotton, kapok, coffee, cinchona, cocoa, pepper, fruits, vegetables; cattle, buffalo; tin, coal, petroleum, bauxite, manganese; rubber goods, chemicals, shipyards, textiles, paper, breweries, glass, handicrafts.
IRAN	Constitutional monarchy governed by a shah, prime minister, cabinet and a bicameral legislature.	rial	Persian Arabic Kurdish	Wheat, cotton, gums, opium, fruit, rice, barley, sugar beets, tobacco, tea, corn, millet, legumes, vegetables, nuts; sheep, goats, cattle, asses, horses, mules; fish; petroleum oil, red oxide, copper, sulphur, arsenic, coal, salt, marble, nickel, manganese, lead, cobalt, turquoise, iron ore; carpets, rugs, textiles, leather, glass, matches, chemicals, jute, tobacco products, oil refining, casings, wood, oils.
IRAQ	Independent republic.	dinar	Arabic Turkish Kurdish	Dates, other fruits, barley, wheat, rice, tobacco, cotton, beans, corn, sorghum, sesame; sheep, goats, asses, camels, horses, buffalo; oil, salt, wool, textiles, cigarettes, distilling.
IRELAND	A republic with a president, premier and an elective, two-house parliament.	pound	English and Gaelic	Hay, potatoes, turnips, fodder, beets, sugar beets, oats, wheat, barley, cabbage, rye, flax; cattle, sheep, pigs, horses, poultry; fish; coal, peat, gypsum; tobacco, dairy products, foodstuffs, beer, malt, clothing, meats, textiles, boots and shoes, wood and paper products.
ISRAEL	Republic with president, prime minister, cabinet and elective unicameral legislature.	Israeli pound	Hebrew Arabic	Dairy products, vegetables, eggs, fruits, green fodder, wheat, hay, barley, corn, durra; goats, sheep, cattle, camels, poultry; fish; textiles, clothing, foods, beverages, tobacco, diamond polishing, shoes, metal and woodwork, furniture, building materials, leather, dairy products, electrical products, paper, printing, false teeth, pharmaceuticals, chemicals, dyes, soap, radios, oil refining, wines.
ITALY	A republic with a president, a two-house, elective legislature and an appointive cabinet.	lira	Italian	Wheat, corn, oats, sugar beets, potatoes, tomatoes, rice, olives, grapes, lemons and other fruits, hemp, tobacco, nuts; fish; sheep and goats, cattle, pigs, horses, donkeys; iron ore, sulphur, zinc, bauxite, lead, mercury, barite, copper, marble, manganese, lignite; textiles, chemicals, wines, automobiles and machinery, electrical goods, beet sugar, olive oil, cheese, clothing, processed foods.
IVORY COAST	Territory of Fr. West Africa with a governor and an elective representative assembly.	franc	Sudanese languages French	Coffee, cocoa, bananas, manioc, corn, rice, yams, kola, coconuts, palm oil, groundnuts, cotton, millet, tobacco; mahogany, caoutchouc; sheep, cattle, goats, pigs; gold, diamonds, manganese, iron ore, ilmenite.
JAMAICA*	British colony with a governor, executive and legislative councils and house of representatives.	pound	English	Sugar cane, bananas, tobacco, coconuts, cacao, pimentoes, coffee, ginger; bauxite; honey; logwood; rum, textiles, cigars.
JAPAN	Constitutional monarchy with the executive power vested in prime minister and cabinet, the legislative power residing in a two-house parliament. The duties of the emperor are merely ceremonial.	yen	Japanese	Rice, wheat, barley, mulberry trees, potatoes, sweet potatoes, fruits, rape, vegetables, oats, tobacco, soy beans, tea, flax, hemp, camphor; timber, bamboo; horses, cattle, sheep, goats, pigs, rabbits; fish, agar, pearl oysters; silk worms; coal, pyrites, gold, copper, pyrethrum, manganese, silver, sulphur, chromite, zinc, salt, tin, lead, iron, petroleum; textiles, steel, paper, porcelain, earthenware, lacquer ware, vegetable oil, toys, slippers, shoes, machinery.
JORDAN	Constitutional monarchy with cabinet and bicameral legislature.	Jordan dinar	Arabic	Wheat, barley, legumes, vegetables, fruits, olives; sheep, goats, camels; salt, phosphate, potash; wool, tobacco products, flour milling, building materials, olive oil.
KENYA	Colony and protectorate of Great Britain with a governor, a council of ministers, an appointive executive and a partly elective legislative council.	East African shilling	Swahili English Sudanese Hamitic Bantu	Sisal, wheat, tea, coffee, pyrethrum, cotton, corn, sugar cane, sesame, groundnuts, wattle; hides and skins; sodium carbonate, gold, kyanite, salt, silver, lime, bags, butter, sugar, sisal products.
KOREA	Divided into two parts by Armistice Line of August, 1953, pending final decisions of peace treaty. Communist "People's Republic" in North Korea; South Korea headed by a president, a prime minister, a cabinet and a bicameral legislature.	hwan	Korean	Rice, barley, millet, wheat, soya beans, red beans, cotton, tobacco, hemp, ginseng, fruit, radishes; timber; draft cattle, pigs, horses, mules, donkeys, sheep, goats, rabbits; fish; gold, iron ore, coal, tungsten, copper, silver, graphite, salt, kaolin, talc, bismuth, flourite, minerals (N. Korea), textiles, fertilizer, chemicals, cement, heavy industries (N. Korea); textiles, cement, tobacco, silkworms, chemicals, machinery, metal, rubber, wood and paper and tobacco products (S. Korea).
KUWAIT	Arab sheikhdom protected by Great Britain and advised by British political agent.	Indian rupee	Arabic	Petroleum, shipbuilding (dhows), pearls, skins, wool.

* Member of The West Indies (British Caribbean Federation)

POLITICAL DIVISION	GOVERNMENT	MONETARY UNIT	LANGUAGE	MAJOR PRODUCTS
LAOS	Constitutional monarchy with a cabinet and a national assembly.	kip	Khmer (Annamese) Lao	Rice, coffee, tea, citrus fruits, corn, cinchona, gum, benzoin, cardamon; stick-lac; teak; tin.
LEBANON	Independent republic governed by a president, cabinet and an elective legislature.	Lebanese pound	Arabic French	Wheat, barley, corn, potatoes, citrus and other fruits, onions, olives, tobacco (Latakia); goats, asses, cattle, buffalo, sheep, horses, mules; iron, lignite; textiles, cement, olive oil, tobacco products, soap, matches, petroleum refining, gasoline, leather.
LIBERIA	Republic with president, cabinet, senate and house of representatives.	dollar	English Sudanese languages	Rubber, rice, coffee, cassava, sugar cane, cacao, palm oil and kernels, piassava, groundnuts; rum; iron ore.
LIBYA	A federal kingdom with a bicameral legislature, constituted under U.N. auspices and comprising the three provinces of Cyrenaica, Tripolitania and the Fezzan.	Libyan pound	Arabic	Barley, wheat, olives, grapes, dates, almonds, figs, tobacco, esparto; goats, sheep, camels, cattle, donkeys, mules and horses; sponge and tuna fishing; matting, carpets, leather articles, embroidered fabrics.
LIECHTENSTEIN	A principality headed by a prince and an elective, one-house legislature.	Swiss franc	German	Grain, fruit, grapes, wood; cattle, pigs, chickens; cotton textiles, wine, leather, false teeth, pottery, wood-carving.
LUXEMBOURG	A grand duchy and hereditary, constitutional monarchy with an elective chamber of deputies and appointive minister of state and cabinet.	franc	Mosel-frankisch (German dialect)	Oats, potatoes, wheat, rye, grapes; livestock; iron ore, slate, gypsum, sand and gravel; iron, steel and metal working; chemicals, non-metallic minerals, beverages, tobacco, leather, wines, dairy products, quarrying.
MACAO	Portuguese overseas province ruled by a governor.	pataca	Chinese Portuguese	Fish; preserves, firecrackers, vegetable oil, cement, metal work, lumber, tobacco (processed), matches, wine.
MADAGASCAR	Autonomous republic within the French Community of Nations.	franc	French Malagasy and Bantu languages	Cassava, rice, corn, potatoes, coffee, sugar cane, haricot beans, groundnuts, sisal, castor oil, tobacco, raffia; cattle, pigs, goats, sheep; graphite, mica, gold, rock crystal, corundum, phosphates, agate; textiles, sugar and rice factories, tapioca.
MALAYA, FEDERATION OF	Fed. of 9 sultanates and 2 settlements within Br. Commonwealth. It is a constitutional monarchy with cabinet and two-house legislature.	Malayan dollar	Malay Chinese English	Rubber, rice, coconuts, pineapples, tapioca, pepper, spices, tobacco, fibers, gambier, vegetables, tea; buffalo, swine, oxen, goats, sheep; fish; guano, tin, coal, iron ore, bauxite, manganese, copra, palm oil, timber, gold, rubber products, gutta percha, wood products, canned pineapples, textiles.
MALDIVE ISLANDS	An independent sultanate, under British protection, with a bicameral legislature.	rupee	Singhalese Arabic Dravidian	Coconuts, copra, coir, fruit, nuts; fish, cowries; cloth, mats, boats.
MALTA	A self-governing colony of Great Britain with a governor. It. governor and an elective legislative assembly.	pound	Maltese and English	Wheat, barley, potatoes, onions, grapes and other fruits, cumin seed, cotton; goats, sheep, pigs, cattle; fish; lace, filigree, wine, footwear, beer, cigarettes, buttons, pipes, gloves.
MARIANA ISLANDS	A group of islands in the United States trust territory of the Pacific administered by a high commissioner.	dollar	Micronesian dialects Spanish	Fruits, corn, sweet potatoes, vegetables, breadfruit, cacao; fish; phosphates.
MARQUESAS ISLANDS	A group of islands in French Polynesia administered from Tahiti	franc	Marquesan French	Bananas, breadfruit, yams, bamboo, coconuts, sugar cane.
MARSHALL ISLANDS	A group of islands in the United States trust territory of the Pacific administered by a high commissioner.	dollar	Micronesian dialects	Arrowroot, breadfruit, coconuts, pandanus, taro, vegetables, copra, bananas; poultry, pigs; fish.
MARTINIQUE	Overseas department of France with a prefect and elective general council.	franc	Creole, French	Sugar cane, cocoa, pineapples, bananas, coffee; rum, sugar.
MAURITANIA	Territory of Fr. West Africa with a governor and an elective representative assembly.	franc	Arabic Hamitic and Sudanese languages French	Millet, gum, dates, corn, watermelons, wheat, henna; sheep and goats, cattle, camels, asses, horses; hides and skins; salt.
MAURITIUS	British colony ruled by a governor, an executive council and a legislative council.	rupee	English Hindustani French	Sugar, aloe fiber, rice, vanilla beans, hemp, sisal, groundnuts, tea, yams, manioc, pineapples, tobacco, coconuts; alcohol, molasses, rum, copra.
MEXICO	Federative republic with a president, council of ministers and a two-house legislature.	peso	Spanish	Corn, wheat, beans, chick peas, sugar, bananas, barley, cotton, coffee, vegetables; cattle; henequen; fish; silver, petroleum, lead, gold, zinc, copper; textiles, sugar, alcohol, foundry products.
MONACO	A principality. The prince's authority exercised through a state ministry and 3 government counsellors. The one-house legislative body is elective.	franc	French	Principal revenue derived from Monte Carlo gambling casino. Tobacco, postage stamps, perfume, liqueurs, olive oil, oranges.
MONGOLIAN REPUBLIC	Communist republic, whose prime minister is also head of communist party politburo, which is the actual ruler.	Tugrik	Mongolian Russian	Stock raising (sheep, goats, cattle, horses, camels); milk, butter, cheese; wool, hides, skins, horns, bricks, machinery; coal, lead, gold.
MOROCCO	Constitutional monarchy with a cabinet and a consultative national assembly.	Moroccan franc	Arabic Berber French	Wheat, barley, olives, almonds, citrus fruits, dates, beans, grapes, vegetables, linseed; cork, cedar; sheep, goats, cattle, asses, camels, horses, mules, pigs; fish; phosphate, iron ore, anthracite, manganese, lead, zinc, cobalt, copper, antimony; leather, carpets.
MOZAMBIQUE	Portuguese overseas province ruled by a governor and a government council.	escudo	Bantu languages Portuguese	Sugar, corn, cotton, copra, sisal, cashew nuts, bananas, coffee, kapok, sorghum, manioc, beeswax, tea, tobacco, vegetable oils; mangrove bark; timber; oxen, goats, pigs, sheep, cattle; gold, silver, asbestos, uranium, bauxite, samerskite.
NAURU	Trust territory of Great Britain, Australia and New Zealand. Administered by Australia.	Australian pound	English Micronesian Chinese	Phosphates; fishing; mats.
NEPAL	An independent kingdom governed by a maharaja, prime minister and a bicameral legislature.	Nepalese rupee	Indo-Aryan languages Tibetan	Rice, grains, jute, sugar cane, tea, vegetables, tobacco, cotton, potatoes, medicinal herbs; timber; cattle, hides, skins, ghee; iron, coal, copper, lead, zinc; cotton cloth, pottery, paper.

POLITICAL DIVISION	GOVERNMENT	MONETARY UNIT	LANGUAGE	MAJOR PRODUCTS
NETHERLANDS	A constitutional, hereditary monarchy governed by the queen, her ministers and a two-house legislature, partly elective and partly chosen by provincial councils.	guilder	Dutch	Potatoes, sugar beets, rye, wheat, oats, barley, flax, legumes, flower bulbs, seeds, vegetables, fruit; cattle, pigs, sheep, horses, poultry; fish; coal, petroleum, salt; leather, rubber, footwear; metal products, textiles, paper, building materials, chemicals, foods and beverages, clothing, shipbuilding, cheese and other dairy products, fertilizers, ceramics, cement, tobacco products.
NEW CALEDONIA	French overseas territory administered by high commissioner assisted by an appointive executive council and an elective general council.	franc	Melanesian dialects French	Coconuts, copra, coffee, cotton, manioc, corn, tobacco, bananas, pineapples, wheat, rice, kauri logs; cattle, pigs, horses, goats, sheep, hides; guano, trochus shell; nickel, chrome, manganese, iron, cobalt, copper, lead, platinum; canned meat.
NEW GUINEA, NETHERLANDS	A Dutch colony, its status undetermined pending negotiations with Indonesian government.	guilder	Papuan Dutch Negrito	Sago, coconuts, sweet potatoes, wild nutmeg, mace, copra; bird of paradise plumes; petroleum.
NEW HEBRIDES	British and French condominium administered by British and French resident commissioners.	Australian currency Bank of Indo-china Notes	Melanesian dialects Pidgin English English French	Coconuts, copra, cocoa, coffee, yams, taro, manioc, fruits; kauri pine; cattle, pigs; trochus shells.
NEW ZEALAND	A member of the British Commonwealth with dominion status governed by a governor-general, cabinet and unicameral assembly.	New Zealand pound	English Maori	Wheat, oats, barley, seeds, kauri, gum; sheep, cattle, pigs, horses; hides, skins; fish; gold, silver, coal, copper, limestone, manganese, iron, tungsten; dairy products, meats, wool, clothing, lumber, woodwork, furniture, electrical and radio goods, motor assembly, printing, publishing, biscuits, confections, footwear, rubber products, chemical fertilizers, tobacco products, brewing.
NICARAGUA	Republic with a president, cabinet and a two-house legislature.	córdoba	Spanish	Coffee, sugar cane, sesame, corn, bananas, rice, cacao, cotton, beans; cattle; hardwoods; gold; silver; sugar, wood products.
NIGER	Territory of Fr. West Africa with a governor and an elective representative assembly.	franc	Sudanese Hamitic Arabic French	Millet, manioc, groundnuts, rice, wheat, cotton, gum arabic, kapoc, kidney beans, corn, onions, sorghum, dates, sugar cane; goats, sheep, cattle, asses, camels, horses; hides and skins, leather; natron, sodium sulphate, salt.
NIGERIA	A federated colony and protectorate of Great Britain with a governor-general, a council of ministers and a federal house of representatives.	pound	Sudanese languages Arabic English	Palm oil and kernels, cacao, groundnuts, cotton, rubber, bananas, benni seeds, shea nuts, yams, cassava, corn, rice, fruits, millet, coffee; cattle, sheep, goats; hides and skins; timber; tin, coal, columbite, lead, gold, silver, zinc; cigarettes, soap, sugar.
NIUE	Dependency of New Zealand administered by a resident commissioner.	New Zealand pound	Mixed Melanesian and Polynesian dialects English	Copra, sweet potatoes, bananas; hats, baskets.
NORFOLK ISLAND	Administered by Australia.	Australian pound	English	Citrus, passion fruits, bananas, cherry guavas; hides; fish.
NORTH BORNEO	British colony ruled by a governor and assisted by executive and legislative councils.	Malayan dollar	Malay Indonesian languages English Chinese	Rubber, coconuts, copra, tobacco, manila hemp, sago, rice, cutch, sugar, pepper, kapok, groundnuts, derris root, vegetables; timber; fish.
NORTHEAST (TERR. OF) NEW GUINEA	Trust territory of Australia governed by administrator of Papua.	Australian pound	Papuan Pidgin English English	Coconuts, copra, cocoa, dairying; timber; gold, silver, platinum; boat making.
NORTHERN IRELAND	Executive power vested in appointed governor and cabinet responsible to legislative two-house parliament.	pound	English and Gaelic	Potatoes, oats, flax, turnips, hay; cattle, sheep, pigs, poultry; basalt and igneous rocks, sand and gravel, grit and conglomerate, chalk, clays; linen, rayon, woolen goods, carpets, hosiery, cotton goods, shirts, collars, underwear, shipbuilding, aircraft, marine machinery, rope, tobacco, whiskey.
NORTHERN RHODESIA*	British protectorate administered by a governor and executive and legislative council.	pound	Bantu languages English	Corn, wheat, potatoes, tobacco, sorghum, millet, groundnuts, cassava, rice, beans, cow-peas, cotton; lumber; cattle and other livestock.
NORWAY	A constitutional, hereditary monarchy headed by the king, his council of state and a two-house, elective legislature.	krone	Norwegian	Hay, potatoes, oats, barley, wheat, rye, fruits, vegetables; dairy products, livestock; herring, cod and other fish; sulphur, iron, copper, zinc, silver, nickel, molybdenum; timber, pulp, cellulose, paper, canned foods, electro-chemical products, transportation equipment, salted, dried and canned fish, leather, basic metals, textiles, fertilizers, shipbuilding.
NYASALAND*	British protectorate administered by a governor and executive and legislative council.	pound	Bantu languages English	Tobacco, tea, cotton, pulses, tung-oil, sisal, corn, cassava, wheat, rice, millet, groundnuts, rubber, beeswax; timber; goats, cattle, pigs, sheep; hides, skins, meat, ghee, soap; gold, mica, corundum.
OMAN AND MUSCAT	An independent sultanate.	rupee (official) Maria Theresa dollar	Arabic	Dates, pomegranates, limes and other fruits, sugar cane; dried fish.
PAKISTAN	Self-governing republic of the British Commonwealth ruled by a president, cabinet and unicameral legislature.	Pakistani rupee	Indo-Aryan languages (Bengali, Urdu, Punjabi, etc.)	Rice, wheat, corn, jute, cotton, sugar cane, fruit, oilseeds, tobacco, tea, fibers; timber; cattle, goats, sheep, horses, camels, poultry; hides, skins, wool; fish; salt, copper, petroleum, chromite, gypsum, magnisite, sulphur, antimony; textiles, flour milling, cement, iron and steel foundries, sugar, leather, chemicals, glass, sportsgoods, handicrafts, surgical instruments.
PALAU ISLANDS	A civil administrative district in the Western Carolines and part of the United States Pacific trust territory.	dollar	Micronesian dialects	Coconuts, manioc, taro, pineapples, sweet potatoes, papayas; poultry, pigs, goats; fish; phosphate; handicrafts.
PANAMA	Republic with a president, two vice-presidents, and a one-house legislature.	balboa	Spanish	Bananas cacao, abaca, coconuts, rice, sugar cane, coffee, pineapples; cattle; hardwoods; gold; hides, sugar, wood products.
PAPUA TERRITORY	Australian colony governed by an administrator.	Australian pound	Papuan Pidgin English English	Coconuts, rubber, sweet potatoes, yams, taro, sago, rice, bananas, coffee, kapok, bamboo, sisal hemp, copra; shells, sponges; cattle, goats, poultry; gold, copper, manganese.
PARAGUAY	A centralized republic with a president, an appointed cabinet and a one-house legislature.	guarani	Spanish, Indian	Cotton, tobacco, sugar cane, rice, cassava, yerba maté, corn, citrus fruits; cattle, hides; lumber, quebracho; iron, manganese, copper; canned meats, vegetable oils, petit-grain oil, tobacco products.
PERU	A republic with a president, two vice-presidents, appointive cabinet and a two-house legislature.	sol	Spanish, Indian	Cotton, sugar, potatoes, barley, corn, rice, wheat, coca, quinoa, cacao, tobacco, coffee, quinine, flax, rubber, balata, guano; fish; livestock; petroleum, lead, zinc, copper, silver, gold, vanadium; textiles, foodstuffs, cement, leather, wool, hides, pharmaceuticals, paper products, clothing, metal products.

*Member of Federation of Rhodesia and Nyasaland.

POLITICAL DIVISION	GOVERNMENT	MONETARY UNIT	LANGUAGE	MAJOR PRODUCTS
PHILIPPINES	Republic governed by a president, cabinet and a bicameral legislature.	peso	Malayan languages (Tagalog, Visayan, etc.) English Spanish	Rice, sugar cane, copra, manila hemp (abacá), corn, tobacco, maguey, rubber, bananas, pineapples, mangoes, papaya, citrus fruits, other fruits; hogs, carabaos, cattle, horses, goats, sheep; fish; timber, gum resins, tan and dye barks, dye woods; gold, iron, copper, chromite, silver, manganese, asbestos, asphalt, guano, silica, coal, petroleum; sugar, textiles, distilling, dessicated coconuts, tobacco products, rice milling, cocoa, coconut oil, embroideries.
PITCAIRN ISLAND	British colony administered by a chief magistrate responsible to the governor of Fiji.	Fiji pound	English Tahitian	Fruits, vegetables, goats, poultry; handicraft.
POLAND	A Soviet-type "People's Republic" headed by a one-party legislative Sejm which elects an executive Council of Ministers. Acutal power in the hands of politburo, highest organ of communist party.	zloty	Polish	Potatoes, straw and hay, rye, sugar beets, mangolds, oats, barley, wheat, peas, beans, flax, hemp, rapeseed; livestock; fish; zinc, lead, coal, salt, iron ore, petroleum, natural gas, phosphates, lignite; iron and steel products, coke, foods and beverages, textiles, cement, lime, bricks, electrical goods, chemicals, wood, timber, paper, cellulose, leather and leather products, glass.
PORTUGAL	A "unitary corporative republic" with a president, premier, and a one-house, elective legislature.	escudo	Portuguese	Wheat, corn, oats, barley, rye, rice, French beans, potatoes, grapes, olives; livestock; cork, lumber, resin; sardines, tuna and other fish; copper pyrites, coal, copper, tin, kaolin, cement, wolfram, sulphur, tungsten, iron; wines, olive oil, canned sardines, textiles, porcelain, tiles, embroideries, lace.
PRINCIPE AND SÃO TOMÉ	Portuguese overseas province administered by a governor.	escudo	Bantu languages Portuguese	Cacao, coffee, coconuts, copra, palm oil, cinchona, bananas.
PUERTO RICO	A self-governing commonwealth associated with the U.S., with a governor, an executive council and a bicameral legislature.	dollar	Spanish, English	Sugar cane, tobacco, fruits, pineapples, grapefruit, coconuts, coffee, cotton, livestock, vegetables; molasses, embroideries, rum, canned fruit and juice, alcohol, cordials, tobacco products.
QATAR	Sheikdom under British protection.	rupee riyal	Arabic	Dates; pearl fishing, dried fish; camels; petroleum.
RÉUNION	French overseas department administered by a prefect and a council-general.	franc	French	Sugar, rum, vanilla, tapioca, essences, fruit and vegetable preserves.
RUANDA—URUNDI	Under United Nations trusteeship, administered by Belgium and governed by a vice-governor general.	franc	Bantu languages Flemish French	Foods; cattle; hides.
RUMANIA	A Soviet-type "People's Republic" with a 17-member presidium, cabinet of ministers and a one-house legislature. Supreme power resides in communist party politburo.	leu	Rumanian	Wheat, barley, rye, corn, oats, potatoes, sugar beets, hemp, flax, grapes, fruits, tobacco; lumber; sheep, cattle, pigs, horses; petroleum, natural gas, salt, coal, lignite, iron and copper ores, gold, silver, bauxite, lead, manganese, zinc; flour, brewing and distilling, iron and steel, metal products, textiles, wood and paper products.
RYUKYU IS.	Administered by the United States.	yen	Luchuan Japanese English	Sweet potatoes, sugar cane, rice, fruits, mulberries; swine, cattle, goats, horses, poultry; silkworms; fish; Panama hats, textiles, lacquer, pottery, china, glassware, tiles.
ST. HELENA	British colony with a governor, an executive and an advisory council.	pound	English	Hemp, lily bulbs, potatoes, tow, rope and twine, lace; sheep, goats, cattle, donkeys, poultry.
ST. PIERRE AND MIQUELON	French territory with a governor, privy council and elective general council.	franc	French	Fish, silver fox; dried cod and cod liver oil; sienna earth, yellow ocher.
SALVADOR	Republic with a president and a one-house legislature.	colón	Spanish	Coffee, cotton, corn, tobacco, henequen, sugar cane, rice; balsam and other woods; gold, silver; cotton textiles, henequen bags, sugar.
SAMOA, EASTERN	Possession of the United States with a governor and a bicameral legislature.	dollar	English Samoan	Copra, taro, breadfruit, yams, bananas, arrowroot, pineapples, oranges; mats.
SAMOA, WESTERN	Under United Nations trusteeship administered by New Zealand.	New Zealand pound	Samoan English	Copra, cocoa beans, bananas, taro; fish; pigs, poultry.
SAN MARINO	Republic with two regents, council of state, one-house legislature.	lira	Italian	Cattle, hides, wines, quarrying.
SARAWAK	British colony administered by a governor and an executive and legislative council.	Malayan dollar	Malay Indonesian languages Chinese English	Rice, rubber, sago, pepper, coconuts, pineapples, tobacco, coffee, fruits, vegetables; timber, rattan cane, guttas; buffalo, cattle, pigs, goats; fish; petroleum, gold, antimony, phosphate, cutch.
SAUDI ARABIA	Absolute monarchy, with premier and cabinet responsible to the king, and advisory councils.	riyal	Arabic	Dates, sorghums, wheat, rice, henna, coffee, fruits, nuts, vegetables, honey, gum, sesame oil; fish; camels, sheep, goats, cattle, donkeys, poultry, horses; hides, wool, clarified butter, charcoal, pottery, tile, salt, soap, weaving; petroleum, gold, pearls.
SCOTLAND	A secretary of state for Scotland in the British cabinet has in his charge four departments for Scotland (agriculture, education, health and home.) Authority in other matters is exercised by other members of the British cabinet.	pound	English and Gaelic	Turnips, potatoes, wheat, barley, sugar beets, flax, vegetables, forage crops, fruits; sheep, cattle, pigs, horses; coal, iron ore, granite, sandstone, limestone, slate, lead, clay; steel, machinery, tools, locomotives, electronic equipment, linoleum, shipbuilding and repair, watches, clocks, jute, bagging, burlap, textiles, hosiery, thread, lace, carpet, yarn, chemicals, whiskey, ale, paper, bricks and other clay products, preserves, boots and shoes, furniture.
SENEGAL	Territory of Fr. West Africa with a governor and an elective representative assembly.	franc	Sudanese languages Arabic French	Millet, groundnuts, manioc, rice, corn, gum arabic, palm nuts, honey, sweet potatoes, sisal, indigo; sheep, goats, cattle, asses, horses; fish; titanium, zircon; brick, pottery, weaving, jewelry, oil cakes.
SEYCHELLES	A British colony ruled by a governor and legislative and executive councils.	rupee	English French	Coconuts, cinnamon, patchouli, copra, vanilla, corn; guano; salted fish, tortoise shell, calipee.
SIERRA LEONE	A British colony and protectorate ruled by a governor and legislative and executive councils.	pound	Sudanese languages English	Palm oil and kernels, kola nuts, ginger, piassava, groundnuts, cocoa; diamonds, iron ore, chrome ore.
SIKKIM	A protectorate of India ruled by a maharaja and a council.	rupee	Nepali Tepcha Bhutia	Millet, corn, pulse, rice, fruits; cattle; woolen cloth.
SINGAPORE	British Crown colony administered by a governor, council of ministers and legislative assembly.	Malayan dollar	Chinese Malay Hindi English	Rubber, coconuts, fruits, vegetables, rice, coffee, tapioca, tobacco, sweet potatoes, pepper, pineapples; pigs, poultry, cattle; fish; tin, tin smelting, rubber milling, coconut milling, soap, beer, pineapple canning, biscuits, brick making, shipping, textiles, palm oil, cigarettes, gasoline, kerosene.

POLITICAL DIVISION	GOVERNMENT	MONETARY UNIT	LANGUAGE	MAJOR PRODUCTS
SOCIETY ISLANDS	Part of Fr. Polynesia governed from Tahiti.	franc	Polynesian	Copra, vanilla, pearls, mother-of-pearl, vanilla, phosphates, sugar, rum.
SOLOMON ISLANDS	A protectorate administered by the British high commissioner of the Western Pacific.	Australian pound	Melanesian Pidgin English English	Copra, pigs, poultry; trochus shell, turtle shell, bêche-de-mer.
SOLOMON ISLANDS (NORTHERN)	Part of the territory of New Guinea and governed as an Australian trust territory.	Australian pound	Melanesian Pidgin English English	Coconuts, copra, bananas, yams, taro, fruits; trochus shell, green snail shell, rubber.
SOMALILAND	Under United Nations trusteeship and administered by Italy with U. N. and local advisory councils.	Somalo	Somali Arabic Italian	Sugar, cotton, tobacco, bananas, aromatic gums, resin, kapok, grains, beans; camels, goats, sheep, cattle; skins, hides; tunny, mother-of-pearl.
SOMALILAND, BRITISH	British protectorate ruled solely by governor, assisted by advisory councils.	Indian rupee East African shilling	Somali Arabic	Millet, sorghum, corn; sheep, goats, camels, cattle; skins, hides; gums, salt.
SOMALILAND, FRENCH	Overseas territory of France with a governor and an elective representative assembly.	Djibouti franc	Hamitic languages Arabic French	Boats, sheep; salt.
SOUTHERN RHODESIA†	A self-governing colony and member of British Commonwealth with governor and elective executive and legislative councils.	pound	Bantu languages English	Corn, tobacco, groundnuts, wheat, potatoes, citrus and other fruits; cattle, sheep, pigs, goats; meats, hides; gold, asbestos, chromite, coal; footwear, apparel, cigarettes, flour, groundnut oil, wood products.
SPAIN	A nominal monarchy governed by a chief of state. The legislative Cortés prepares laws subject to the veto of the chief of state. A king is to be chosen by a regency council upon the death or incapacitation of the chief of state.	peseta	Spanish Catalan	Wheat, barley, potatoes, oranges, olives, oats, rye, rice, corn, peas, beans, grapes, onions, sugar beets, esparto, flax, hemp, pulse, cork, nuts; pigs, sheep, goats, donkeys, mules, horses, poultry; sardines, tuna, cod and other fish; coal, lignite, iron ore, lead, iron pyrites, potash, zinc, mercury, sulphur, copper; textiles, wines, olive oil, paper, cement, hides, preserved and canned fish and shellfish, paper products.
SPANISH SAHARA	Spanish territory, consisting of Saguia el Hamra and Río de Oro, ruled by sub-governors.	peseta	Arabic Spanish	Barley, corn; goats, sheep, camels; fish.
SUDAN	A republic with a bicameral parliament and council of ministers. Executive power resides temporarily in a council of state.	Egyptian pound	Arabic Sudanese Hamitic languages English	Cotton, cotton seed, gum arabic, Senna leaves and pods, groundnuts, sesame, millet, dates, dom nuts (vegetable ivory), wheat, shea nuts; sheep, goats, cattle, camels, asses; mahogany; hides and skins, ivory, gold, salt, trochus shell, mother-of-pearl.
SURINAM (see Guiana, Neth.)				
SWAZILAND	British protectorate governed by a resident commissioner under the High Commissioner for Basutoland, Bechuanaland and Swaziland.	pound	Bantu languages English	Tobacco, corn, groundnuts, kaffir-corn, wheat, oats, rye, barley, fruits; cattle, goats, sheep, pigs; butter; hides, skins; asbestos, gold, tin.
SWEDEN	A constitutional hereditary monarchy with a prime minister, council of state and a two-house, elective legislature.	krona	Swedish	Hay, sugar beets, potatoes, fodder crops, oats, wheat, rye, barley; forest products, cattle, pigs, sheep, horses, poultry; fish; iron ore, sulphur, arsenic, zinc, copper, silver, gold, lead, manganese; lumber and wood products, machinery, textiles, iron and steel and metal goods, chemicals, dairy products, electric power, tobacco products, brick, porcelain and glass, shipbuilding, matches.
SWITZERLAND	A republic with a president, vice-president, an executive federal council and a two-house, elective legislature.	franc	German, French, Italian, Romansch	Wheat, potatoes, sugar beets, rye, oats barley, fruits, tobacco; livestock; salt, iron, manganese; dairy products, textiles, watches and clocks, chemicals, foods, wines, dyes, instruments.
SYRIA (See United Arab Republic)	Province of United Arab Republic.	Syrian pound	Arabic Turkish Kurdish	Wheat, barley, sorghum, corn, cotton, lentils, chickpeas, sesame, vegetables, olives, grapes, tobacco (Latikia); sheep, goats, cattle, donkeys, camels, horses, poultry; wool, hides, skins; gypsum; leather, textiles, food, tobacco, wine, flour.
TANGANYIKA TERRITORY	Under United Nations trusteeship and administered by Great Britain. Ruled by a governor and a legislative and executive council.	East African shilling	Bantu languages Swahili English	Sisal, cotton, coffee, bananas, tobacco, papain, beeswax, grains, sugar; cattle, goats, sheep; hides, skins; wood, timber, wax, gum arabic; diamonds, gold, tin, mica, salt, camphor, tungsten.
TANGIER	International zone of Tangier was dissolved in 1956 and joined to independent Morocco.	franc peseta	Arabic French Spanish English	Wheat, barley, chickpeas; soap, canned fish, essential oils.
THAILAND (SIAM)	Constitutional monarchy ruled by a king, prime minister and a legislative assembly.	baht	Thai Khmer	Rice, rubber, coconuts, tobacco, cotton, corn, beans; teak and other woods; bullocks, buffalo, horses, elephants; fish; tin, wolfram.
TIBET	Theocracy. Nominally independent but under effective Chinese Communist control. Religious affairs are directed by the Dalai Lama.	sang	Tibetan	Barley, wheat, pulse, corn, vegetables, rice; yaks, asses, sheep, goats, donkeys; hides, wool, furs, musk; borax, salt, gold; cult objects.
TIMOR, PORTUGUESE	Portuguese overseas province ruled by a governor.	escudo	Malay Portuguese	Coffee, copra, sandalwood, wax, cocoa; hides, shells.
TOGO	Under United Nations trusteeship administered by France as an autonomous republic.	franc	Sudanese languages French	Palm oil and kernels, tapioca, cocoa, yams, coffee, plantains, corn, groundnuts, cotton, copra, kola, cassava, rubber; sheep, goats, pigs, cattle, asses, horses.
TOKELAU ISLANDS	An island territory of New Zealand administered by a high commissioner.	New Zealand pound	Samoan	Coconuts, fiber, taro, copra; pigs, chickens; fish; hats, mats.
TONGA	Constitutional monarchy under Br. protection ruled by queen with cabinet and legislative assembly.	Tongan pound	Tongan English	Copra, bananas, fungus, candlenuts; pigs, cattle, goats.
TRIESTE	Former free territory was dissolved in 1954 and joined to Italy and Yugoslavia respectively.	lira	Italian and Slovene	Vineyards, shipyards, oil refineries, steel, vegetable oils, fishing.
TRINIDAD AND TOBAGO *	British colony with a governor and executive and legislative councils.	B.W.I. dollar	English	Coffee, cocoa, sugar cane, citrus fruits; cattle; petroleum, asphalt; rum, canned grapefruit juice, sugar.
TRISTAN DA CUNHA	Possession of Great Britain governed by an administrator and an island council responsible to St. Helena.	pound	English	Potatoes, fruit; cattle, sheep; fish.

* Member of The West Indies (British Caribbean Federation)   † Member of Federation of Rhodesia and Nyasaland

POLITICAL DIVISION	GOVERNMENT	MONETARY UNIT	LANGUAGE	MAJOR PRODUCTS
TRUCIAL OMAN	Seven sheikhdoms under British protection with a British agent.	rupee riyal	Arabic	Dates, grains, vegetables; fishing, pearl fishing.
TUAMOTU ARCHIPELAGO	Part of Fr. Polynesia governed from Tahiti.	franc	Polynesian dialects French	Copra, pearls, pearl shell.
TUBUAI ARCHIPELAGO	Part of Fr. Polynesia governed from Tahiti.	franc	Roman Catholic Tribal religions	Copra, arrowroot.
TUNISIA	A republic with a president, a cabinet of secretaries of state, and an assembly.	franc	Arabic French Berber	Wheat, barley, oats, corn, sorghum, beans, grapes, olives, citrus fruits, dates, alfa grass, almonds, oranges, shaddocks, pistachios, cork; sheep, goats, cattle, horses, asses, mules, camels, pigs; fish, sponges; flour milling, oil refining, wool spinning, pottery, leather, silk weaving; phosphates, iron ore, lignite, lead, zinc.
TURKEY	A republic with a president and a one-house, elective legislature.	pound	Turkish	Tobacco, cereals, olives, cotton, figs, nuts, fruits; cattle, livestock; fish; chromium, iron ore, copper, coal, lignite, meerschaum, manganese; textiles, iron and steel, paper, rugs, olive oil.
UGANDA	British protectorate controlled by a governor with executive and legislative councils. Native kings and their assemblies rule locally.	East African shilling	Bantu and Sudanese languages English	Cotton, coffee, plantains, millet, cotton seed, tobacco, chilies, sugar cane, rubber; cattle, sheep, goats; hides, skins; tin; cigarettes.
UNION OF SOUTH AFRICA	Member of British Commonwealth with a governor general, cabinet, elective senate and house of assembly.	pound	Afrikaans English Bantu languages Bushman	Corn, wheat, potatoes, oats, kaffir-corn, barley, tobacco, sugar cane, tea, citrus fruits, rye, groundnuts, grapes, pineapples; cattle, sheep, goats, pigs, horses, donkeys, mules; gold, coal, diamonds, copper, asbestos, manganese, lime, limestone, platinum, chrome, iron, silver, tungsten, mercury, vanadium, tin, antimony, silver, scheelite, talc; hides, chemicals, wool, footwear, rubber, machinery, clothing, textiles, food, vehicles, printing, furniture, building materials.
U.S.S.R.	A federation of 15 socialist republics with a two-chamber legislative assembly (Supreme Soviet) which elects the executive presidium and council of ministers. The policy of the state is largely defined by the Central Committee of the communist party, the only legal party.	ruble	Russian, Ukrainian, White Russian, Uzbek, Tatar, Azerbaizhani, Georgian, Lithuanian, Armenian, Yiddish, Latvian, Mordvinian, Chuvash, Tadzhik, Esthonian, Kazakh.	Wheat, rye, oats, barley, corn, sugar beets, sunflower seeds, cotton, forage crops, flax, hemp, potatoes, tobacco; cattle, sheep, goats, pigs, horses; lumber, furs; fish; coal, peat, petroleum, iron, lignite, copper, lead, zinc, nickel, aluminum, phosphates, manganese, gold, sulphur, potash, asbestos, platinum, salt, chromite; steel, machinery, textiles, sugar, flour, meats, automobiles, paper, synthetic rubber, foods, wines, chemicals.
UNITED ARAB REPUBLIC	The union of Egypt and Syria as the United Arab Republic was proclaimed on February 1, 1958 in Cairo. The new state possesses a president, cabinet and unicameral legislature with its capital located at Cairo.	Egyptian and Syrian pound	See Egypt and Syria	See Egypt and Syria.
UNITED STATES	Federal republic with a president, vice-president and two-house legislature.	dollar	English	Corn, hay, tobacco, wheat, cotton, oats, soy beans, potatoes, barley, sorghums, peanuts, rye, rice, citrus fruits, fruits, sugar beets, sugar cane, vegetables, tree nuts, feed grains and hay; livestock; fish; lumber; petroleum, coal, cement, iron, natural gas, copper, sand and gravel, zinc, lead, stone, gold, silver, molybdenum, bauxite, phosphates, mica, sulphur; foods, transportation equipment, machinery, primary metal products, electrical machinery, textiles, chemicals, paper and wood products, beverages, dairy products.
UPPER VOLTA	Territory of Fr. West Africa with a governor and an elective representative assembly.	franc	Sudanese languages French	Millet, groundnuts, corn, karite nuts and butter (shea nut), vegetables, rice, tapes, cotton, kapok, sesame, sorghum, tea; sheep, goats, cattle, asses, pigs; gold, manganese, copper, silver, chrome, lignite, iron.
URUGUAY	A republic governed (as of March, 1955) by a National Council, an appointed cabinet and a two-house elective legislature.	peso	Spanish	Wheat, corn, linseed, oats, sunflower seeds, peanuts, barley, rice, citrus fruits, peaches, grapes, vegetables, tobacco; sheep, cattle; gold; meat, hides, wool, textiles, leather, boots and shoes, wines.
VATICAN CITY	The Pope, who is elected for life by the cardinals of the Roman Catholic Church, exercises absolute legislative, executive and judicial power. He appoints a governor of the state and delegates diplomatic and judicial power.	lira	Italian Latin	
VENEZUELA	A republic with a president, appointive cabinet, and elective two-house legislature.	bolivar	Spanish	Coffee, cacao, sugar cane, cotton, tobacco, coconuts, tonka beans; balata, dividivi, rubber; livestock; fish and pearls; petroleum, iron, gold, coal, copper, phosphates, magnesite, asphalt, salt, diamonds; textiles, leather, sugar, cement, wood products, foodstuffs, beverages, soap, tobacco products, meats, milk; refined petroleum.
VIETNAM	Divided in two parts by Armistice Line Sept. 1954. North of 17th parallel is Communist controlled "republic". South is a republic with a president and an assembly.	piaster	Khmer (Annamese) Lao	Rice, corn, sugar, tobacco, coffee, fruits, manioc, betel nuts, arrowroot, tea, cotton, areca nut, medicinal plants, cardamom, soya, rubber, copra, groundnuts, haricots, sweet potatoes, cinnamon; mulberries, bamboo, silk; cattle, buffalo, pigs; lumber; gold, tin, copper, coal, zinc, iron, cement, limestone, calamine, tungsten, manganese, phosphate, lead, bauxite.
VIRGIN ISLANDS (U. S.)	Territory of the U. S. with an appointed governor.	dollar	English, Creole	Sugar cane, vegetables, citrus fruits, coconuts; cattle; fish; rum, bay rum, bay oil, molasses, handicrafts, sugar, lime juice, hides, bitters.
VOLCANO ISLANDS	Administered by the United States.	dollar yen	Japanese	Sugar cane; fish; sulphur.
WEST INDIES	A federation of colonies within the Br. Commonwealth with a governor-general, council of state and bicameral legislature.	B.W.I. dollar	English	Sugar cane, cocoa, coffee; citrus fruit, bananas, coconuts, pimentos, ginger; edible oil, margarine, honey, nutmeg; sugar, molasses, rum, bitters; petroleum, asphalt, charcoal.
YAP	Administered by a civil administrator of the Palau district as a part of the United States Pacific trust territory.	dollar	Micronesian dialects	Coconuts, breadfruit, sweet potatoes, taro, manioc, vegetables; poultry, pigs; fish.
YEMEN†	Independent kingdom.	riyal	Arabic	Coffee, barley, wheat, millet, sesame; cattle, hides; fish.
YUGOSLAVIA	A Soviet-type republic combining 6 republics under a central government with a president, fed. executive council and two-house elective legislature. Actually ruled by Communist League.	dinar	Serbian-Croatian, Slovenian Macedonian	Wheat, barley, rye, oats, corn, sugar beets, hemp, hops, opium, tobacco, flax, alfalfa, vegetables, fruits; sheep, cattle, pigs, goats, horses, poultry; coal, lignite, iron, copper, lead, salt, zinc, mercury, antimony, petroleum, bauxite, chrome, cement; lumber; textiles, foods, beverages, sugar, wood-distillates, wines.
ZANZIBAR	British protectorate nominally ruled by a sultan but under the effective control of a governor and a legislative and executive council.	East African shilling	Bantu languages Swahili English	Sisal, cotton, coffee, bananas, tobacco, papain, beeswax, grains, sugar; cattle, goats, sheep; hides, skins; wood, gum arabic; diamonds, gold, tin, mica, salt, camphor, tungsten.

† Allied member of the United Arab Republic.

WHAT A MAP IS ...

A *map* is like a picture of the earth taken from high in the air.

A *globe* is the only true map of the earth because it shows us the roundness of the earth. A globe shows us all the lands and seas in their true shapes and positions. A globe is really a *model* or small copy of our earth.

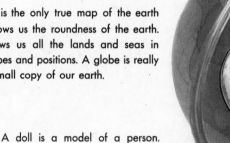

A doll is a model of a person.

A toy airplane is a model of a real airplane.

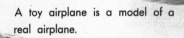

ROUTES

MAN-MADE FEATURES

NATURAL FEATURES

A map can show us many things that are located upon the earth. A few of them are shown here.

WHAT A MAP DOES ...

HOW TO

1. A map tells you in which *direction* one object or place is from another.

You can find direction on the ground in the following ways.....

YOUR SHADOW: At noon, if you face the sun, you are looking *south*. Your shadow will point *north*. If you raise your arms, your right arm will point *west* and your left arm will point *east*.

THE NORTH STAR: If you face the North Star, you are facing *north*.

NORTH STAR

BIG DIPPER

The two pointer stars of the Big Dipper point to the North Star.

A MAGNETIC COMPASS

The needle of compass points to ward *north*.

The compass-rose tells you where *north* is located on your map.

USE A MAP...

TO FIND YOUR WAY: You should turn the map so that *N* on the compass rose will point *north*. When this is done the position of the features on the map will be the same as on the earth.

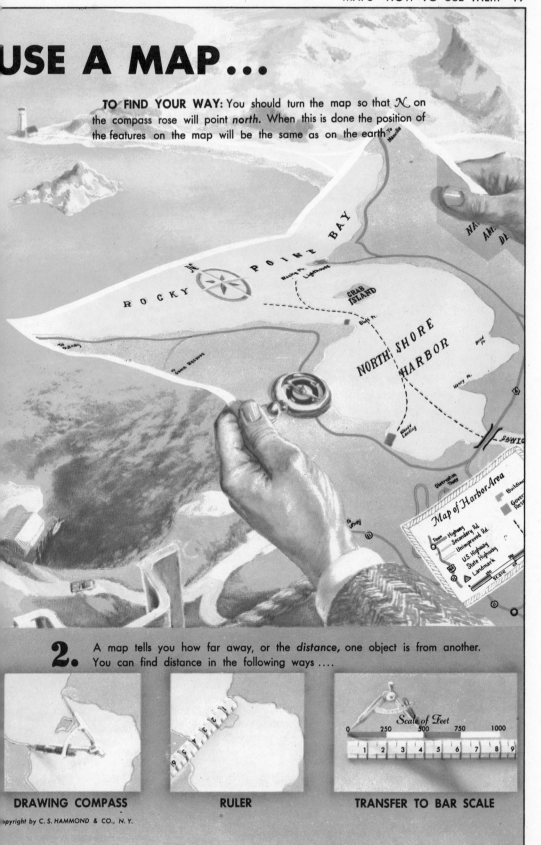

2. A map tells you how far away, or the *distance*, one object is from another. You can find distance in the following ways....

DRAWING COMPASS

RULER

TRANSFER TO BAR SCALE

WHAT SCALE MEANS...

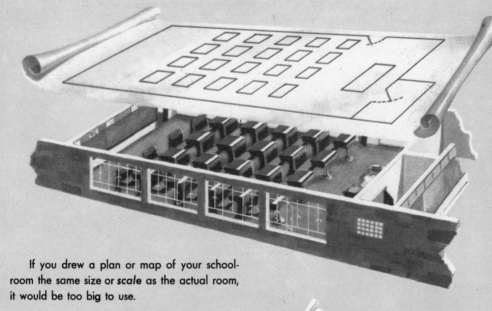

If you drew a plan or map of your schoolroom the same size or *scale* as the actual room, it would be too big to use.

If you drew the plan or map somewhat smaller, it still would be too large to use easily.

A still smaller plan or map could be drawn to a convenient size or scale.

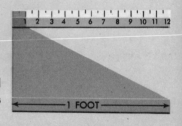

We do this by making a small length, such as an inch, stand for a large one, such as a foot or a mile. This diagram shows one inch equaling a foot.

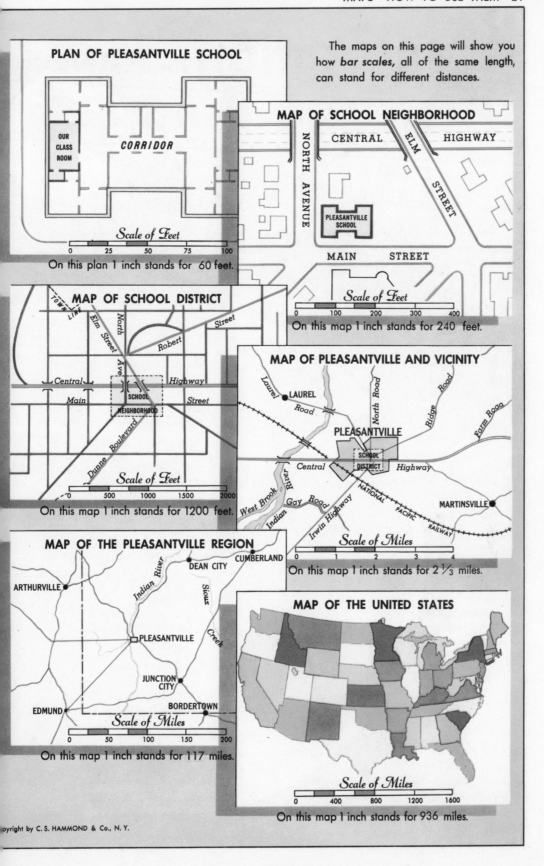

PLAN OF PLEASANTVILLE SCHOOL

OUR CLASS ROOM

CORRIDOR

Scale of Feet

0   25   50   75   100

On this plan 1 inch stands for 60 feet.

The maps on this page will show you how *bar scales*, all of the same length, can stand for different distances.

MAP OF SCHOOL NEIGHBORHOOD

CENTRAL   ELM   HIGHWAY

NORTH AVENUE

STREET

PLEASANTVILLE SCHOOL

MAIN   STREET

Scale of Feet

0   100   200   300   400

On this map 1 inch stands for 240 feet.

MAP OF SCHOOL DISTRICT

TOWN LINE

Elm Street   North   Street

Robert

Central   Highway

Main   SCHOOL NEIGHBORHOOD   Street

Dunne Boulevard

Scale of Feet

0   500   1000   1500   2000

On this map 1 inch stands for 1200 feet.

MAP OF PLEASANTVILLE AND VICINITY

Laurel   LAUREL

Road   North Road   Ridge Road   Farm Road

PLEASANTVILLE

SCHOOL DISTRICT   Highway

Central

West Brook   Indian River   Gay Road   Irwin Highway   NATIONAL PACIFIC RAILWAY   MARTINSVILLE

Scale of Miles

0   1   2   3   4

On this map 1 inch stands for 2 1/3 miles.

MAP OF THE PLEASANTVILLE REGION

CUMBERLAND

DEAN CITY

ARTHURVILLE

Indian River   Sioux   Creek

PLEASANTVILLE

JUNCTION CITY

EDMUND   BORDERTOWN

Scale of Miles

0   50   100   150   200

On this map 1 inch stands for 117 miles.

MAP OF THE UNITED STATES

Scale of Miles

0   400   800   1200   1600

On this map 1 inch stands for 936 miles.

PROJECTION: CHANGIN

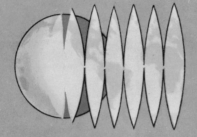

We can peel a globe as we can peel an orange. However, a map separated in this manner is difficult to use.

A better way to make a world map is to *project* features of the round globe onto a flat surface. We something like this when we make shadow pictures on wall with our hands.

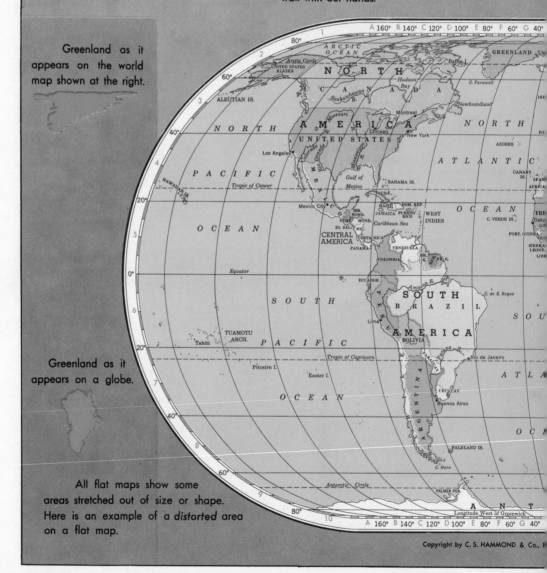

Greenland as it appears on the world map shown at the right.

Greenland as it appears on a globe.

All flat maps show some areas stretched out of size or shape. Here is an example of a *distorted* area on a flat map.

A GLOBE INTO A FLAT MAP

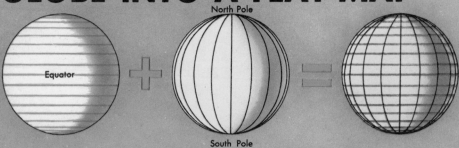

North Pole

Equator

South Pole

Latitude–imaginary lines that extend around the globe in the same direction as the equator.

Longitude–imaginary half-circles that extend from the North Pole to the South Pole.

When placed together they form a *grid* which helps to find the location of any place on earth.

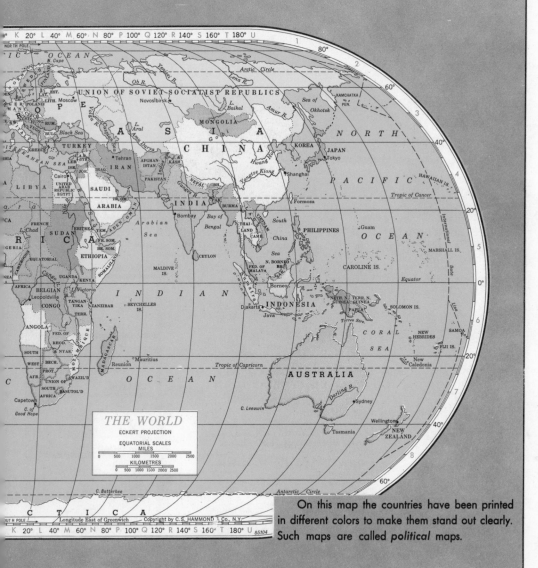

THE WORLD

ECKERT PROJECTION

EQUATORIAL SCALES
MILES
0   500 1000 1500 2000 2500

KILOMETRES
0 500 1000 1500 2000 2500

On this map the countries have been printed in different colors to make them stand out clearly. Such maps are called *political* maps.

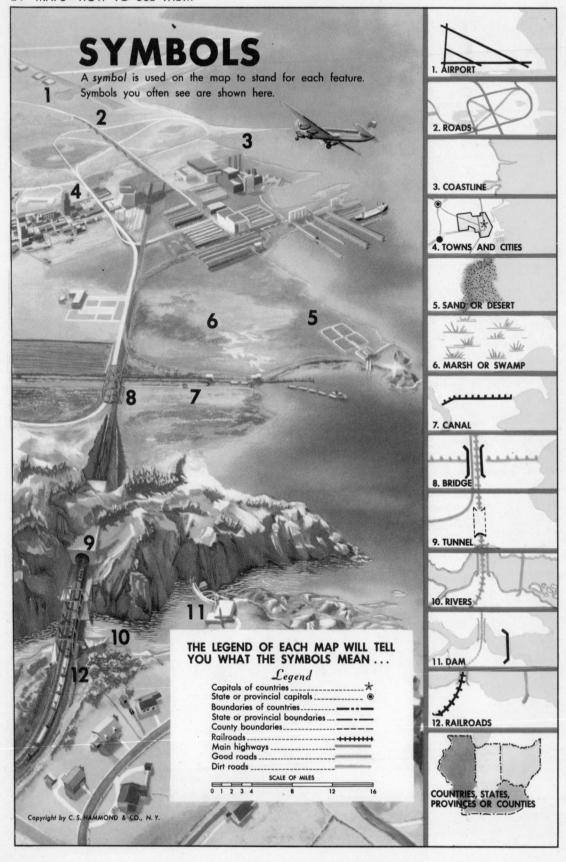

SYMBOLS

A *symbol* is used on the map to stand for each feature. Symbols you often see are shown here.

1. AIRPORT

2. ROADS

3. COASTLINE

4. TOWNS AND CITIES

5. SAND OR DESERT

6. MARSH OR SWAMP

7. CANAL

8. BRIDGE

9. TUNNEL

10. RIVERS

11. DAM

12. RAILROADS

COUNTRIES, STATES, PROVINCES OR COUNTIES

THE LEGEND OF EACH MAP WILL TELL YOU WHAT THE SYMBOLS MEAN . . .

Legend

Capitals of countries	☆
State or provincial capitals	◎
Boundaries of countries	▬ ▪ ▬ ▪
State or provincial boundaries	▬ ▪ ▬ ▪
County boundaries	▬ ▬ ▬
Railroads	＋＋＋＋＋
Main highways	▬▬▬
Good roads	▬▬▬
Dirt roads	▬▬▬

SCALE OF MILES

0 1 2 3 4   8   12   16

CONTOURS: WHAT THEY ARE... HOW TO USE THEM...

Some maps show highlands and lowlands. There are many ways of doing this on a map. One important way of showing the height and shape of land on a map is by means of *contour lines*. A contour is a line drawn on a map to connect all points that are the same height or *altitude* above the sea.

Sea-level means the level of the ocean. We start measuring from sea-level because it is the same all over the world.

If you made a clay model of the mountain shown above and sliced it into layers of the same thickness, the cuts would show on the surface as lines or *contour lines*.

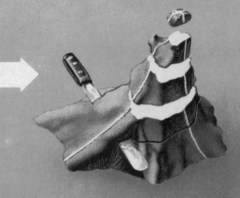

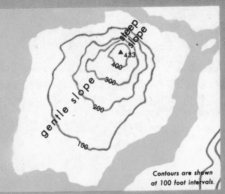

If you traced the outline of each layer on a piece of paper, your drawing would look something like this. Contour lines spaced closely together indicate a steep slope. Lines spaced far apart indicate a gentle slope.

A finished contour map may appear as ...

OR

Contours are shown at 100 foot intervals.

Lines with altitudes given in feet.

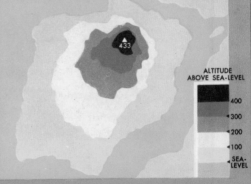

ALTITUDE ABOVE SEA-LEVEL

400
300
200
100
SEA-LEVEL

Colored areas with an altitude scale

FACTS ABOUT OUR

MARCH-
beginning of spring

JUNE-
beginning of summer

ORBIT OF EARTH

This picture shows the trip our earth takes around the sun every year. The circular path that it follows in *revolving* around the sun is known as its *orbit*.

HOW WE KNOW THE EARTH IS ROUND...

HORIZON

We know that our earth is round because we can see a ship go out of sight as it sails below the horizon.

NIGHT AND DAY

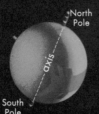
North Pole
axis
South Pole

Our earth turns or *rotates* on its *axis* once every 24 hours. We are carried by the spinning earth from daylight into darkness and, about 12 hours later, into daylight again.

Earth

The sun is much larger than the earth. This is how our earth would look if it were placed next to the sun.

EARTH...

Our earth receives its *light* and *heat* from the sun.

The moon *revolves* around the earth in its own *orbit*.

DECEMBER -
beginning of winter

SEPTEMBER -
beginning of fall

JULY
Summer

Winter

JANUARY
Winter

Summer

When the top half of the earth, or the *Northern Hemisphere,* leans toward the sun, the weather is warmer and the days longer. The *Southern Hemisphere* is then tilted away from the sun, thus receiving less heat and light. When the Southern Hemisphere leans toward the sun, warmer and longer days are experienced there, while it is cooler in the Northern Hemisphere.

JULY

JANUARY

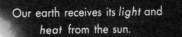

POLAR REGION
always cold
Arctic Circle

NORTH MID-LATITUDE REGION
seasons change

Tropic of Cancer

TROPICAL REGION
- Equator -
always hot

Tropic of Capricorn

SOUTH MID-LATITUDE REGION
seasons change
Antarctic Circle
POLAR REGION

JULY

JANUARY

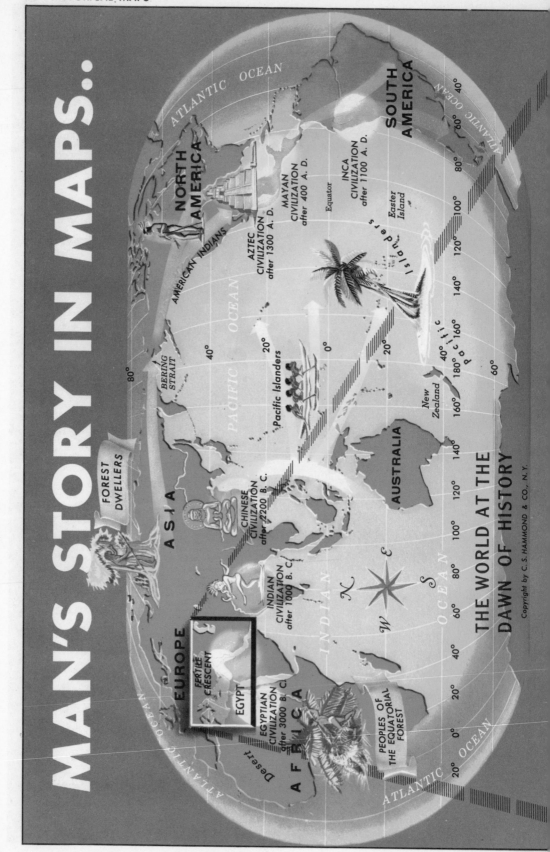

MAN'S STORY IN MAPS..

FOREST DWELLERS

AMERICAN INDIANS

NORTH AMERICA

ATLANTIC OCEAN

AZTEC CIVILIZATION after 1300 A. D.

MAYAN CIVILIZATION after 400 A. D.

Equator

INCA CIVILIZATION after 1100 A. D.

SOUTH AMERICA

Easter Island

Islanders

PACIFIC OCEAN

Pacific Islanders

BERING STRAIT

ASIA

CHINESE CIVILIZATION after 2200 B. C.

INDIAN CIVILIZATION after 1000 B. C.

New Zealand

AUSTRALIA

Pacific

INDIAN OCEAN

EUROPE

FERTILE CRESCENT

EGYPT

EGYPTIAN CIVILIZATION after 3000 B. C.

Desert

AFRICA

PEOPLES OF THE EQUATORIAL FOREST

ATLANTIC OCEAN

THE WORLD AT THE DAWN OF HISTORY

Copyright by C. S. HAMMOND & CO., N.Y.

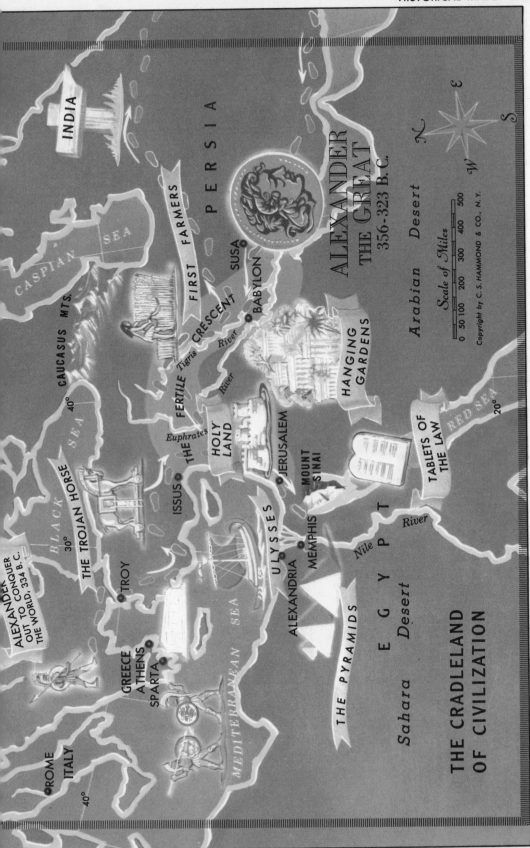

THE CRADLELAND
OF CIVILIZATION

ALEXANDER
THE GREAT
356-323 B.C.

Arabian Desert

Scale of Miles

0 50 100 200 300 400 500

Copyright by C. S. HAMMOND & CO., N.Y.

PERSIA

INDIA

FIRST FARMERS

FERTILE CRESCENT

Tigris River

Euphrates River

SUSA

BABYLON

HANGING
GARDENS

THE HOLY LAND

JERUSALEM

MOUNT
SINAI

TABLETS OF
THE LAW

RED SEA

20°

CASPIAN SEA

CAUCASUS MTS.

BLACK SEA

40°

30°

ISSUS

ULYSSES

THE TROJAN HORSE

TROY

GREECE
ATHENS
SPARTA

ROME
ITALY

40°

MEDITERRANEAN SEA

ALEXANDRIA

MEMPHIS

Nile River

E G Y P T

THE PYRAMIDS

Sahara Desert

ALEXANDER
OUT TO CONQUER
THE WORLD, 334 B.C.

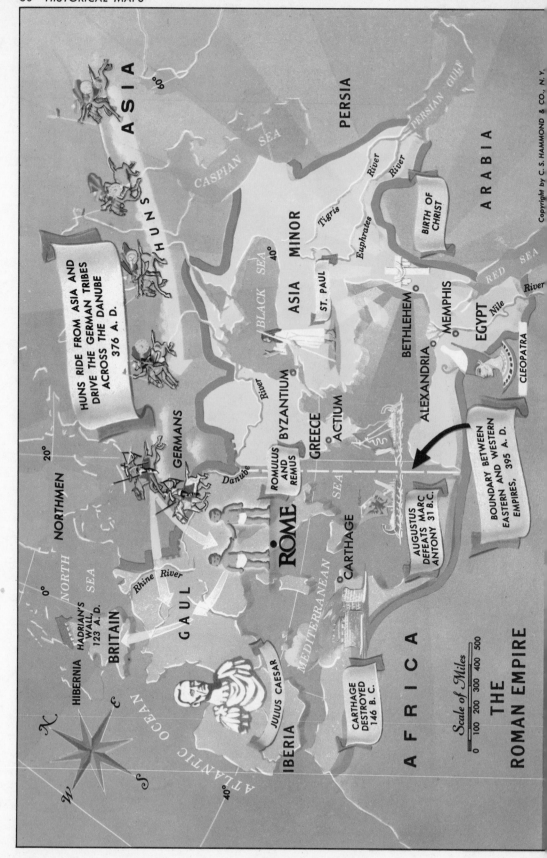

THE
ROMAN EMPIRE

Scale of Miles
0 100 200 300 400 500

Copyright by C. S. HAMMOND & CO., N.Y.

THE OLD WORLD
IN THE MIDDLE AGES
570 to 1400 A.D.

Scale of Miles
0 250 500 750 1000

Copyright by C.S. HAMMOND & CO., N.Y.

MONGOLS BREAK THROUGH THE GREAT WALL

MARCO POLO GOES FROM VENICE TO PEKIN 1271-1275

MARCO POLO SAILS BACK FROM PEKIN TO VENICE 1292-1295

SMALL GERMAN STATES

ASIA

CHINA

PEKIN

Yellow River

Yangtze River

Amur River

KARAKORUM

MONGOLS—1200's

TIBET

INDIA

Bay of Bengal

TURKESTAN
SAMARKAND

PERSIA

ORMUZ

PERSIAN GULF

ARABIA

MECCA

RED SEA

MOHAMMED 570-632

CASPIAN SEA

Volga River

BLACK SEA

CONSTANTINOPLE

BYZANTINE EMPIRE

Tigris R.

Euphrates R.

JERUSALEM

Danube River

VENICE

ROME

FRANCE

TOURS

EUROPE

ENGLAND

SPAIN

ATLANTIC OCEAN

ARCTIC OCEAN

MEDITERRANEAN SEA

BERBERS

Sahara Desert

AFRICA

ETHIOPIA

Nile River

PACIFIC OCEAN

INDIAN OCEAN

40°

20°

0°

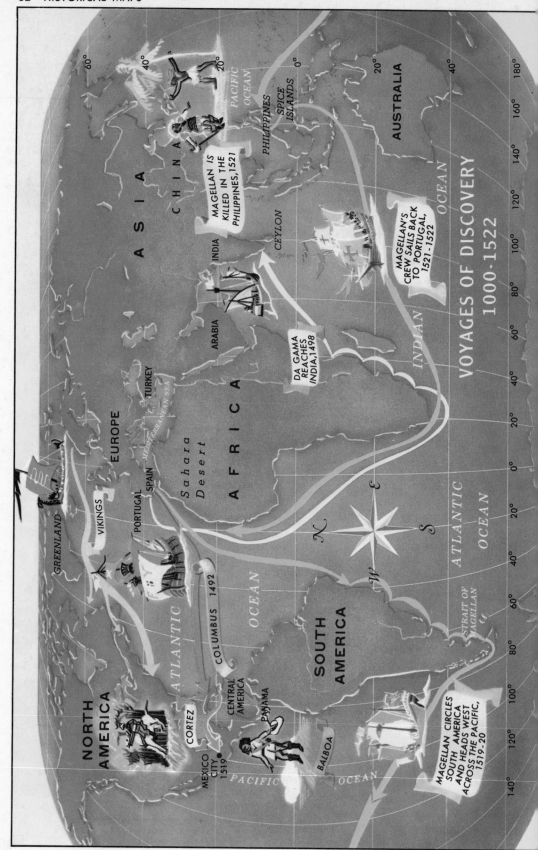

VOYAGES OF DISCOVERY
1000-1522

NORTH AMERICA

SOUTH AMERICA

EUROPE

ASIA

AFRICA

AUSTRALIA

CHINA

INDIA

ARABIA

CEYLON

TURKEY

SPAIN

PORTUGAL

GREENLAND

VIKINGS

CORTEZ

MEXICO CITY 1519

CENTRAL AMERICA

PANAMA

BALBOA

COLUMBUS 1492

Sahara Desert

MEDITERRANEAN SEA

PHILIPPINES

SPICE ISLANDS

PACIFIC OCEAN

ATLANTIC OCEAN

ATLANTIC OCEAN

PACIFIC OCEAN

INDIAN OCEAN

STRAIT OF MAGELLAN

MAGELLAN IS KILLED IN THE PHILIPPINES, 1521

MAGELLAN'S CREW SAILS BACK TO PORTUGAL, 1521-1522

DA GAMA REACHES INDIA, 1498

MAGELLAN CIRCLES SOUTH AMERICA AND HEADS WEST ACROSS THE PACIFIC, 1519-20

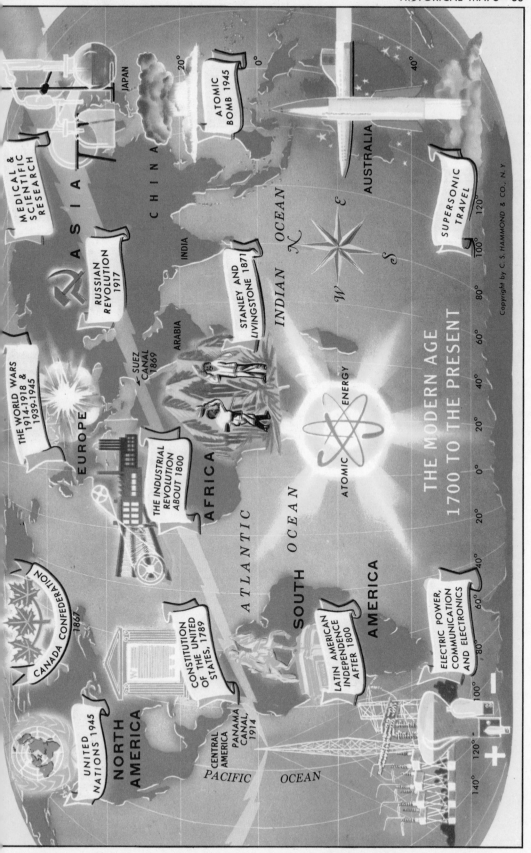

THE MODERN AGE
1700 TO THE PRESENT

Copyright by C. S. HAMMOND & CO., N.Y.

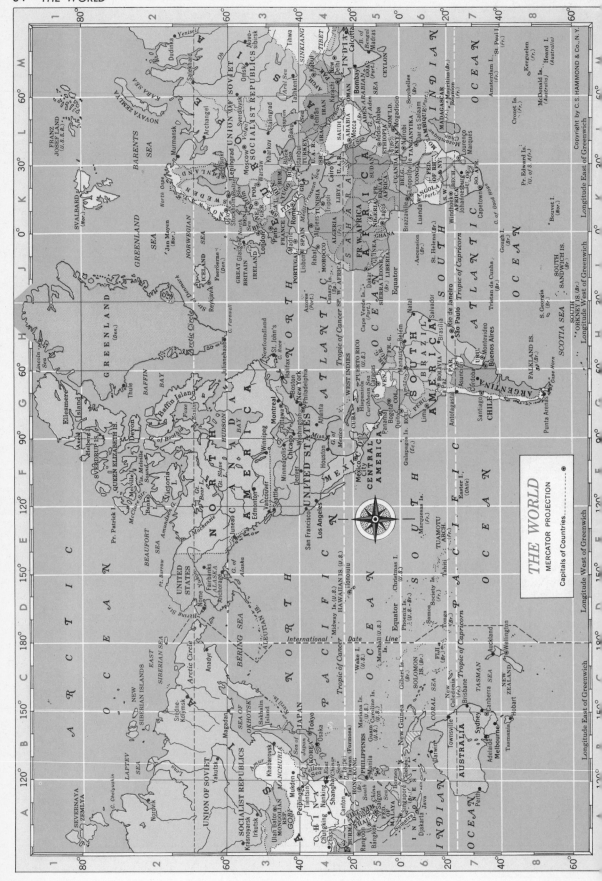

THE WORLD

MERCATOR PROJECTION

Capitals of Countries............●

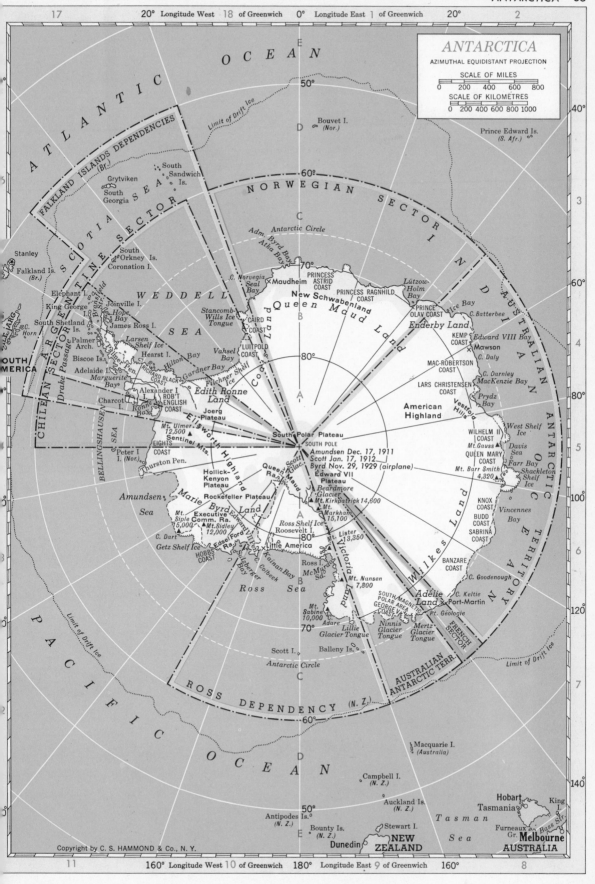

ANTARCTICA
AZIMUTHAL EQUIDISTANT PROJECTION

SCALE OF MILES
0 200 400 600 800

SCALE OF KILOMÉTRES
0 200 400 600 800 1000

17   20° Longitude West 18 of Greenwich   0° Longitude East 1 of Greenwich   20°   2

40°

ATLANTIC   OCEAN   E
50°
Bouvet I.
(Nor.)
D
Prince Edward Is.
(S. Afr.)

FALKLAND ISLANDS DEPENDENCIES (Br.)

South
Sandwich
Is.
60°
NORWEGIAN SECTOR
C

Grytviken
South
Georgia

SCOTIA SEA

Antarctic Circle
Adm. Byrd Bay
Atka Bay
70°
PRINCESS
ASTRID
COAST
Lützow-
Holm
Bay
Ice Bay
C. Batterbee

Stanley
Falkland Is.
(Br.)

South
Orkney Is.
Coronation I.

C. Norvegia
Seal
Bay
Maudheim
New Schwabenland
PRINCESS RAGNHILD
COAST
PRINCE
OLAV COAST

Enderby Land
KEMP
COAST
Edward VIII
Mawson
C. Daly

WEDDELL
SEA

Elephant I.
King George
South Shetland
Is.
Joinville I.
Hope
Bay
James Ross I.

Stancomb-
Wills Ice
Tongue
CAIRD
COAST
Queen Maud Land
60°

C. Horn
Palmer
Arch.
Larsen
Shelf Ice
Hearst I.
LUITPOLD
COAST
80°
MAC-ROBERTSON
COAST
C. Darnley
MacKenzie Bay
Prydz
Bay

SOUTH
AMERICA
Biscoe Is.
Adelaide I.
Vahsel
Bay
Filchner
Ice Shelf
Gardner Bay
LARS CHRISTENSEN
COAST
American
Highland
Vestfold
Hills

Marguerite
Bay
RICHARD BLACK
COAST
Edith Ronne
Land
ROB'T
ENGLISH
COAST
80°
WILHELM II
COAST
West Shelf
Ice
Davis
Sea

Charcot
I.
Alexander I
Ronne
Bay
Joerg
Plateau
QUEEN MARY
COAST
Farr Bay
Shackleton
Shelf
Ice

Peter I
I. (Nor.)
Mt. Ulmer
12,500
Sentinel Mts.
EIGHTS
COAST
South Polar Plateau
SOUTH POLE
Amundsen Dec. 17, 1911
Scott Jan. 17, 1912
Byrd Nov. 29, 1929 (airplane)
Mt. Barr Smith
4,320
100°

Thurston Pen.
Ellsworth Highland
Hollick-
Kenyon
Plateau
Queen Maud
Ra.
Scott Glac.
Edward VII
Plateau
Beardmore
Glacier
Mt. Kirkpatrick 14,600
Mt.
Markham
15,100
KNOX
COAST
BUDD
COAST
SABRINA
COAST
Vincennes
Bay

Amundsen
Sea
Marie
Byrd Land
Mt.
Executive Comm. Ra.
15,000
Mt.Sidley
12,000
Rockefeller Plateau
Ross Shelf Ice
Roosevelt I.
Mt. Lister
13,350
BANZARE
COAST

C. Dart
Getz Shelf Ice
HOBBS
COAST
Edsel Ford Ra.
Little America
Kainan Bay
Ross I.
McMurdo
Sd.
Victoria Land
Mt. Nansen
7,800
C. Goodenough
C. Keltie

BELLINGSHAUSEN SEA
80°
Siple
PACIFIC OCEAN
Colbeck
Bay
Ross
Sea
B
SOUTH
MAGNETIC
POLAR AREA
GEORGE V
COAST
Adélie
Land
Port-Martin
Pt. Géologie

ROSS DEPENDENCY (N. Z.)
Mt.
Sabine
10,000
C. Adare
Lillie
Glacier Tongue
Ninnis
Glacier
Tongue
Mertz
Glacier
Tongue
FRENCH
SECTOR

70°
C
Scott I.
Balleny Is.
AUSTRALIAN
ANTARCTIC TERR.
Limit of Drift Ice

Antarctic Circle
60°

D
Macquarie I.
(Australia)
140°

PACIFIC OCEAN
Campbell I.
(N. Z.)

50°
Auckland Is.
(N. Z.)
Tasman
King
I.
Hobart
Tasmania

Antipodes Is.
(N. Z.)
E
Bounty Is.
(N. Z.)
Stewart I.
Sea
Furneaux
Gr.
Melbourne

Dunedin
NEW
ZEALAND
AUSTRALIA

Copyright by C. S. Hammond & Co., N.Y.

11   160° Longitude West 10 of Greenwich   180° Longitude East 9 of Greenwich   160°   8

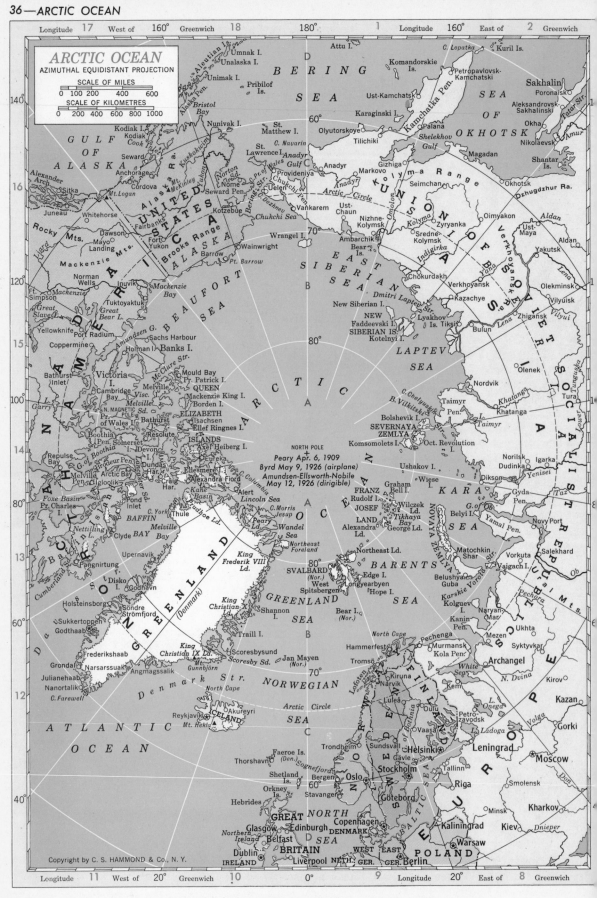

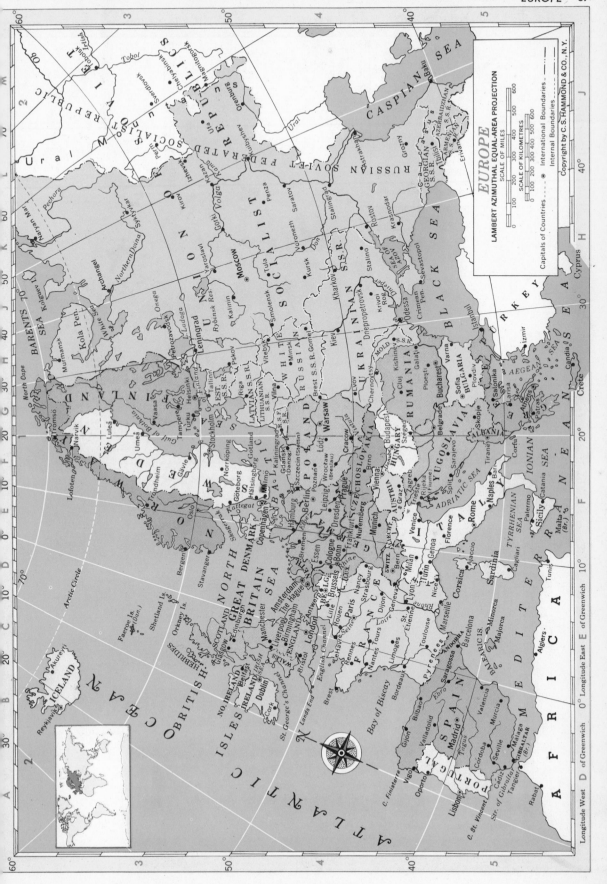

EUROPE

LAMBERT AZIMUTHAL EQUAL-AREA PROJECTION

SCALE OF MILES

0   100   200   300   400   500   600

SCALE OF KILOMETRES

0 100 200 300 400 500 600

Capitals of Countries · · · · · ·   International Boundaries · · · · · ·
Internal Boundaries · · · · · ·

Copyright by C. S. HAMMOND & CO., N.Y.

ATLANTIC OCEAN

ARCTIC OCEAN

BARENTS SEA

North Cape

NORWAY

SWEDEN

FINLAND

ICELAND

Reykjavik

Akureyi

Faeroe Is. (Dan.)

Shetland Is.

Orkney Is.

HEBRIDES

BRITISH ISLES

SCOTLAND

Glasgow

Edinburgh

NO. IRELAND

Belfast

IRELAND

Dublin

Cork

WALES

ENGLAND

GREAT BRITAIN

Liverpool

Manchester

Birmingham

London

IRISH SEA

St. George's Channel

Lands End

Bristol

English Channel

Brest

Bay of Biscay

c. Finisterre

PORTUGAL

Oporto

Lisbon

C. St. Vincent

SPAIN

Madrid

Vigo

Gijon

Valladolid

Bilbao

Ebro

Saragossa

Barcelona

BALEARIC IS.

Minorca

Majorca

Valencia

Cordoba

Seville

Cadiz

Str. of Gibraltar

GIBRALTAR (Br.)

Tangier

Rabat

Murcia

Malaga

Algiers

Tunis

AFRICA

MEDITERRANEAN SEA

FRANCE

Paris

Rouen

Le Havre

Rennes

Nantes

Tours

Loire

Bordeaux

Toulouse

Pyrenees

Marseille

Lyon

St. Etienne

Limoges

Dijon

Nancy

Strasbourg

Nice

Rhône

Seine

Corsica (Fr.)

Ajaccio

Sardinia

Cagliari

DENMARK

Copenhagen

Kattegat

Skagerrak

Oslo

Stavanger

Bergen

Trondheim

Narvik

Lofoten Is.

Tromsö

Arctic Circle

Stockholm

Göteborg

Malmö

Gotland

Hälsingborg

Norrköping

Gävle

Umeå

Luleå

Gulf of Bothnia

Vaasa

Turku

Tampere

Helsinki

BALTIC SEA

NORTH SEA

NETHERLANDS

Amsterdam

The Hague

Antwerp

BELGIUM

Brussels

LUX.

GERMANY

Cologne

Bonn

Essen

Bremen

Hamburg

Elbe

Berlin

Leipzig

Dresden

Frankfurt

Nuremberg

Munich

Rhine

Stuttgart

SWITZ.

Bern

Geneva

Milan

Turin

Genoa

ITALY

Rome

Florence

Venice

Trieste

Naples

TYRRHENIAN SEA

Sicily

Palermo

Catania

Malta (Br.)

AUSTRIA

Vienna

Graz

Danube

POLAND

Warsaw

Cracow

Lódz

Poznań

Wrocław (Breslau)

Gdańsk (Danzig)

Stettin (Szczecin)

Brno

Prague

CZECHOSLOVAKIA

HUNGARY

Budapest

Szeged

YUGOSLAVIA

Zagreb

Rijeka (Fiume)

Split

Belgrade

Sarajevo

Skoplje

ADRIATIC SEA

Bari

Tirane

ALBANIA

Corfu

IONIAN SEA

GREECE

Athens

Larisa

Patras

AEGEAN SEA

Crete

Candia

Corinth

Salonika

RUMANIA

Bucharest

Ploesti

Cluj

Galati

BULGARIA

Sofia

Varna

Plovdiv

BLACK SEA

Istanbul

TURKEY

Izmir

Cyprus

Crimean Pen.

SEA OF AZOV

Sevastopol

Odessa

Dnieper

UKRAINIAN S.S.R.

Kiev

Dnepropetrovsk

Krivoi Rog

Stalino

Chernovtsy

Kishinev

MOLD. S.S.R.

Lvov

WHITE RUSSIAN S.S.R.

Minsk

Gomel

Brest

Vitebsk

Smolensk

LITHUANIAN S.S.R.

LATVIAN S.S.R.

Riga

EST. S.S.R.

Tallinn

Pskov

Kaliningrad

KARELO FINNISH S.S.R.

Leningrad

Ladoga

Onega

Petrozavodsk

White Sea

Kola Pen.

Murmansk

Archangel

Kolguev I.

Narian Mar

Pechora

Syktyvkar

Northern Dvina

Sukhona

RUSSIAN SOVIET FEDERATED SOCIALIST REPUBLIC

Moscow

Kalinin

Rybinsk Res.

Yaroslavl

Gorki

Volga

Kazan

Kuibyshev

Penza

Saratov

Stalingrad

Don

Voronezh

Kursk

Tula

Kharkov

Rostov

Krasnodar

CASPIAN SEA

Astrakhan

Ural

Baku

AZERBAUDZHAN S.S.R.

ARMENIAN S.S.R.

Erivan

GEORGIAN S.S.R.

Tbilisi

Grozny

Ufa

Perm

Kama

Kirov

UNION

Kotlas

Molotov

Sverdlovsk

Chelyabinsk

Magnitogorsk

URAL

Tobol

Tobolsk

Irtish

FINLAND

Longitude West   D   of Greenwich   0° Longitude East   E   of Greenwich   10°

60°   50°   40°   30°   20°   10°

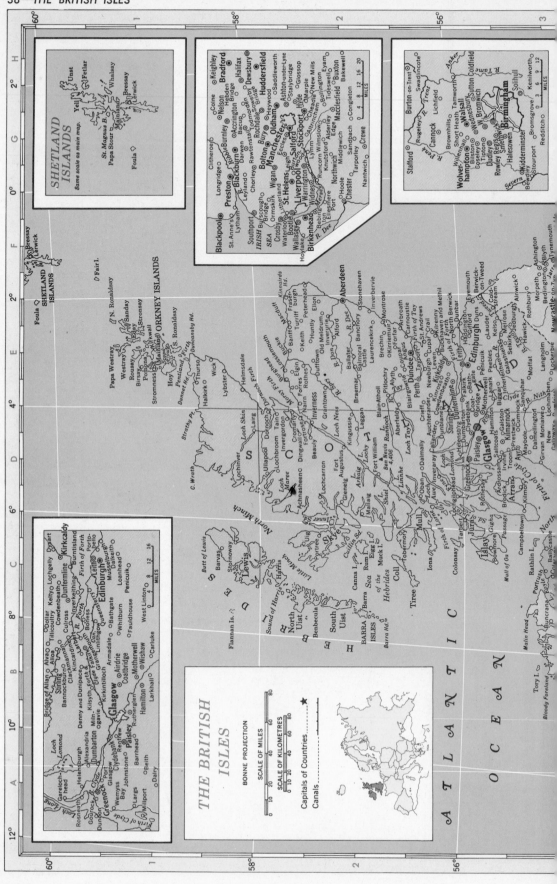

SHETLAND ISLANDS

Same scale as main map.

Yell
Unst
Fetlar
Whalsay
Bressay
Lerwick
Mainland
St. Magnus B.
Papa Stour
Foula

THE BRITISH ISLES

BONNE PROJECTION

SCALE OF MILES

SCALE OF KILOMETRES

Capitals of Countries
Canals

SHETLAND ISLANDS
Foula
Fair I.

ORKNEY ISLANDS
Papa Westray
Westray
Rousay
Sanday
N. Ronaldsay
Stronsay
Birsay
Stromness
Kirkwall
Hoy
S. Ronaldsay
Pentland Firth
Duncansby Hd.

SCOTLAND

C. Wrath
Durness
Strathy Pt.
Tongue
Thurso
Dunnet Hd.
Wick
Lochinver
Ullapool
Loch Shin
Lairg
Helmsdale
Lybster
Halkirk
Dornoch
Tain
Dingwall
Cromarty
Invergordon
Fortrose
Nairn
Forres
Elgin
Lossiemouth
Buckie
Banff
Fraserburgh
Peterhead
Keith
Huntly
Ellon
Old Meldrum
Dufftown
Rothes
Kinnairds Hd.

Loch Maree
Achnasheen
Lochcarron
Kyle
Loch Ness
Inverness
Grantown
Ballater
Balmoral Castle
Braemar
Alford
R. Don
R. Dee
Aberdeen
Stonehaven
Inverbervie

Gairloch
Portree
Skye
Cuillin Sd.
Glenelg
Fort Augustus
Arkaig
Loch Lochy
Loch Ness
Kingussie
Blair-Atholl
Ben Nevis 4,406
Fort William
Laggan
Pitlochry
Brechin
Montrose

Rum I.
Muck I.
Eigg
Mallaig
Loch Shiel
Loch Linnhe
Ballachulish
Oban
Dalmally
Crieff
Taymouth
Killin
Aberfeldy
R. Tay
Perth
Blairgowrie
Forfar
Arbroath
Carnoustie
Firth of Tay
Dundee
Cupar
St. Andrews
Newburgh
Auchterarder

Coll
Tobermory
Mull
Loch Awe
Inveraray
Lochgilphead
Loch Lomond
Callander
Stirling
Dunfermline
Dunblane
Bridge of Allan

Tiree
Iona
Colonsay
Jura
Gigha
Tarbert
Islay
Campbeltown
Mull of Oa
Mull of Kintyre

Inner Hebrides
North Minch
Little Minch
North Uist
South Uist
Benbecula
Barra
BARRA ISLES
Sound of Harris
Harris
Lewis
Stornoway
Barvas
Butt of Lewis
Flannan Is.
OUTER HEBRIDES

Eyemouth
Berwick-on-Tweed
Coldstream
Kelso
Jedburgh
Hawick
Langholm
Lockerbie
Moffat
Sanquhar
New Cumnock
Dalmellington
Maybole
Girvan
Ballantrae
Stranraer
Newton Stewart
Wigtown
Whithorn
Dumfries
R. Nith
Kirkcudbright
Gatehouse
Castle Douglas
Dalbeattie

Tory I.
Bloody Foreland
Gweebarra
Malin Head
Inishowen
Buncrana
Moville
Portrush
Coleraine
Ballycastle
Rathlin I.

ATLANTIC OCEAN

ATLANTIC OCEAN

Inset: Glasgow region

Loch Lomond
Loch Long
Gareloch
Helensburgh
Rosneath
Garelochhead
Gourock
Greenock
Port Glasgow
Dumbarton
Alexandria
Kilsyth
Denny and Dunipace
Bonnybridge
Falkirk
Grangemouth
Bo'ness
Linlithgow
Bathgate
Whitburn
Fauldhouse
West Linton
Penicuik
Loanhead
Musselburgh
Leith
Edinburgh
Queensferry
Dalkeith
Inverkeithing
Dunfermline
Cowdenbeath
Kelty
Kinross
Dollar
Tillicoultry
Alloa
Alva
Clackmannan
Culross
Burntisland
Porto-bello
Dysart
Kirkcaldy
Leslie
Markinch
Bridge of Allan
Stirling
Bannockburn
Kincardine
Firth of Forth
Firth of Clyde
Wemyss Bay
Largs
Millport
Dunoon
Kirn
Johnstone
Barrhead
Beith
Dalry
Paisley
Renfrew
Clydebank
Glasgow
Rutherglen
Cambuslang
Coatbridge
Airdrie
Bathgate
Motherwell
Hamilton
Wishaw
Carluke
Larkhall
Kintilloch
Armadale

MILES

Inset: Liverpool / Manchester region

Clitheroe
Longridge
Colne
Keighley
Nelson
Bradford
Preston
Ribble
Burnley
Hebden Bridge
Halifax
Blackburn
Accrington
Bacup
Darwen
Rawtenstall
Todmorden
Dewsbury
Lytham
Leyland
Chorley
Bury
Rochdale
Huddersfield
St. Anne's
Blackpool
Southport
Ormskirk
Wigan
Bolton
Heywood
Oldham
Eccles
Manchester
Saddleworth
Ashton-under-Lyne
Stalybridge
IRISH SEA
Crosby
Bootle
Waterloo
Liverpool
St. Helens
Leigh
Warrington
Stockport
Hyde
Glossop
Cheadle
Wilmslow
New Mills
Marple
Bollington
Buxton
Birkenhead
Wallasey
Hoylake
Bebington
Widnes
Runcorn
Lymm
Knutsford
Alderley Edge
Macclesfield
Eyam
Bakewell
Hoole
R. Dee
Ellesmere Port
Northwich
Middlewich
Sandbach
Congleton
Tarporley
Chester
Nantwich
Crewe
MILES

Inset: Birmingham region

Burton-on-Trent
Swadlincote
R. Trent
R. Tame
Anker
Stafford
Tamworth
Rugeley
R. Penk
Cannock
Lichfield
Brownhills
Shot Heath
Sutton Coldfield
Walsall
Wolverhampton
Willenhall
Wednesbury
W. Bromwich
Bilston
Coseley
Smethwick
Birmingham
Solihull
Kenilworth
Dudley
Rowley Regis
Halesowen
Bewdley
Stourport
Kidderminster
Bromsgrove
Redditch
R. Severn
MILES

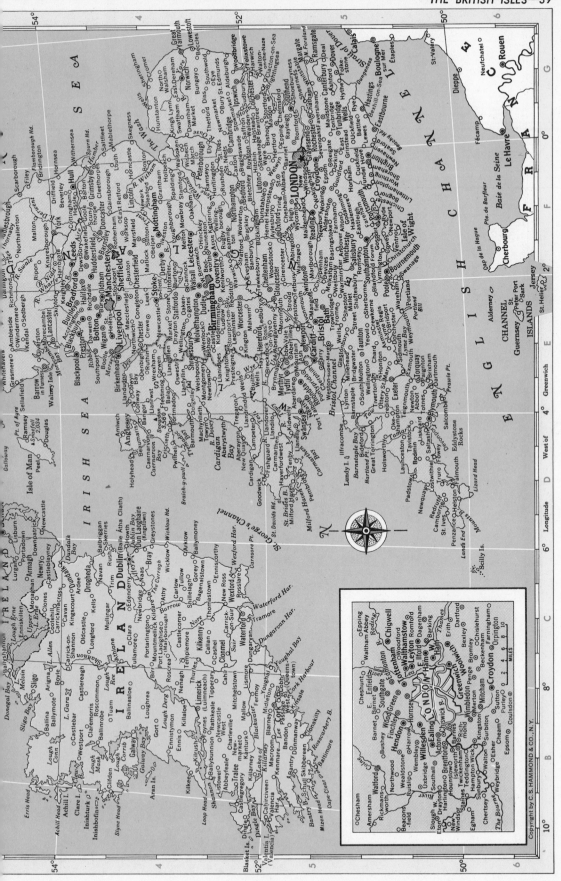

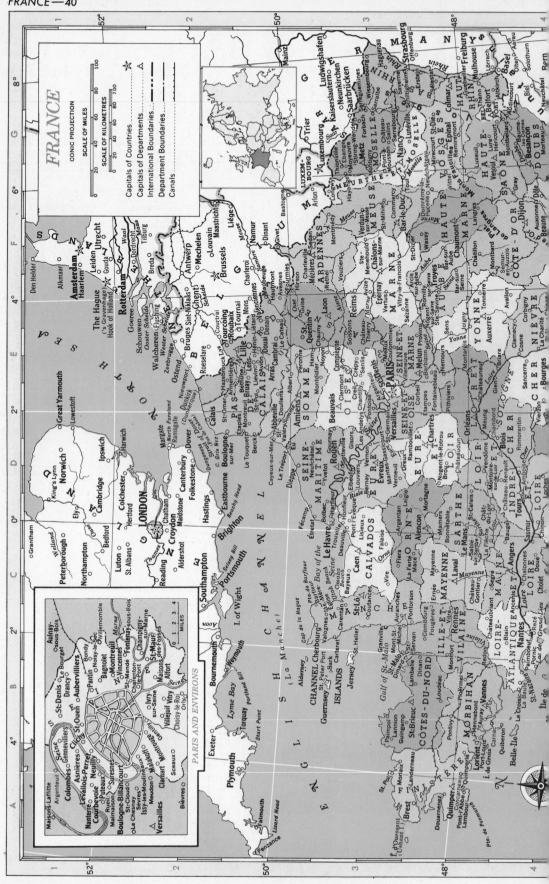

FRANCE

CONIC PROJECTION

SCALE OF MILES

SCALE OF KILOMETRES

Capitals of Countries ....
Capitals of Departments ....
International Boundaries ....
Department Boundaries ....
Canals ....

PARIS AND ENVIRONS

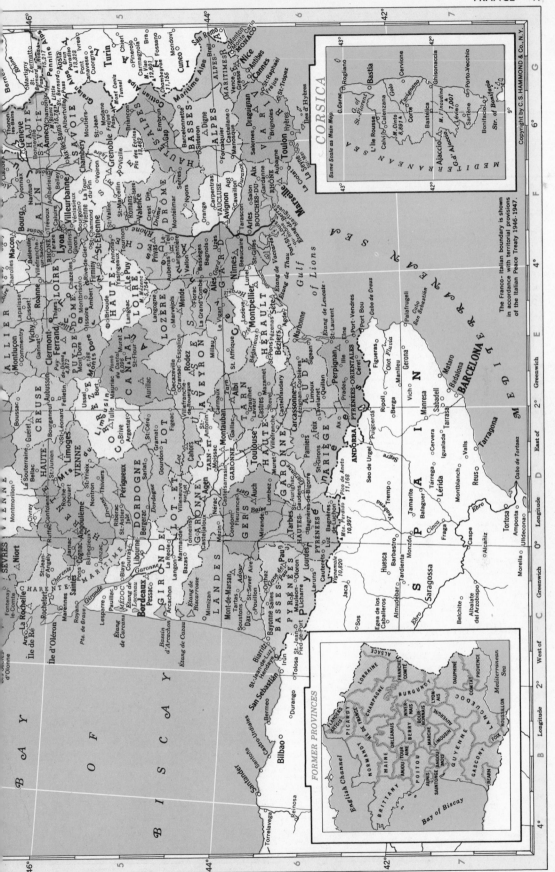

Copyright by C. S. HAMMOND & CO., N.Y.

The Franco-Italian boundary is shown in accordance with territorial provisions of the Italian Peace Treaty 1946-1947.

GERMANY

CONIC PROJECTION

SCALE OF MILES
0 10 20   40   60

SCALE OF KILOMETRES
0 10 20   40   60

Capitals of Countries ☆
State and District Capitals △
Canals

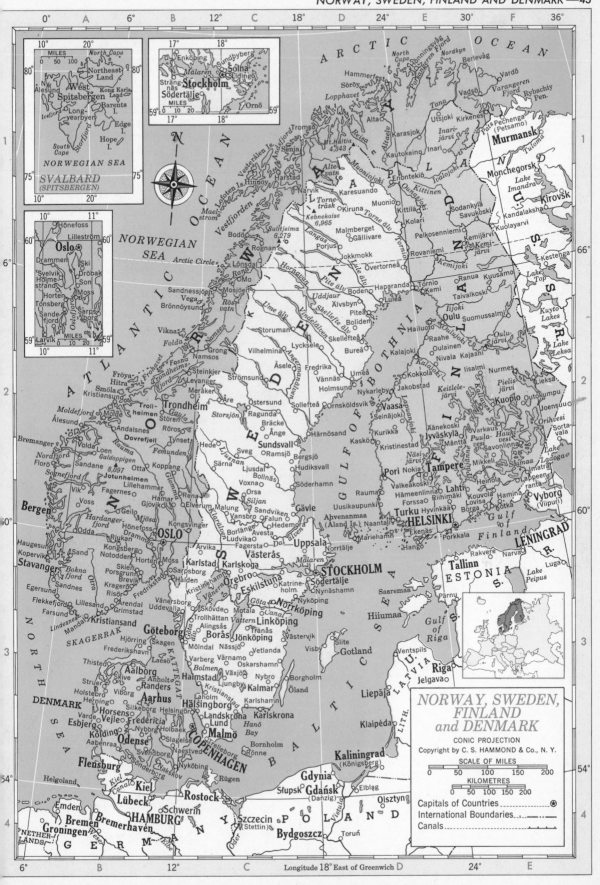

NORWAY, SWEDEN,
FINLAND
and DENMARK

CONIC PROJECTION

Copyright by C. S. HAMMOND & Co., N. Y.

SCALE OF MILES

0   50   100   150   200

KILOMETRES

0   50   100   150   200

Capitals of Countries .... ⊛
International Boundaries .... ———
Canals .... ———

Longitude 18° East of Greenwich

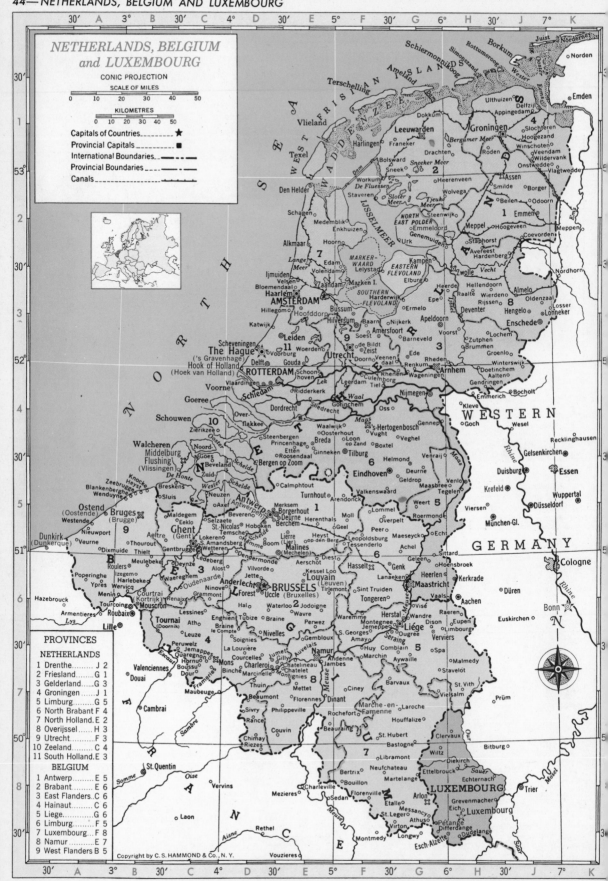

NETHERLANDS, BELGIUM
and LUXEMBOURG

CONIC PROJECTION

SCALE OF MILES

0 10 20 30 40 50

KILOMETRES

0 10 20 30 40 50

Capitals of Countries............★
Provincial Capitals............■
International Boundaries........
Provincial Boundaries..........
Canals.........................

PROVINCES

NETHERLANDS
1 Drenthe..........J 2
2 Friesland........G 1
3 Gelderland.......G 3
4 Groningen........J 1
5 Limburg..........G 5
6 North Brabant....F 4
7 North Holland....E 2
8 Overijssel.......H 3
9 Utrecht..........F 3
10 Zeeland.........C 4
11 South Holland...E 3

BELGIUM
1 Antwerp..........E 5
2 Brabant..........E 6
3 East Flanders....C 6
4 Hainaut..........E 6
5 Liege............G 6
6 Limburg..........F 5
7 Luxembourg.......F 8
8 Namur............E 7
9 West Flanders....B 5

Copyright by C. S. HAMMOND & Co., N.Y.

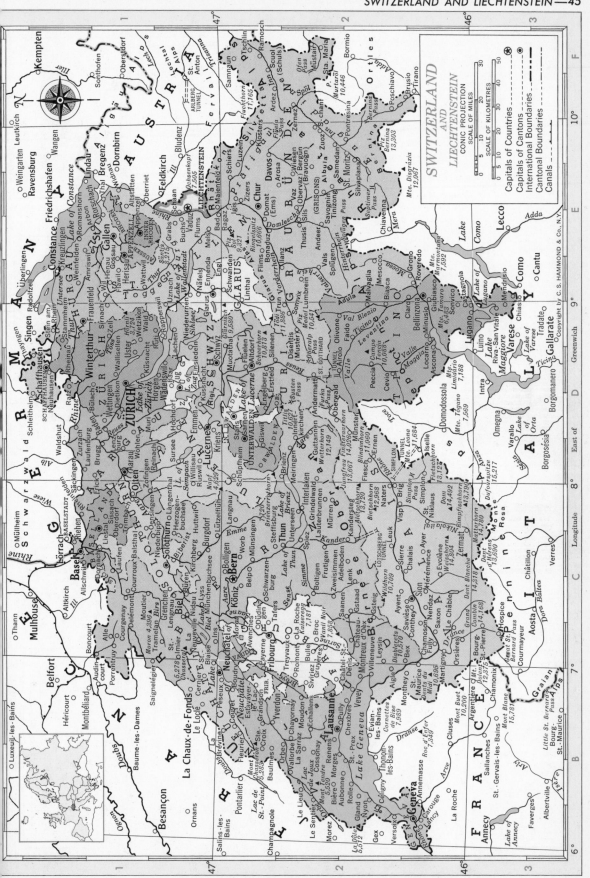

SWITZERLAND
AND
LIECHTENSTEIN
CONIC PROJECTION
SCALE OF MILES

SCALE OF KILOMETRES

Capitals of Countries
Capitals of Cantons
International Boundaries
Cantonal Boundaries
Canals

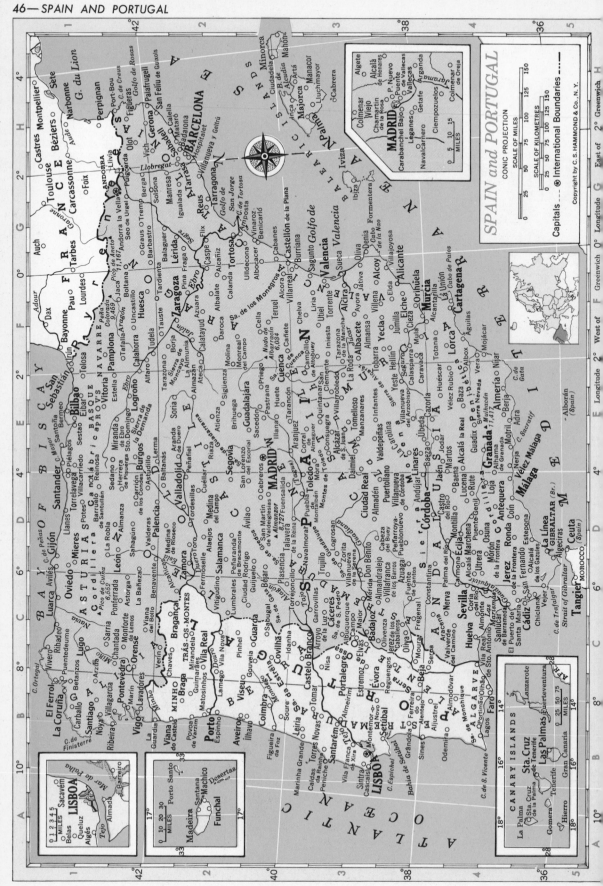

SPAIN and PORTUGAL

CONIC PROJECTION

SCALE OF MILES

SCALE OF KILOMETRES

Capitals ---- ⊛ International Boundaries ------

Copyright by C. S. HAMMOND & Co., N.Y.

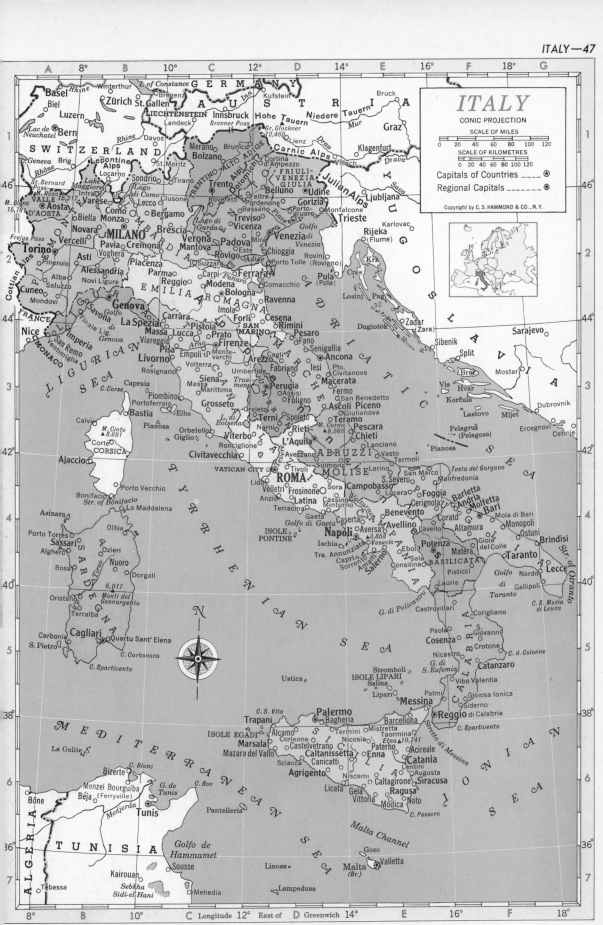

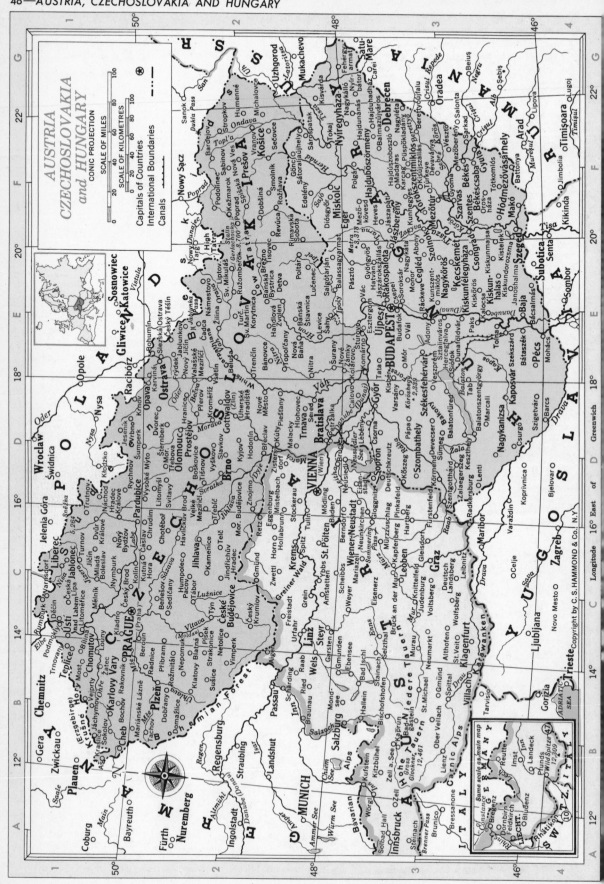

AUSTRIA
CZECHOSLOVAKIA
and HUNGARY
CONIC PROJECTION

SCALE OF MILES

SCALE OF KILOMETRES

Capitals of Countries ⊕
International Boundaries
Canals

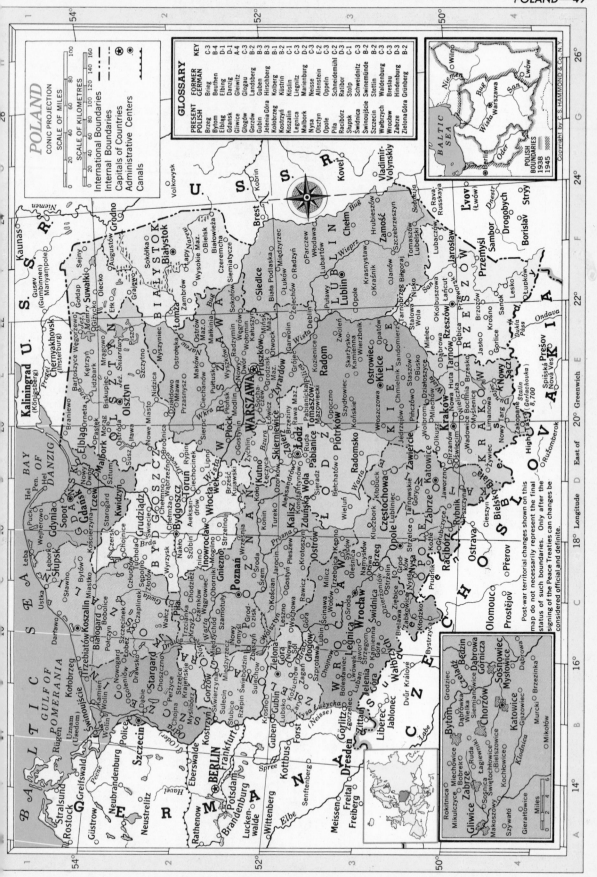

POLAND
CONIC PROJECTION
SCALE OF MILES
SCALE OF KILOMETRES

International Boundaries
Internal Boundaries
Capitals of Countries
Administrative Centers
Canals

GLOSSARY

PRESENT POLISH	FORMER GERMAN	KEY
Brzeg	Brieg	C-3
Bytom	Beuthen	B-4
Elbląg	Elbing	D-1
Gdańsk	Danzig	D-1
Gliwice	Gleiwitz	A-4
Głogów	Glogau	C-3
Gorzów	Landsberg	B-2
Gubin	Guben	B-3
Jelenia Góra	Hirschberg	B-3
Kołobrzeg	Kolberg	B-2
Kostrzyń	Küstrin	B-2
Koszalin	Köslin	C-1
Legnica	Liegnitz	C-3
Malbork	Marienburg	C-1
Nysa	Neisse	C-3
Olsztyn	Allenstein	E-2
Opole	Oppeln	C-3
Piła	Schneidemühl	C-2
Racibórz	Ratibor	D-3
Słupsk	Stolp	C-1
Świdnica	Schweidnitz	C-3
Świnoujście	Swinemünde	B-2
Szczecin	Stettin	B-2
Wałbrzych	Waldenburg	C-3
Wrocław	Breslau	C-3
Zabrze	Hindenburg	D-3
Zielona Góra	Grünberg	B-2

Copyright by C.S. HAMMOND & Co., N.Y.

POLISH BOUNDARIES 1938
1945

Post-war territorial changes shown on this
map do not necessarily represent the final
status of such boundaries. Only after the
signing of the Peace Treaties can changes be
considered official and definite.

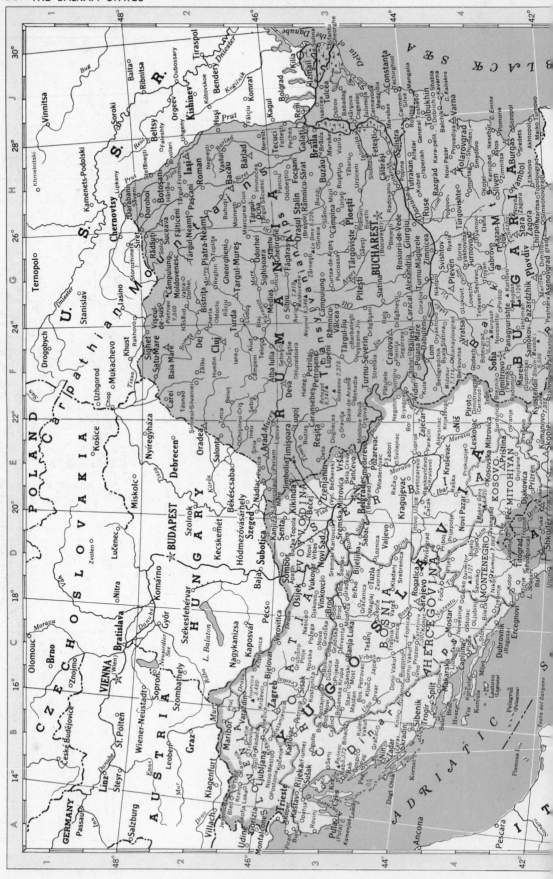

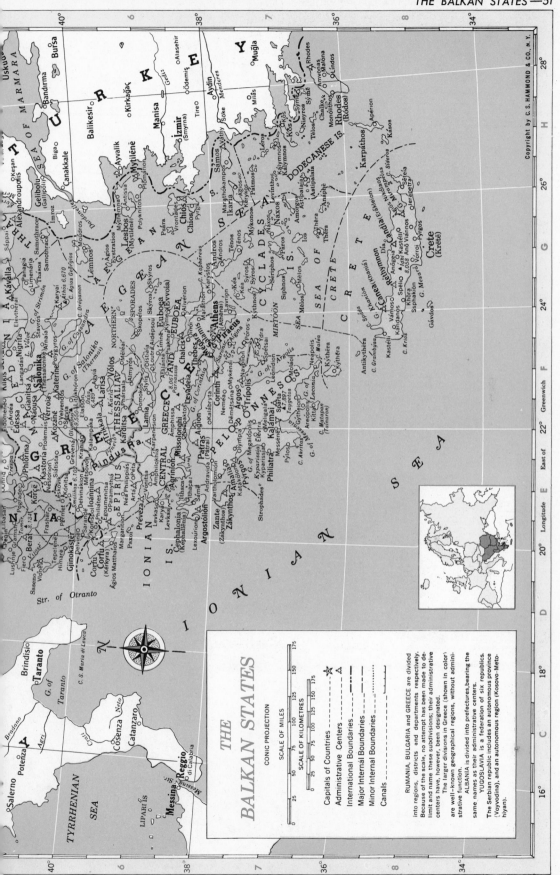

THE
BALKAN STATES

CONIC PROJECTION

SCALE OF MILES

0   25   50   75   100   125   150   175

SCALE OF KILOMETRES

0   25   50   75   100   125   150   175

Capitals of Countries ....⊛
Administrative Centers ....⊛
International Boundaries ....
Major Internal Boundaries ....
Minor Internal Boundaries ....
Canals ....

RUMANIA, BULGARIA and GREECE are divided into regions, districts and departments respectively. Because of the scale, no attempt has been made to delimit and name these subdivisions; their administrative centers have, however, been designated.

The larger divisions in Greece (shown in color) are well-known geographical regions, without administrative function.

ALBANIA is divided into prefectures, bearing the same names as their administrative centers.

YUGOSLAVIA is a federation of six republics. The Serbian republic includes an autonomous province (Voyvodina), and an autonomous region (Kosovo-Metohiyan).

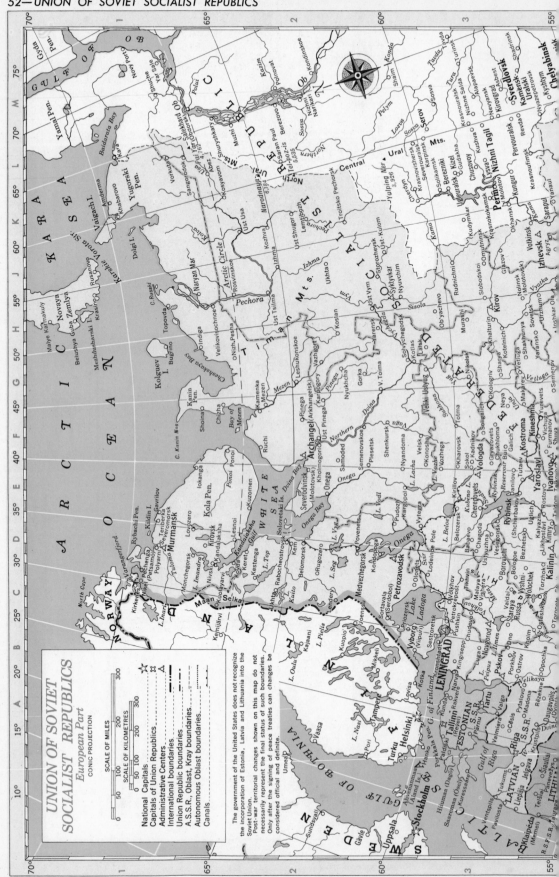

UNION OF SOVIET SOCIALIST REPUBLICS
European Part
CONIC PROJECTION

SCALE OF MILES
0   50 100   200   300

SCALE OF KILOMETRES
0 50 100   200   300

National Capitals..................★ ☆
Capitals of Union Republics.......◉ ◍
Administrative Centers............△ ▵
International boundaries...........————
Union Republic boundaries.........—·—·—
A.S.S.R., Oblast, Kray boundaries.—··—··—
Autonomous Oblast boundaries......·······
Canals...........................————

The government of the United States does not recognize
the incorporation of Estonia, Latvia and Lithuania into the
Soviet Union.
Post-war territorial changes shown on this map do not
necessarily represent the final status of such boundaries.
Only after the signing of peace treaties can changes be
considered official and definite.

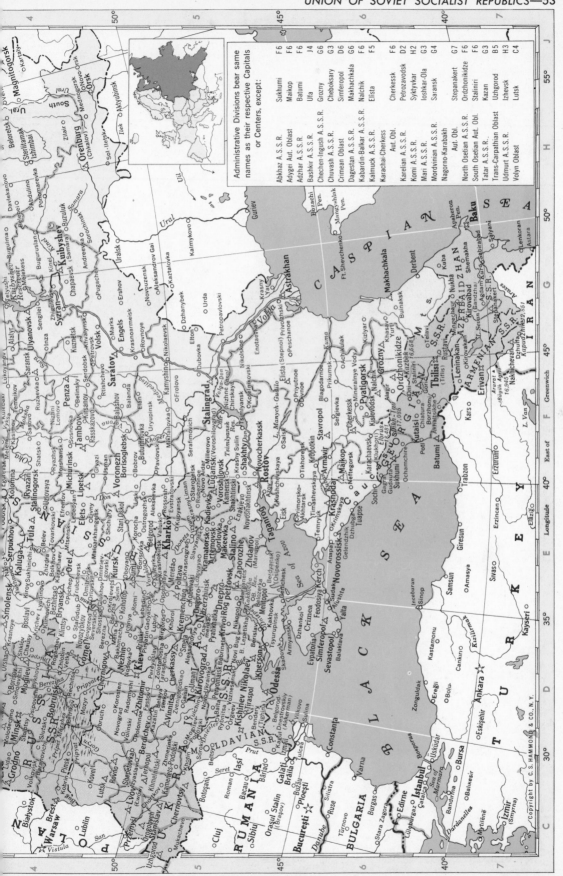

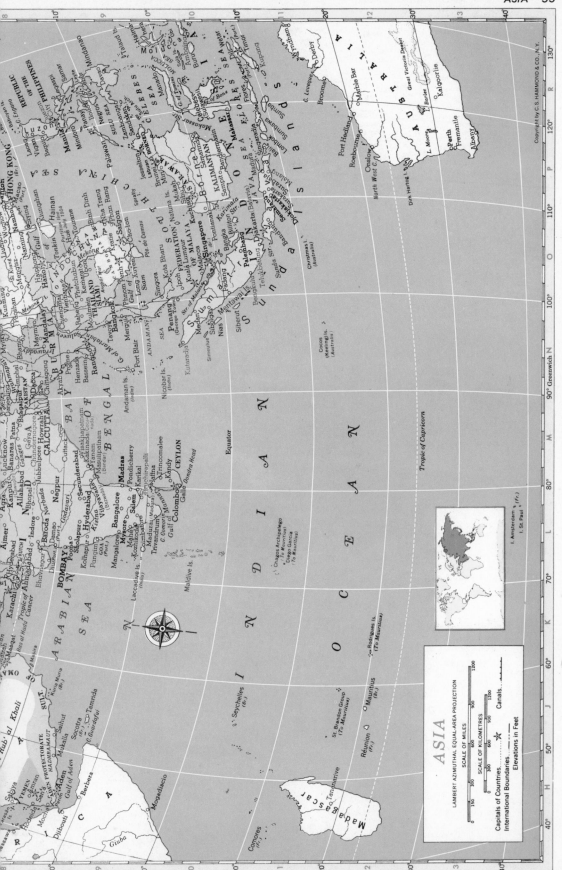

ASIA

LAMBERT AZIMUTHAL EQUAL-AREA PROJECTION

SCALE OF MILES

0   150   300   600   900   1200

SCALE OF KILOMETRES

0   300   600   900   1200

Capitals of Countries..........⭑
International Boundaries..........
Canals..........
Elevations in Feet

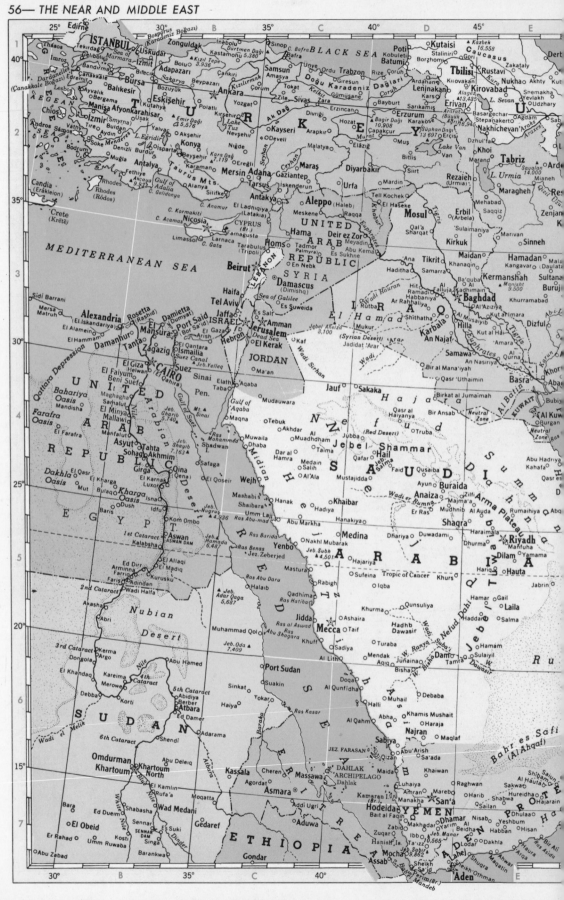

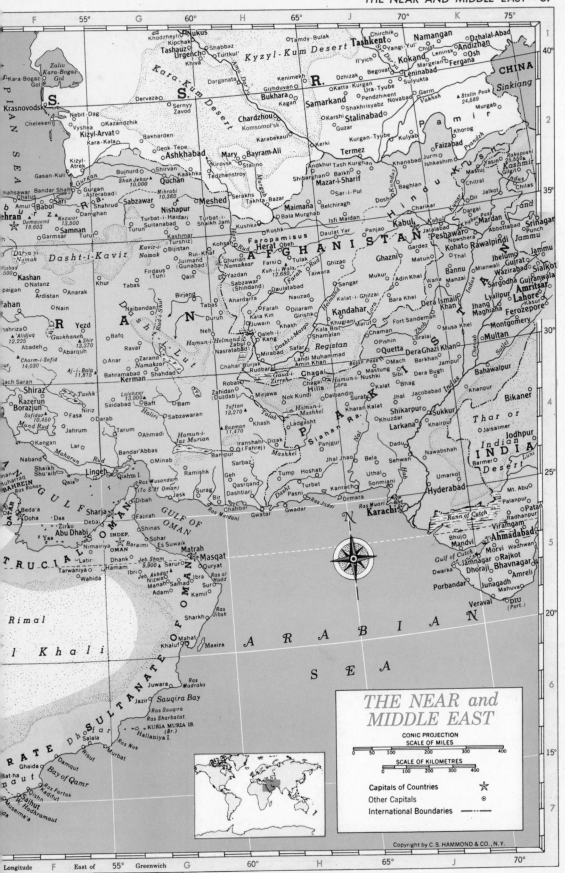

THE NEAR and MIDDLE EAST

CONIC PROJECTION
SCALE OF MILES

0   50   100   200   300   400

SCALE OF KILOMETRES

0   100   200   300   400

Capitals of Countries   ★
Other Capitals   ⊙
International Boundaries   - - - - - -

Copyright by C.S. HAMMOND & CO., N.Y.

Longitude   F   East of   55°   Greenwich   G   60°   H   65°   J   70°

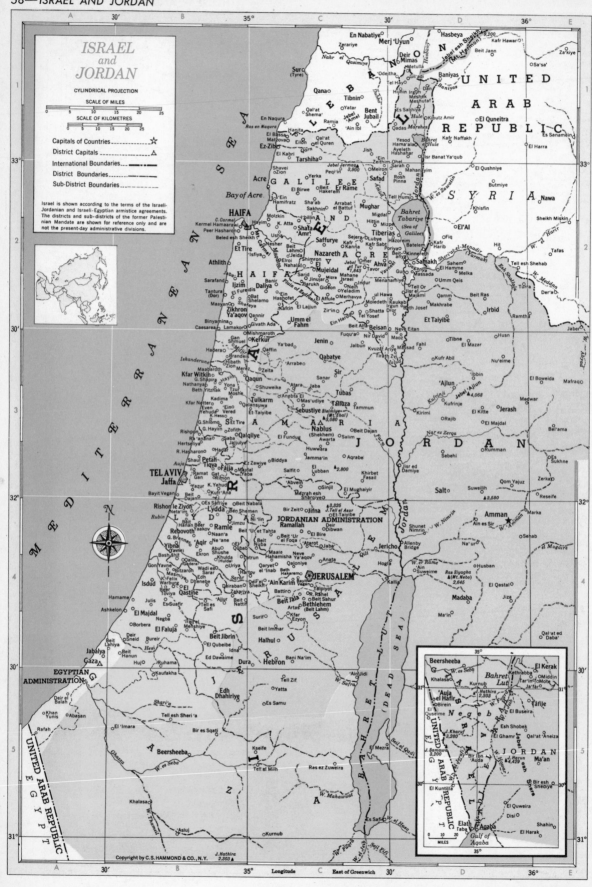

ISRAEL
and
JORDAN

CYLINDRICAL PROJECTION

SCALE OF MILES
0   5   10   15   20   25

SCALE OF KILOMETRES
0   5   10   15   20   25

Capitals of Countries .... ☆
District Capitals .... △
International Boundaries _____
District Boundaries _____
Sub-District Boundaries _____

Israel is shown according to the terms of the Israeli-
Jordanian and Israeli-Egyptian armistice agreements.
The districts and sub-districts of the former Palesti-
nian Mandate are shown for reference only and are
not the present-day administrative divisions.

MEDITERRANEAN SEA

UNITED ARAB REPUBLIC

SYRIA

JORDAN

TEL AVIV
Jaffa

JERUSALEM

HAIFA

Amman

Beersheeba

EGYPTIAN ADMINISTRATION

JORDANIAN ADMINISTRATION
Ramallah

(DEAD SEA)
BAHRET LUT

Gulf of 'Aqaba

Copyright by C. S. HAMMOND & CO., N.Y.

Longitude   East of Greenwich

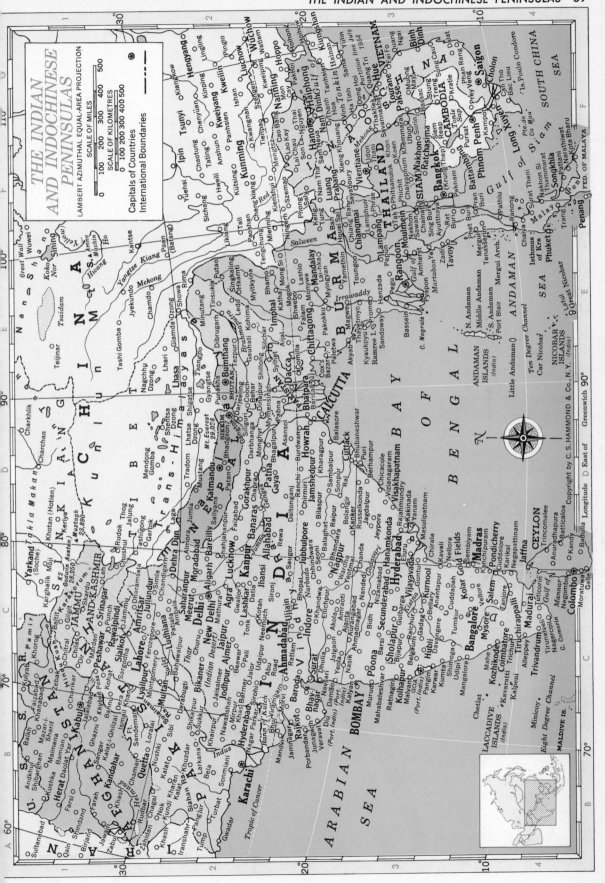

THE INDIAN
AND INDOCHINESE
PENINSULAS

LAMBERT AZIMUTHAL EQUAL-AREA PROJECTION

SCALE OF MILES

0   100   200   300   400   500

SCALE OF KILOMETRES

0   100 200 300 400 500

Capitals of Countries
International Boundaries

EASTERN CHINA,
JAPAN & KOREA

CONIC PROJECTION

SCALE OF MILES

SCALE OF KILOMETRES

Capitals of Countries
Provincial Capitals
Trade Routes
Canals

Copyright by C. S. HAMMOND & Co., N. Y.

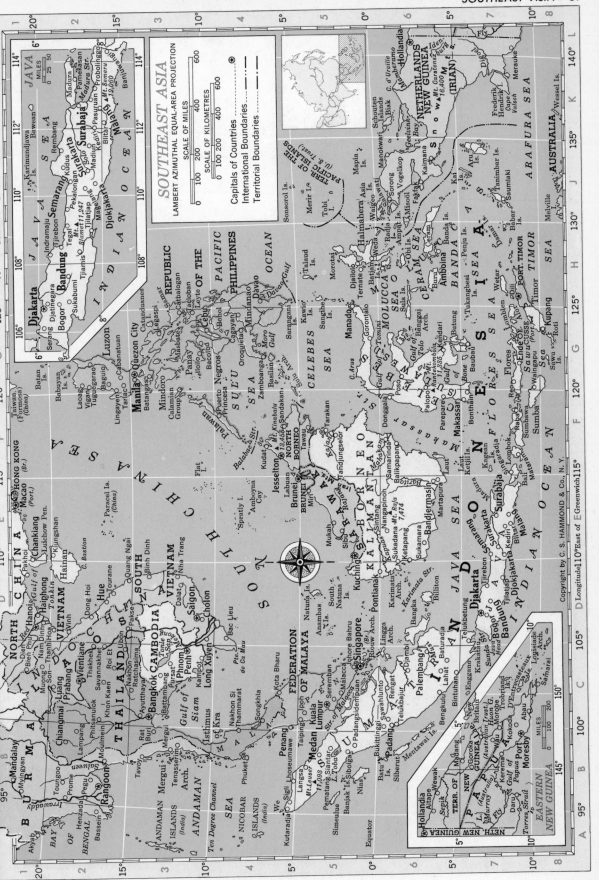

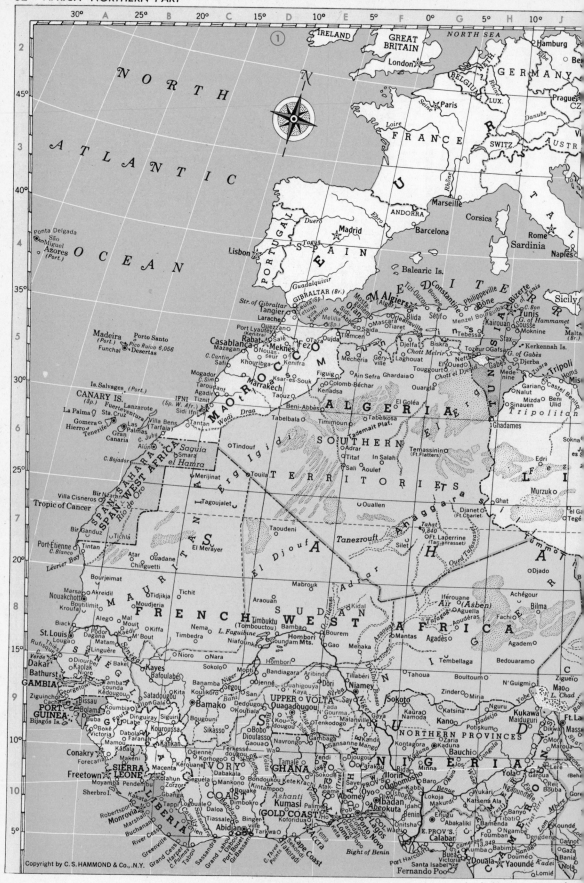

Map continued on

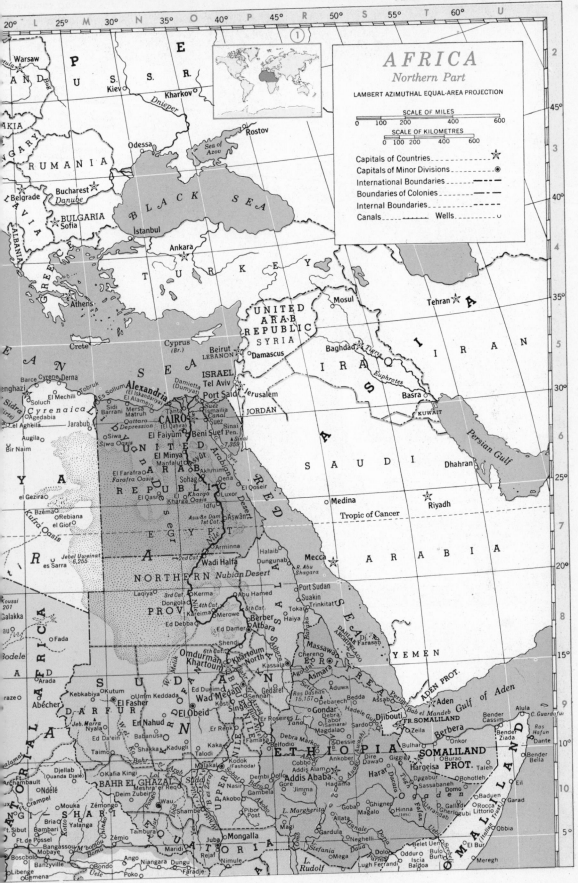

GULF OF GUINEA

Equator

(Sp. Guinea)
Bight of Biafra
Kribi○
Campo○
Dja
Ber
Santo Antonio○
Bata↑
○Ebolova
○Molou
SP.
GUINEA
Rio Muni
○Oyem
Ouess
Príncipe
(Port.)
Los
Elobeyes
I. Corisco○
○Makokou
Makō
Ft. Roust
São Tomé✕
Libreville
Ogoué
São Tomé✕
(Port.)
○N'Djolé
GABON
FRENCH

SOUTH

Annobón •
(Sp. Guinea)
C. Lopez○
Port Gentil○
Sindara○
Lastours-
ville○
Franceville○

Fernand-Vaz○
Bongo○
Setté Cama○
○Dikoudou
Pang
Nyanga○
Mayumba○
○Makabana
M. Brazzavil

• Ascension
(Br.)

A T L A N T I C

Loango○
Loudima○
Luzo
Pointe-Noire○
Landana○
○Ishela
Thys
Cabinda○
Boma○
Matadi○
São
Salvador○
Madi
Santo Antonio○
○Lojé
○Damt
Ambrízete○
Bembe○
Ambríz○
○U
Luanda ✕
○Vila
N
Cuan
G

Porto Amboim○
Novo Redondo○
Lobito○
Benguela○
Nova Lisb
C. de Sta. María○
Cuol
A
Vila da

Sa da Bandeira◉
Capelon
Moçâmedes○
(Mossamedes)
H U I
Porto Alexandre○
Humbe
Pen. de Tigres○
Cunene

O C E A N

C. Frio○
Kaoko
Etosha Pa
St. Helena ○
(Br.)

Tropic of Capricorn

○Otjiwan
SOU
Omaruru
Karibi
Swakopmund○
Walvis B.
U
Walvis Bay○
Re
A
Hollam's Bird I. •
○Mal

Lüderitz○

Port

N

19°
Wolseley○   ○Ceres
Kasteel
Mts.
Malmesbury○
○Hermon
Hex River Mts.
Abbotsdale○
De Doorns○
Kalabaskraal○
Porseleein Berg
Berg
Breede
Goudini Road○
Wellington
Worcester
Groot
Brandvlei○
Nuy○
Tygerberg
Kliphemvel○
Hocks
○Langvlei
SCALE OF MILES
0 5 10   30
Durban-
ville○
○Muldersvlei
Paarl
Robben I.○
Table Bay
Kraaifontein○
Groot Drakenstein○
34°
○Frenchhoek
34°
Capetown✕
○Bellville
Boschjesveld Ra.
Woodstock○
Maitland○
Stellenbosch○
Villiersdorp○
Duiker Pt. △3,582
Wynberg○
5,212△
○Genadendal
○Greyton
Table Mt. △
Somerset
Sneeuw Kop△
Zonder
Einde
Muizenberg○
W.○
○Strand
Seal I.○
○Elgin
Houw Hoek○
Slangkop Pt.○
Fish Hoek○
Gordon○
Bay
○Caledon
○Krige
Simonstown○
False Bay
Bot
River
C. Maclear○
Cape Pt.
Hawston○
Hermanus○
Cape of Good Hope
C. Hangklip○
Sandown
Bay
Mossel River○
Walker Bay

Longitude East of Greenwich 19°

Longitude West of Greenwich   Longitude East of Greenwich

A   25°   B   20°   C   15°   D   10°   E   5°   F   0°   G   5°   H   10°   J   15

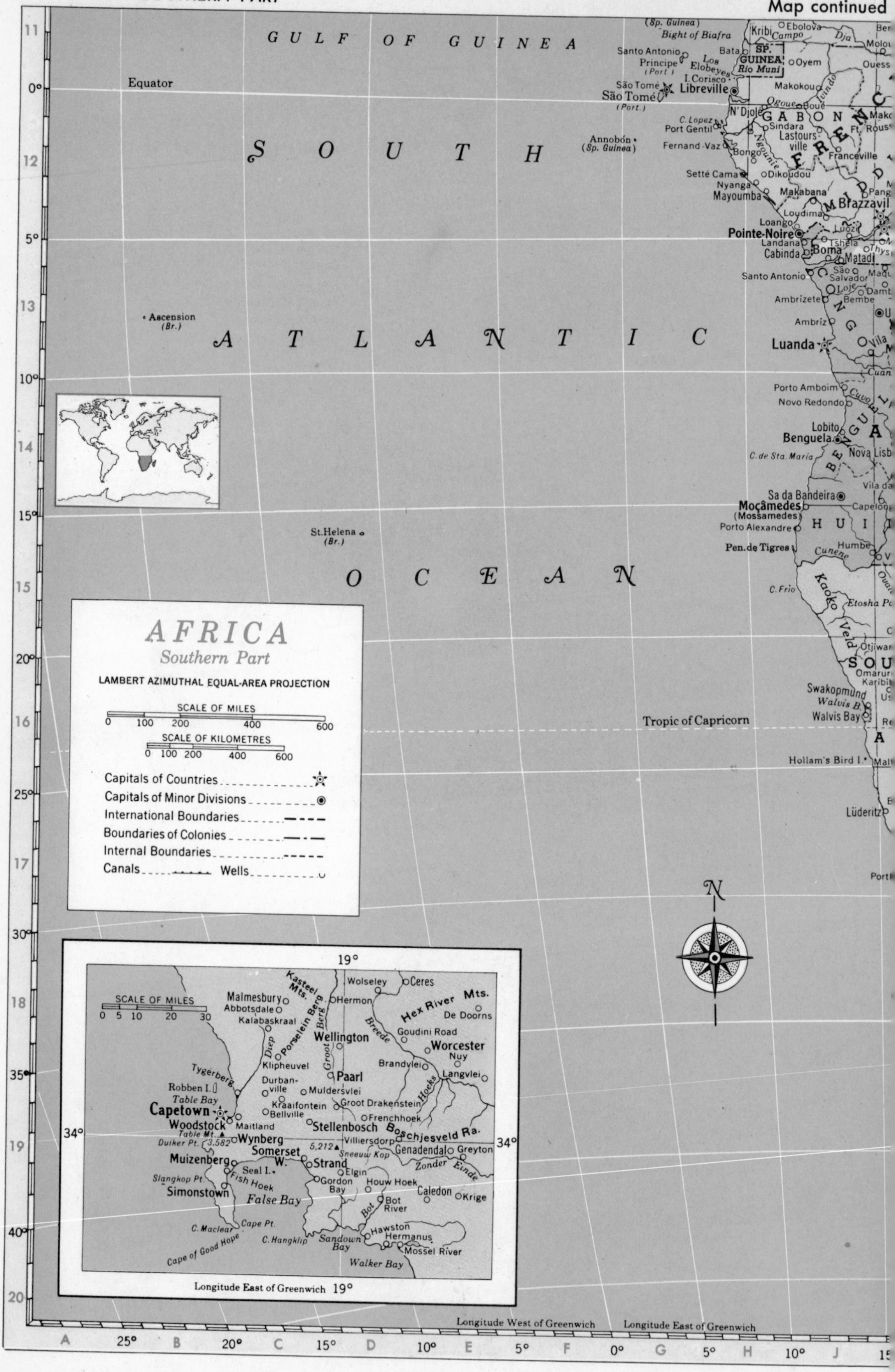

KENYA

UGANDA

BELGIAN CONGO

ORIENTALE

EQUATEUR

KIVU

RUANDA-URUNDI

TANGANYIKA TERR.

KATANGA

ANGOLA

FEDERATION OF RHODESIA

NORTHERN RHODESIA

NYASALAND

SOUTHERN RHODESIA

MOZAMBIQUE

NIASSA

ZAMBEZIA

BECHUANALAND PROT.

Kalahari

SOUTH WEST AFRICA

UNION OF SOUTH AFRICA

CAPE OF GOOD HOPE

ORANGE FREE STATE

BASUTOLAND

SWAZILAND

MADAGASCAR

COMORO IS. (Fr.)

Mozambique Channel

INDIAN OCEAN

Equator

Tropic of Capricorn

Mogadiscio

Marsabit

Nairobi

Mombasa

Zanzibar (Br.)

Dar es Salaam

Lake Tanganyika

Lake Nyasa

Elisabethville

Lusaka

Salisbury

Bulawayo

Livingstone

Johannesburg

Pretoria

Lourenço Marques

Bloemfontein

Kimberley

Durban

Pietermaritzburg

Port Elizabeth

East London

Tananarive

Antsirabe

Fianarantsoa

Tuléar

Fort-Dauphin

Diego Suarez

Majunga

Morondava

11
0°
12
5°
13
10°
14
15°
16
17°
18
19°
20

20° 25° 30° 35° 40° 45° 50° 55° 60°
L   M   N   O   P   R   S   T   U

INSET:

SCALE OF MILES
0   25   50   100

INDIAN OCEAN

MAURITIUS (Br.)

Port Louis

Curepipe

Mahébourg

Morne Brabant 2,711

RÉUNION (Fr.)

St. Denis

Le Port

St. Benoit

Piton des Neiges 10,069

Le Volcan 8,612

St. Pierre

St. Joseph

St. Philippe

55°   56°   57°   58°
Longitude 56° East of Greenwich 57°

20°
35°
21°
40°
20

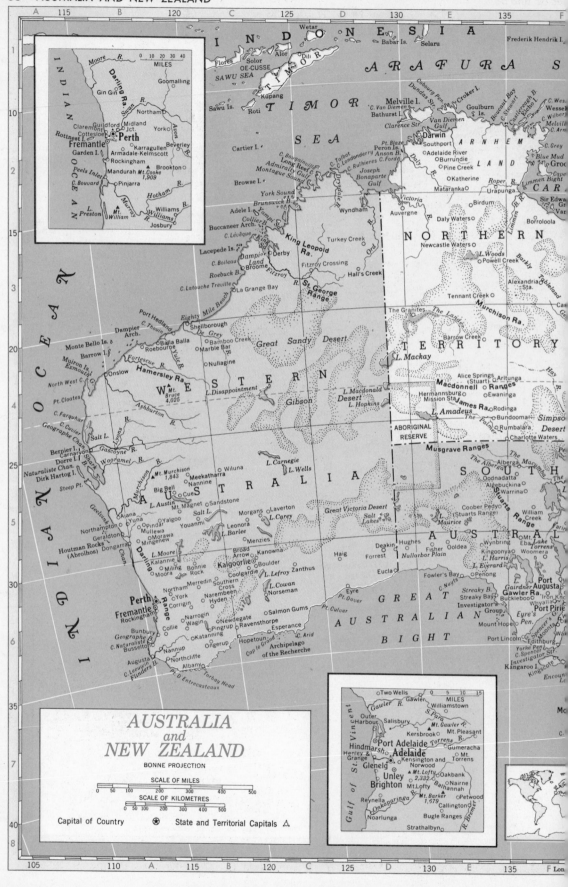

AUSTRALIA
and
NEW ZEALAND

BONNE PROJECTION

SCALE OF MILES

SCALE OF KILOMETRES

Capital of Country ✪   State and Territorial Capitals △

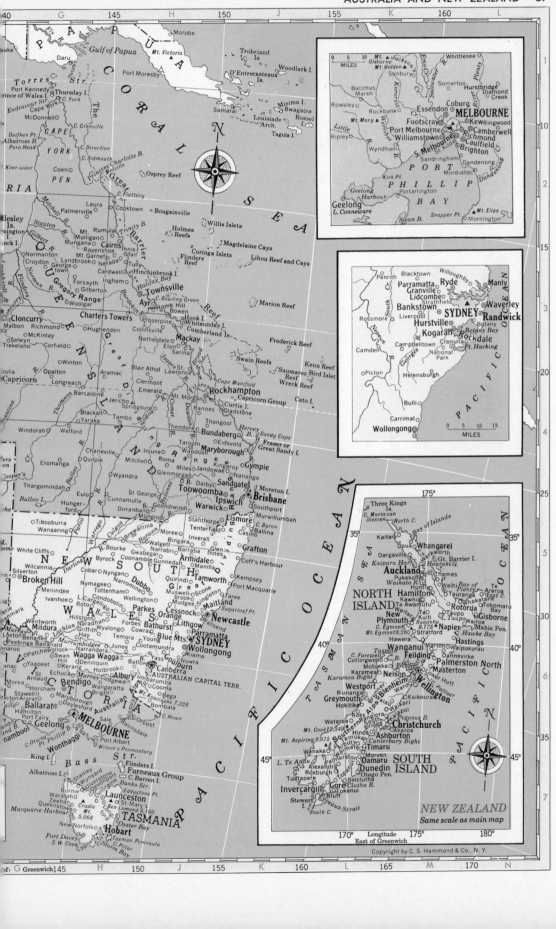

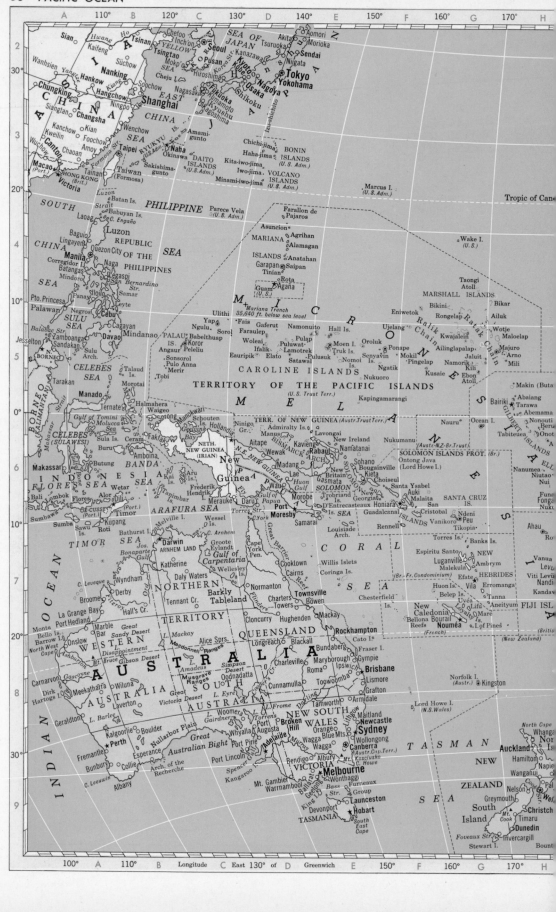

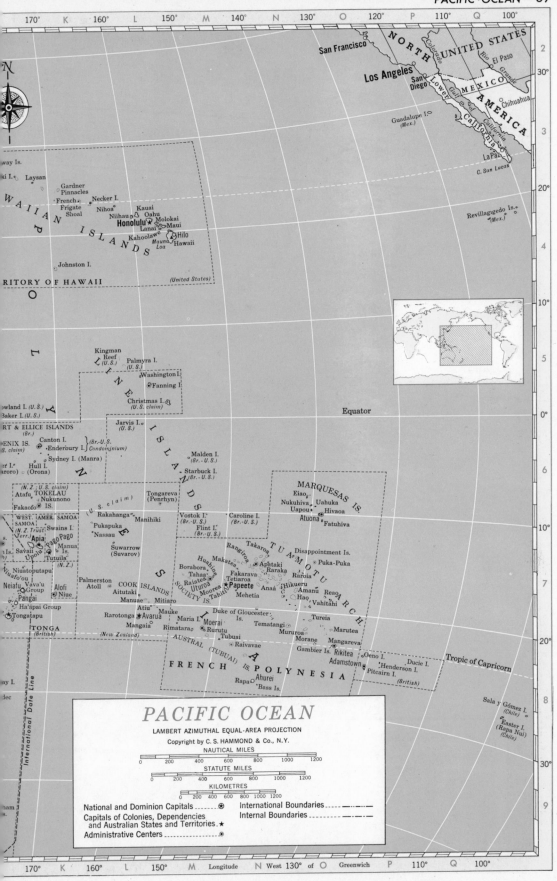

N

170° K 160° L 150° M 140° N 130° O 120° P 110° Q 100°

NORTH UNITED STATES

San Francisco

Los Angeles

San Diego

MEXICO

El Paso

Chihuahua

AMERICA

Lower California

Gulf of California

La Paz

C. San Lucas

Guadalupe I. (Mex.)

Revillagigedo Is. (Mex.)

way Is.

ki I. Laysan

Gardner Pinnacles

French Frigate Shoal

Necker I.

Nihoa

Kauai

Niihau Oahu

Honolulu

Lanai Molokai

Maui

Kahoolawe

Mauna Loa

Hilo

Hawaii

HAWAIIAN ISLANDS

Johnston I.

RITORY OF HAWAII

(United States)

Kingman Reef (U.S.)

Palmyra I. (U.S.)

Washington I.

Fanning I.

Christmas I. (U.S. claim)

owland I. (U.S.)

Baker I. (U.S.)

Jarvis I. (U.S.)

LINE ISLANDS

Equator

RT & ELLICE ISLANDS (Br.)

ENIX IS. (S. claim)

Canton I.

Enderbury I.

(Br.-U.S.) Condominium

Sydney I. (Manra)

er I. (aroro)

Hull I. (Orona)

Malden I. (Br.-U.S.)

Starbuck I. (Br.-U.S.)

(N.Z., U.S. claim)

Atafu TOKELAU

Nukunono

Fakaofo IS.

WEST. SAMOA

AMER. SAMOA

(N.Z. Trust) Terr.

Apia

Upolu

Savaii

Pago Pago

Manua Is.

Tutuila (N.Z.)

Is.

Niuatoputapu

Neiafu Vava'u Group

Niue

Alofi

Pangai

Ha'apai Group

Tongatapu

TONGA (British)

Tongareva (Penrhyn)

Rakahanga

Manihiki

Pukapuka

Nassau

Suwarrow (Suvarov)

Palmerston Atoll

COOK ISLANDS

Aitutaki

Manuae

Mitiaro

Atiu

Mauke

Avarua

Rarotonga

Mangaia

Rimatara

Vostok I. (Br.-U.S.)

Flint I. (Br.-U.S.)

Caroline I. (Br.-U.S.)

SOCIETY IS.

Huahine

Borabora

Tahaa

Raiatea

Moorea

Tetiaroa

Papeete

Tahiti

Mehetia

Maria I.

Moerai

Rurutu

Tubuai

Raivavae

MARQUESAS IS.

Eiao

Nukuhiva

Uapou

Uahuka

Hivaoa

Atuona

Fatuhiva

Takaroa

Rangiroa

Makatea

Apataki

Raraka

Fakarava

Anaa

Hikueru

Amanu

Hao

Vahitahi

Duke of Gloucester Is.

Tematangi

Mururoa

Morane

Gambier Is.

Raroia

Reao

Puka-Puka

Disappointment Is.

TUAMOTU ARCH.

Tureia

Marutea

Mangareva

Rikitea

Adamstown

Pitcairn I.

Oeno I.

Henderson I.

Ducie I.

(British)

Tropic of Capricorn

FRENCH POLYNESIA

AUSTRAL (TUBUAI) IS.

(New Zealand)

Rapa

Ahurei

Bass Is.

Sala y Gómez I. (Chile)

Easter I. (Rapa Nui) (Chile)

PACIFIC OCEAN

LAMBERT AZIMUTHAL EQUAL-AREA PROJECTION

Copyright by C.S. HAMMOND & Co., N.Y.

NAUTICAL MILES

0 200 400 600 800 1000 1200

STATUTE MILES

0 200 400 600 800 1000 1200

KILOMETRES

0 200 400 600 800 1000 1200

National and Dominion Capitals .... ⊗

Capitals of Colonies, Dependencies and Australian States and Territories ..★

Administrative Centers ....

International Boundaries _____

Internal Boundaries ____ ____

International Date Line

170° K 160° L 150° M Longitude N West 130° of O Greenwich P 110° Q 100°

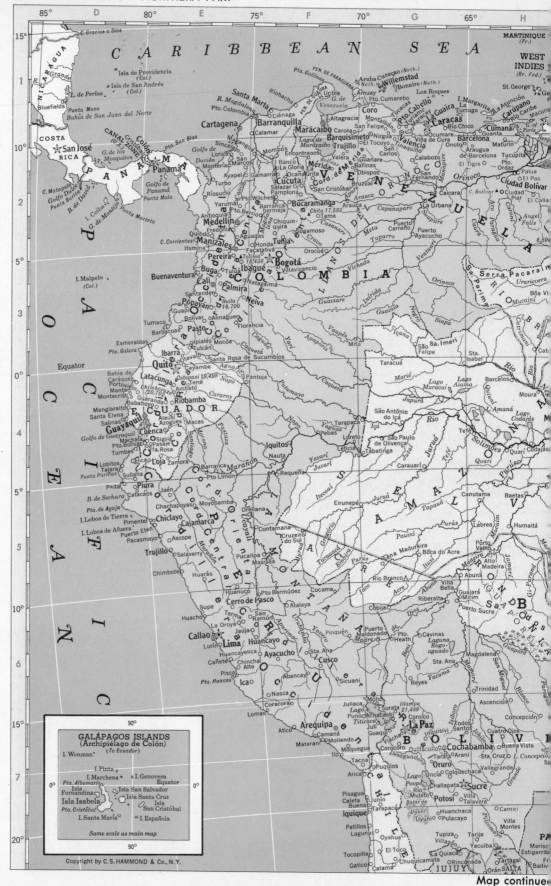

GALÁPAGOS ISLANDS
(Archipiélago de Colón)
(To Ecuador)

I. Wenman

I. Pinta
I. Marchena   I. Genovesa
Pta. Albemarle   Equator
Isla
Fernandina   Isla San Salvador
Isla Isabela   Isla Santa Cruz
Pta. Cristóbal   Isla
I. Santa María   San Cristóbal
I. Española

Same scale as main map

Copyright by C. S. HAMMOND & Co., N.Y.

Map continue

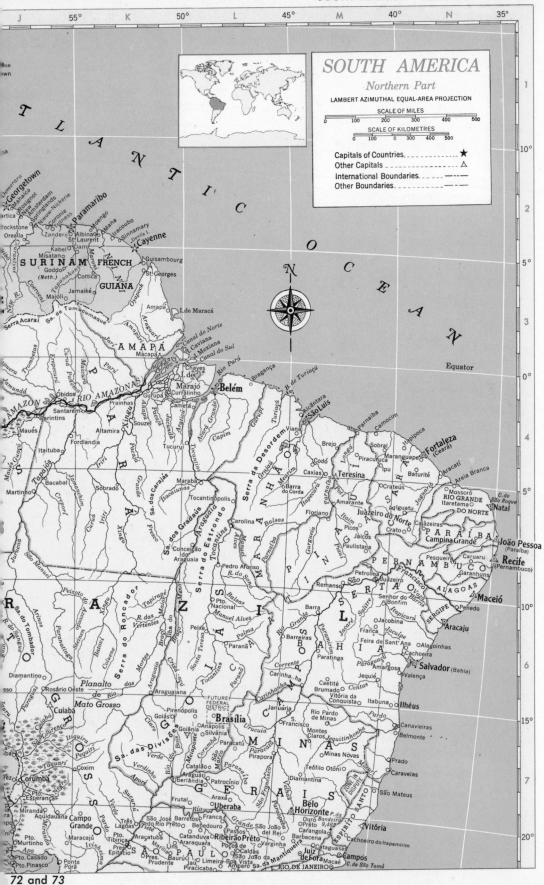

SOUTH AMERICA
Northern Part
LAMBERT AZIMUTHAL EQUAL-AREA PROJECTION
SCALE OF MILES
0   100   200   300   400   500
SCALE OF KILOMETRES
0   100   0   300   400   500

Capitals of Countries............★
Other Capitals.....................△
International Boundaries.........
Other Boundaries.................

ATLANTIC OCEAN

Georgetown
Paramaribo
Cayenne
SURINAM FRENCH
(Neth.)
GUIANA

Equator

AMAPÁ
Macapá
Belém
Marajó
RIO AMAZONAS
AMAZON
Santarém
Óbidos
Maués
Parintins
Itaituba

São Luís
Fortaleza (Ceará)
Teresina
RIO GRANDE DO NORTE
Natal
PARAÍBA
João Pessoa (Paraíba)
Campina Grande
Recife (Pernambuco)
PERNAMBUCO
ALAGOAS
Maceió
SERGIPE
Aracaju
Salvador (Bahia)
Ilhéus

MARANHÃO
PIAUÍ
CEARÁ
Juàzeiro do Norte

SERTÃO
BAHIA

PARÁ

MATO GROSSO
Cuiabá
Corumbá
Campo Grande

GOIÁS
Brasília
FUTURE FEDERAL DISTRICT

MINAS GERAIS
Belo Horizonte
Vitória
ESPÍRITO SANTO
Campos

SÃO PAULO
Ribeirão Prêto
RIO DE JANEIRO

PACIFIC OCEAN

Tropic of Capricorn

8

25°

9

30°

10

35°

11

40°

12

45°

13

50°

55°

15

95° — A

90° — B

85° — C

80° — D

75° — E

70° — F Longitude 65° We

I. de San Félix (Chile) · I. San Ambrosio (Chile)

IS. JUAN FERNÁNDEZ (Chile)
I. Más Afuera · I. Más a Tierra
I. Santa Clara

Mejillones
Antofagasta
Caleta Coloso
Aguas Blancas
Taltal

Chañaral
Pueblo Hundido
Caldera
Copiapó
Juan Godoy
Huasco
Cabo Bascuñan
Vallenar
Cruz Grande Totoral
La Serena
Coquimbo
Tongoy
Ovalle
Illapel
Los Vilos

Viña del Mar
Valparaíso
Santiago
Rancagua
Pichilemu
San Fernando
Curepto
Constitución
Talca
Cauquenes
Quirihue
Linares
Parral
Talcahuano
Concepción Chillán
Arauco
Lota
Lebu
Los Angeles
Cañete
Mulchén
Traiguen
Curacautín
Nueva Imperial
Temuco
Villarrica
Valdivia
Corral
La Unión
Osorno
Puerto Varas
Maullín
Ancud
Castro
Isla de Chiloé
Cabo Quilán
ARCHIPIÉLAGO de los CHONOS
PEN. DE TAITAO
C. Tres Montes
G. de Penas
I. Campana
I. Wellington
I. Madre de Dios
I. Hanover
Estrecho Nelson
ARCHIPIÉLAGO REINA ADELAIDA
Strait of Magellan
I. Desolación
B. Otway
I. Sta. Inés
I. Clarence
I. Stewart
I. Londonderry I. Hoste
I. Hermite
Is. Diego Ramírez

Embarcación
El Chorro
Jujuy Gen. San Martín Rivadavia
Salta
El Quebrachal
Rosario de la Frontera
Alemania
Carlos
Llullaillaco 22,145
Salina de Arizaro
Puna de Atacama
Tucumán
Tintina
Andalgalá Santiago
Catamarca SANTIAGO DEL ESTERO
La Rioja
Patquia Deán Funes
Jachal
Serrezuela
Mar Chiquita
Cruz del Eje
SAN JUAN
San Juan
Villa Dolores
Córdoba
CÓRDOBA
Alta Gracia
Villa María
Aconcagua 22,834
Uspallata Pass
Mendoza
Godoy Cruz Río Cuarto
MENDOZA
San Luis SAN LUIS
Mercedes
Tunuyán Venado Tuerto
Maipu 17,388
San Carlos
San Rafael
Soltue
Gral. Alvear
Laboulaye
Ing. Luiggi
Lago Llancanelo
Telén
Gen. Pico
Sta. Rosa
LA PAMPA
Victorica
Gen. Acha Doblas
NEUQUÉN
Gen. Roca
Bernasconi
Pl. Huincul
Zapala
Picun Leufú
Neuquén
Junín de los Andes
El Cuy
Sierra Colorada
RÍO NEGRO
San Carlos de Bariloche
Nahuel Huapi
Maquinchao
Norquinco
Viedma
Gastre
Telsen
Puerto Madryn
Trelew
Gaiman
Rawson
CHUBUT
Colhué Huapi
Camarones
Comodoro Rivadavia
Golfo San Jorge
Colonia Las Heras
L. Buenos Aires
SANTA CRUZ
Deseado
Puerto Deseado
L. San Martín
L. Cardiel
San Julián
L. Viedma
Santa Cruz
L. Argentino
Bahía Grande
El Turbio
Río Gallegos
Cabo Vírgenes
Pto. Natales
Springhill
Pto. Porvenir
TIERRA DEL FUEGO
Punta Arenas
Río Grande
San Diego
Ushuaia
I. Navarino
B. Nassau
I. Wollaston
Cape Horn

DRAKE PAS

SOUTH AMERICA
Southern Part

LAMBERT AZIMUTHAL EQUAL-AREA PROJECTION

SCALE OF MILES
0   100   200   300   400   500

SCALE OF KILOMETRES
0   100   200   300   400   500

Capitals of Countries .... ★
Other Capitals .... △
International Boundaries .....
Other Boundaries ....

Main map

PARAGUAY · PARANÁ · SANTA CATARINA · RIO GRANDE DO SUL · URUGUAY

Horqueta · San Pedro · Villa · Pto. Guaira · Jacarèzinho · Londrina · Tomasina · Botucatú · Campinas · Jundiaí · Petrópolis · Niterói · Cabo Frio

Bernardino · Pto. Mendes · Ivaí · A. Bernardes · Tibaji · Juquiá · Tietê · Taubaté · S. Sebastião · RIO DE JANEIRO · Tropic of Capricorn

Tacuarú · Ponta Grossa · Foz · Guarapuava · Castro · Ribeira · SÃO PAULO · Santos · Rio dos Reis · Sorocaba

Villarrica · Caazapú · do Iguaçú · Iguaçu · Paranagua · Curitiba

Encarnación · Posadas · MISSIONES · Pto. União · São Francisco do Sul · Joinville · Blumenau · Itajaí

Pilar · Humaitá · Gral. Artigas · Sto. Angelo · Palmeira das Missões · Lajes · Florianópolis · I. Sta. Catarina

Corrientes · Paso I. · Libres · Uruguaiana · Sta. Maria · Ijuí · Cruz Alta · Passo Fundo · Tubarão · Laguna

Artigas · Livramento · Alegrete · Rio Pardo · Verânopolis · Caxias do Sul · Araranguá · Tacuarembó

URUGUAY · Rivera · Bagé · S. Leopoldo · Pôrto Alegre

RIO GRANDE DO SUL · Cachoeira · Lagoa dos Patos · Pelotas · Rio Grande

Bella Unión · Salto · Paysandú · Mercedes · Durazno · Trinidad · Florida · Minas · Jaguarão · Lagoa Mirim · Lagoa da Mangueira

Dolores · Carmelo · San José · Canelones · Rocha · Santa Vitória do Palmar

Colonia · Lacaze · MONTEVIDEO · Maldonado · C. San Antonio

Rio de la Plata · La Plata · Gen. Juan Madariaga · Cucho

Mar del Plata · Gen. Alvarado (Miramar) · Nequén

ATLANTIC OCEAN · PACIFIC OCEAN

NDS · I. · East Falkland · Stanley · Choiseul Sd. · ly I. · ture Sd.

AND IS. · Elephant I. · Clarence I. · SOUTH ORKNEY IS. (Br.) · Coronation I. · Laurie I.

N · wich 55° K · 50° L · 45° M · 40° N · 35° O · 30° P · 25° Q

Inset: Chile — Valparaíso / Santiago region

72°   70°

Petorca · Longotoma · Papudo · La Ligua · Putaendo · Aconcagua 22,834 · La Calera · Llay Llay · San Felipe

Quintero · Quillota · Los Andes · Viña del Mar · P. de Caraumilla · Limache

VALPARAISO · SANTIAGO · B. del Algarrobo · Curacaví · Melipilla · San Bernardo

Cartagena · San Antonio · P. Toro · Paine · El Volcán

P. Topocalma · Rancagua · El Teniente · Maipú 17,388

Las Cabras · Peumo · San Fernando · Santa Cruz · Pichilemu

PACIFIC OCEAN · ARGENTINA · 34° · 30° · 9° · 10°

0 15 30 MILES

Inset: Buenos Aires region

60°   58°

El Socorro · La Violeta · San Pedro · Baradero · ENTRE RÍOS · URUGUAY

Pergamino · Ing. Moneta · Alsina · G'ral F. Uriburu · Carmelo

Carabelas · Rancagua · Arrecifes · V. Lía · Lima · I. M. García · Colonia

Rojas · Salto · Cap. Sarmiento · S.A. d'Areco · Cap. del Señor · Las Conchas · San Isidro · BUENOS AIRES

Los Indios · C'nl. Isleño · C. d. Areco · S.A. de Giles · Gral. Sarmiento · Avellaneda · de la Plata

Junín · Rawson · Rivas · Gral. · Mercedes · Merlo · Lanús · Lomas · Quilmes

Irala · C'nl. Mom · Suipacha · Luján · M. Paz · de Zamora · Adrogué · Ensenada · La Plata

G'ral. O'Brien · Alberti · Chacabuco · J. J. Almeyra · G'ral. · Las Heras · San Vicente · Magdalena

G'ral Viamonte · Navarro · Cañuelas · C'nl. Brandsen

Bragado · Ola · Salado · Ernestina · Lobos · Oliden

Gob. Udaondo · Altamirano

BUENOS AIRES

SCALE OF MILES · 0 20 40 60

34° · 34° · 40° · 12°

Inset: Rio de Janeiro (Distrito Federal)

43° 20'   43° 10'

SCALE OF MILES · 0 2 4 6

Baía de Guanabara · Pta. do Tubiacanga · Ilha do Boque · Freguesia

Meríti · Pavuna · Savaratá · Ilha do Governador · Cocotá

Anchieta · Areal · Ilha Tavares · Ilha do Engenho

Ricardo de Albuquerque · Colégio · Iraja · Penha · Olaria · Pta. do Galeão · I. do Fundão · Baía de

Vila Nova · Deodoro · Bom Sucesso · Ramos · I. do Bom Jesus · Guanabara

Bangú · Realengo · Vila Militar · Inhaúma · I. da Sapucaia · Niterói · Icaraí

Sa. do Barata · Sa. do Engenho · Largo do Tanque · Eng. Novo · Aeropôrto S. Dumont · Cais do Pôrto

DISTRITO FEDERAL · RIO DE JANEIRO

Tijuca 3,350 · Corcovado 2,309 · Botafogo · Pão de Açúcar 1,279

Vargem Pequena · Morro da Taquara · L. Rodrigo de Freitas · Alto da Boa Vista · Copacabana

L. Jacarepaguá · Lagoa Marapendi · L. da Tijuca · Cabo Dois Irmãos · Pta. do Arpoador

ATLANTIC OCEAN · Pta. do Marisco · Ilha do Meio · Ilha das Palmas · Ilha Cagarra · Ilha Comprida

Ilha Pontuda · Ilha Alfavaca

22° 50' · 23° · 22° 50' · 23°

13° · 14° · 15° · 45° · 50° · 55°

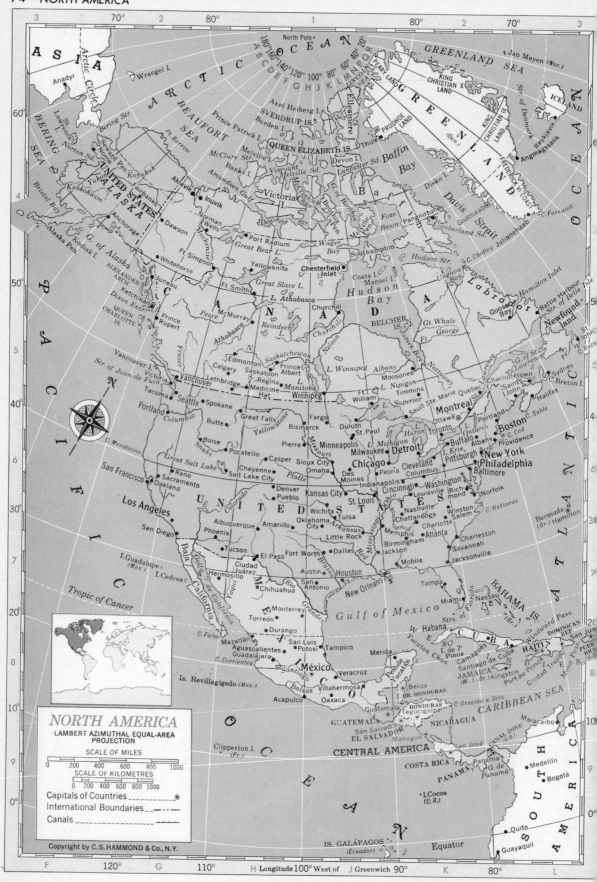

ASIA

Anadyr

ARCTIC OCEAN

North Pole

GREENLAND SEA

Jan Mayen (Nor.)

Wrangel I.

BEAUFORT SEA

Axel Heiberg I.
SVERDRUP IS.
Borden I.
Prince Patrick I.
QUEEN ELIZABETH IS.
Melville I.
Banks I.
Viscount Melville Sd.
Victoria I.

KING CHRISTIAN X LAND
PEARY LAND
KING CHRISTIAN LAND

GREENLAND (Den.)

ICELAND
Reykjavik
Angmagssalik

Bering Str.
Pt. Barrow
Seward Pen.
Nome
Kotzebue
Norton Sd.
Fairbanks
Yukon
UNITED STATES
ALASKA
Anchorage

Bristol Bay
Alaska Pen.
Kodiak I.
G. of Alaska
Seward
Dawson
Whitehorse
Juneau

Aklavik
Inuvik
Norman Wells
Port Radium
Great Bear L.
Yellowknife
Ft. Simpson

CANADA

Baffin Bay
Thule
Devon I.
Lancaster Sd.
Gulf of Boothia
Melville Pen.
Foxe Basin
Southampton I.
Wager Bay
Coats I.
Mansel I.

Davis Strait
Godthaab
C. Farewell

Cumberland Sd.
Pangnirtung
Disko I.

Hudson Str.

Ft. Smith
Great Slave L.
L. Athabasca
McMurray
Athabasca
Reindeer L.
Churchill

Chesterfield Inlet

Hudson Bay

BELCHER IS.
Gt. Whale
George
Ft.

Ungava Bay
Labrador
Gt. Whale
Hamilton Inlet
Goose Bay
Battle Harbour
Str. of Belle Isle
Newfound-land

PACIFIC

Queen Charlotte Is.
Prince Rupert
Ketchikan
Dixon Entrance
ALEXANDER ARCH.
Vancouver I.
Victoria

Edmonton
Calgary
Lethbridge
Medicine Hat
Regina
Saskatoon
Prince Albert
Saskatchewan
L. Manitoba
Winnipeg
L. Winnipeg

Nelson
Churchill
Fraser

Vancouver
Tacoma
Seattle
Spokane
Portland
Columbia
Butte
Boise
Great Falls
Yellowstone
Bismarck
Pierre
Fargo
Duluth

Albany
Nottaway
James Bay
Moosonee
Timmins
L. Nipigon
Sault Ste. Marie
Ft. William
L. Superior

Quebec
L. Ontario
Ottawa
Toronto
Montreal
Portland
Boston
Charlottetown
Saint John
C. Breton I.
Sydney
Halifax
C. Sable
C. Cod
Providence

Snake
Pocatello
Reno
Sacramento
Oakland
San Francisco
C. Mendocino

Great Salt Lake
Salt Lake City
Cheyenne
Casper
Sioux City
Omaha
Platte
Denver
Pueblo

UNITED STATES

St. Paul
Minneapolis
Milwaukee
Chicago
Des Moines
Peoria
L. Michigan
L. Huron
Detroit
Cleveland
L. Erie
Buffalo
Pittsburgh
Columbus
Cincinnati
Indianapolis
St. Louis
Louisville
Washington
Richmond
Norfolk

New York
Philadelphia
Baltimore
Albany

ATLANTIC OCEAN

Bermuda (Br.) Hamilton

Los Angeles
San Diego
Colorado

Kansas City
Wichita
Oklahoma City
Tulsa
Little Rock
Memphis
Nashville
Chattanooga
Atlanta
Birmingham
Jackson
Mobile
Charlotte
Winston-Salem
C. Hatteras
Charleston
Savannah
Jacksonville

Albuquerque
Amarillo
Phoenix
Tucson
El Paso
Fort Worth
Dallas
Arkansas
Red
Mississippi

I. Guadalupe (Mex.)
I. Cedros

Baja California
Hermosillo
Ciudad Juárez
Chihuahua
Yaqui
Golfo de California
C. Falso

Tropic of Cancer

Austin
San Antonio
Houston
New Orleans
Tampa
Miami
Nassau
BAHAMA IS. (Br.)

Gulf of Mexico

Mazatlán
Durango
San Luis Potosí
Tampico
C. Corrientes
Aguascalientes
Guadalajara
Santiago

MÉXICO
Monterrey
Torreón
Rio Grande

Mérida
Yucatan Chan.
Pen. de Yucatan

Habana
Strs. of Florida
CUBA
I. de Pinos
Camagüey
Santiago de Cuba
JAMAICA (W.I.-Br.) Kingston
Windward Pass.
HAITI
Port-au-Prince
Ciudad Trujillo
DOMINICAN REP.
San Juan
PUERTO RICO (U.S.)
Mona Pass.

Veracruz
Balsas
Villahermosa
Acapulco
Oaxaca
Belize
BR. HONDURAS
Guatemala
Tegucigalpa
HONDURAS
C. Gracias a Dios
CARIBBEAN SEA
Maracaibo

Is. Revillagigedo (Mex.)

Clipperton I. (Fr.)

GUATEMALA
San Salvador
EL SALVADOR
NICARAGUA
Managua
San José
CANAL ZONE (U.S.)
COSTA RICA
PANAMA
Panama
G. de Panamá

CENTRAL AMERICA

Medellín
Bogotá

SOUTH AMERICA

I. Cocos (C.R.)

Quito
Guayaquil

IS. GALÁPAGOS (Ecuador)

Equator

OCEAN

N

W E

N

NORTH AMERICA

LAMBERT AZIMUTHAL EQUAL-AREA PROJECTION

SCALE OF MILES

0   200   400   600   800   1000

SCALE OF KILOMETRES

0   200   400   600   800   1000

Capitals of Countries _____⊙
International Boundaries _._._._._
Canals _____

Copyright by C. S. HAMMOND & Co., N.Y.

70°   80°   80°   70°
120°   110°   Longitude 100° West of   Greenwich 90°   80°

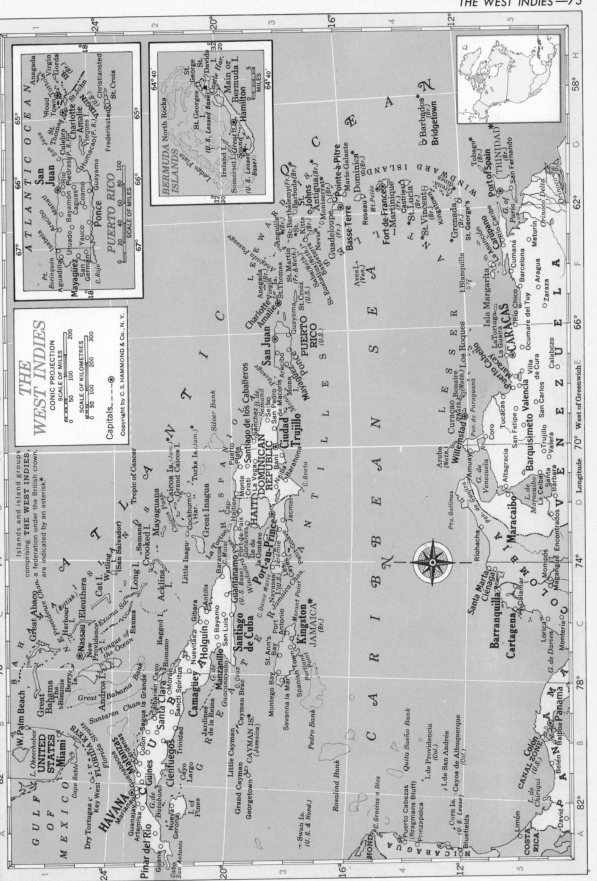

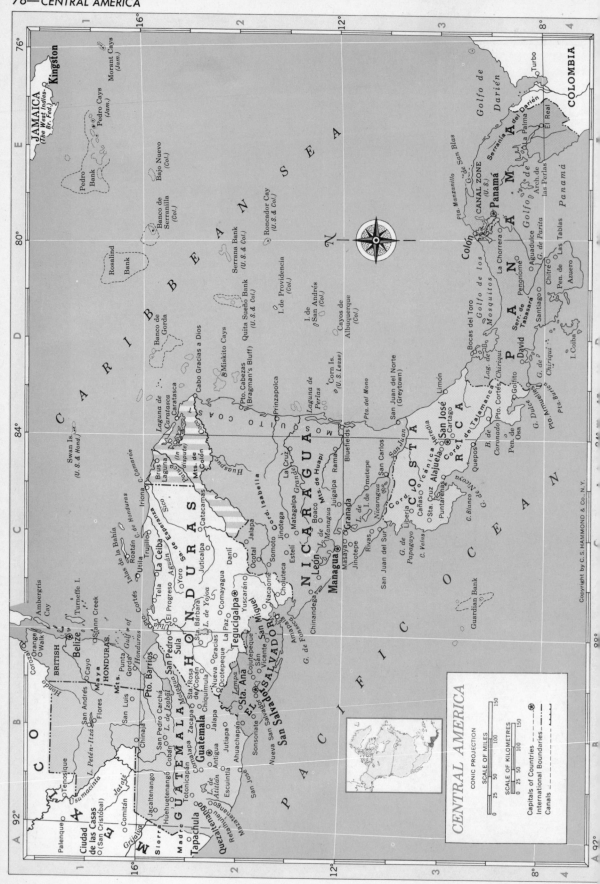

CENTRAL AMERICA

CONIC PROJECTION

SCALE OF MILES
0   25   50   100   150

SCALE OF KILOMETRES
0 25 50   100   150

Capitals of Countries ⊛
International Boundaries
Canals

Copyright by C. S. HAMMOND & CO., N.Y.

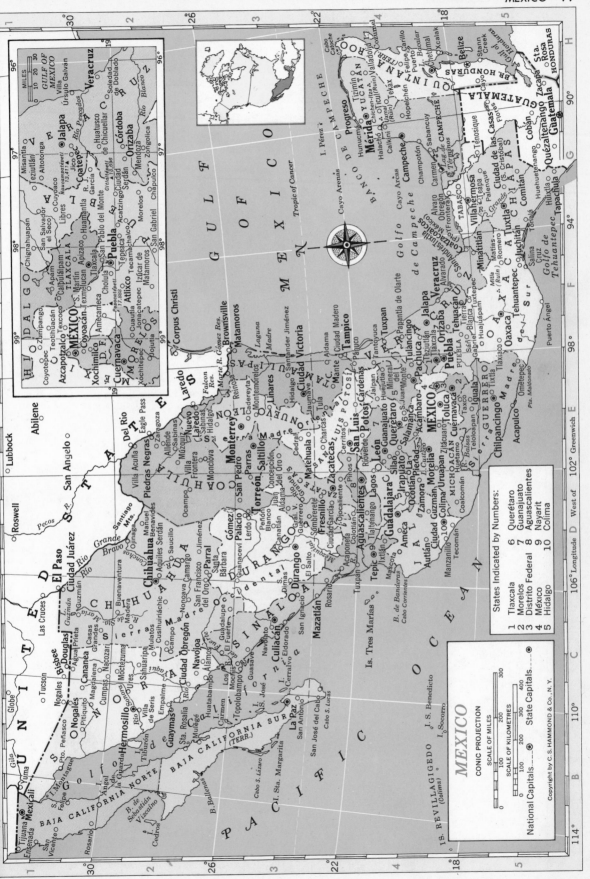

MEXICO
CONIC PROJECTION

SCALE OF MILES

SCALE OF KILOMETRES

National Capitals......... ◉

State Capitals......... ◉

Copyright by C. S. HAMMOND & CO., N. Y.

States Indicated by Numbers:

1 Tlaxcala   6 Querétaro
2 Morelos   7 Guanajuato
3 Distrito Federal   8 Aguascalientes
4 México   9 Nayarit
5 Hidalgo   10 Colima

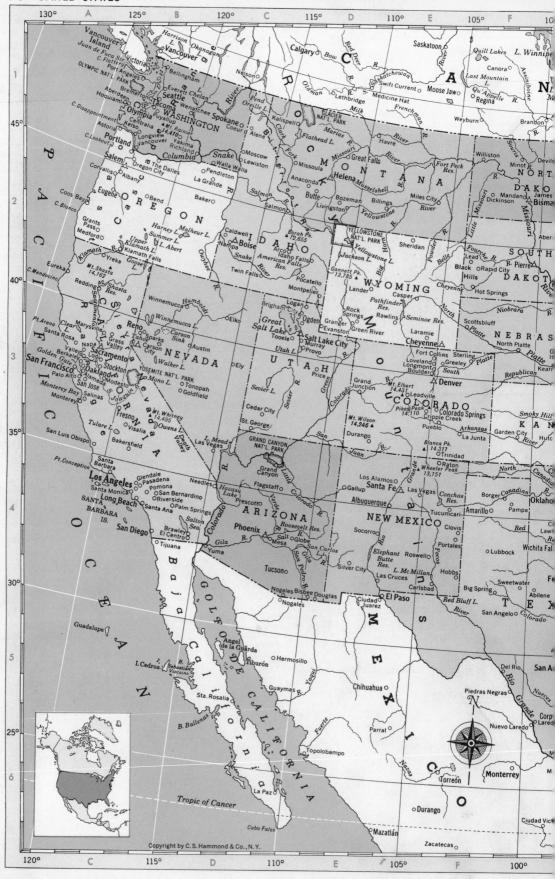

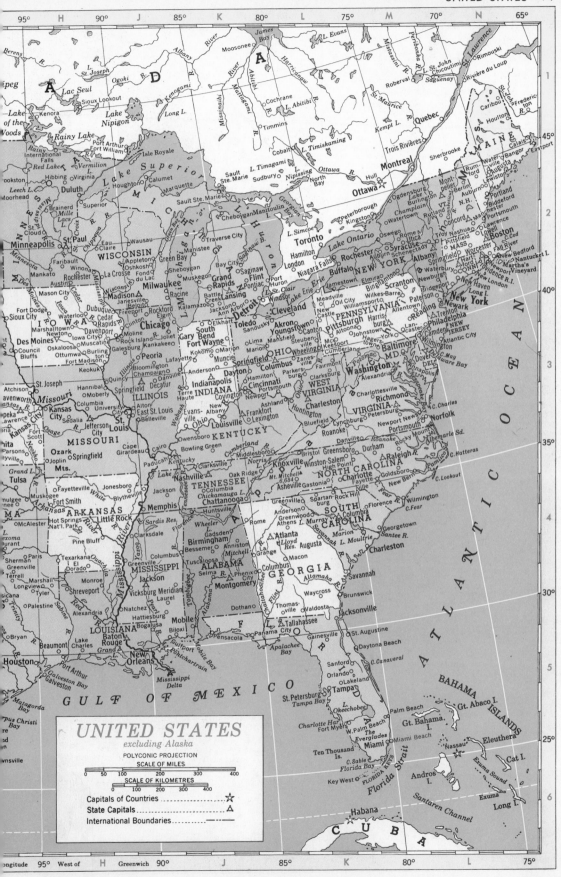

UNITED STATES
excluding Alaska

POLYCONIC PROJECTION

SCALE OF MILES

0   50   100   200   300   400

SCALE OF KILOMETRES

0   100   200   300   400

Capitals of Countries .... ☆
State Capitals .... △
International Boundaries ....

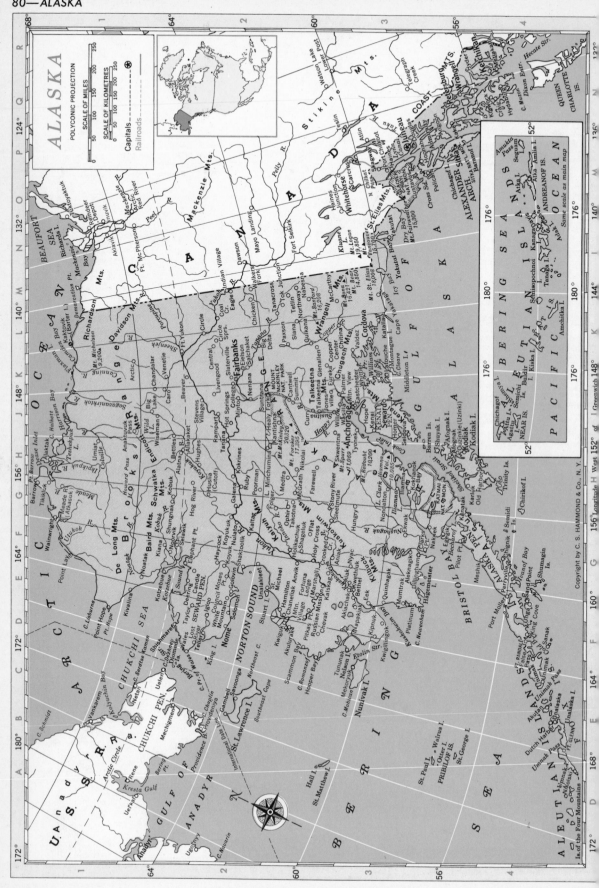

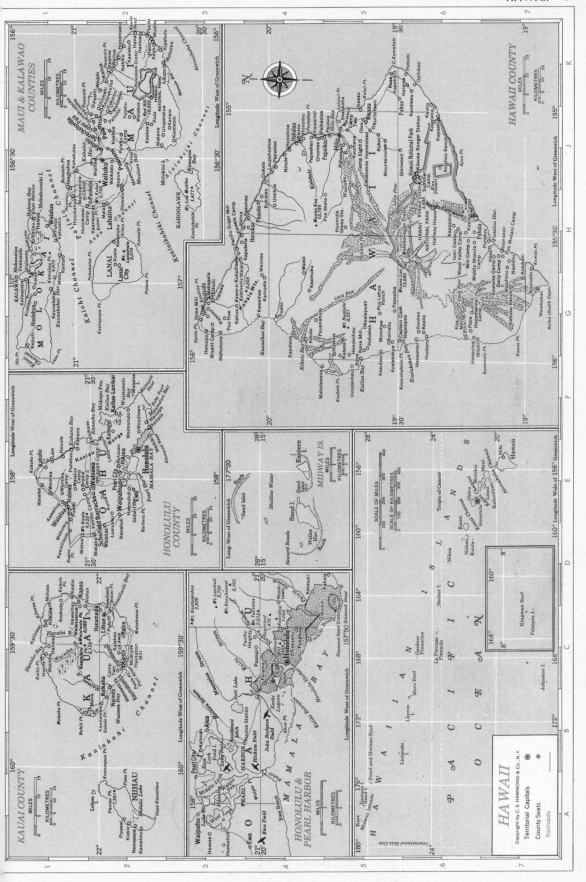

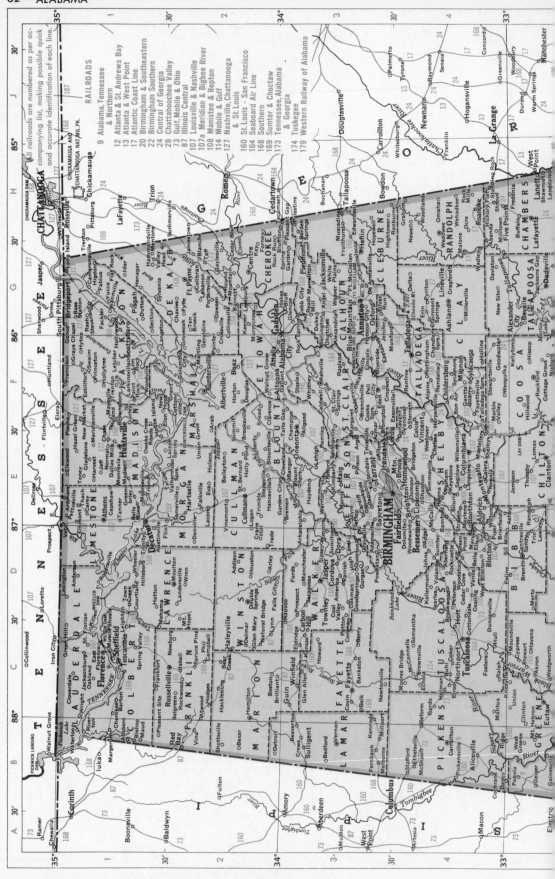

RAILROADS

All railroads are numbered as per accompanying list, making possible quick and accurate identification of each line.

9 Alabama, Tennessee & Northern
12 Atlanta & St. Andrews Bay
13 Atlanta & West Point
17 Atlantic Coast Line
20 Birmingham & Southeastern
22 Birmingham Southern
24 Central of Georgia
28 Chattahoochee Valley
73 Gulf, Mobile & Ohio
87 Illinois Central
107 Louisville & Nashville
107a Meridian & Bigbee River
108 Manistee & Repton
114 Nashville, Chattanooga & St. Louis
127 Nashville, Chattanooga & St. Louis
160 St. Louis - San Francisco
164 Seaboard Air Line
168 Southern
169 Sumter & Choctaw
173 Tennessee, Alabama & Georgia
174 Tuskegee
179 Western Railway of Alabama

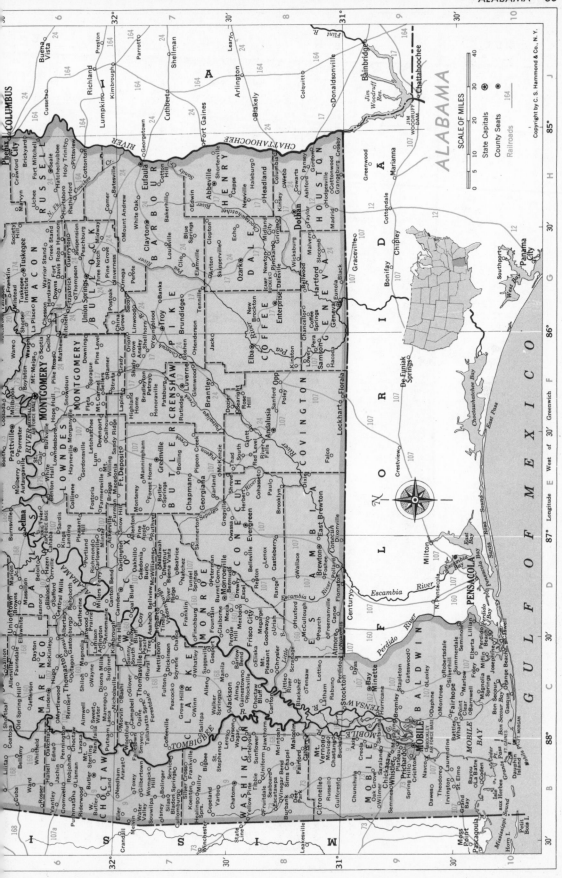

ALABAMA

SCALE OF MILES

State Capitals
County Seats
Railroads

Copyright by C. S. Hammond & Co., N.Y.

GULF OF MEXICO

FLORIDA

MISSISSIPPI

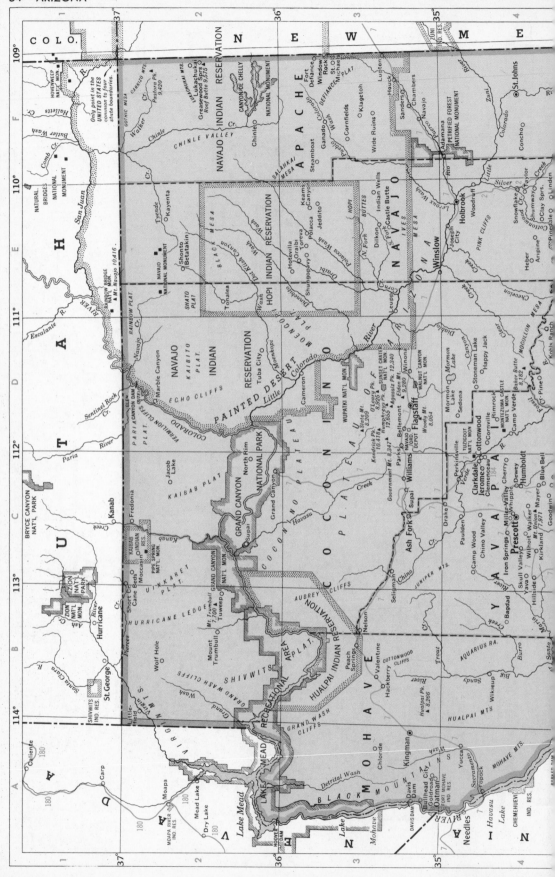

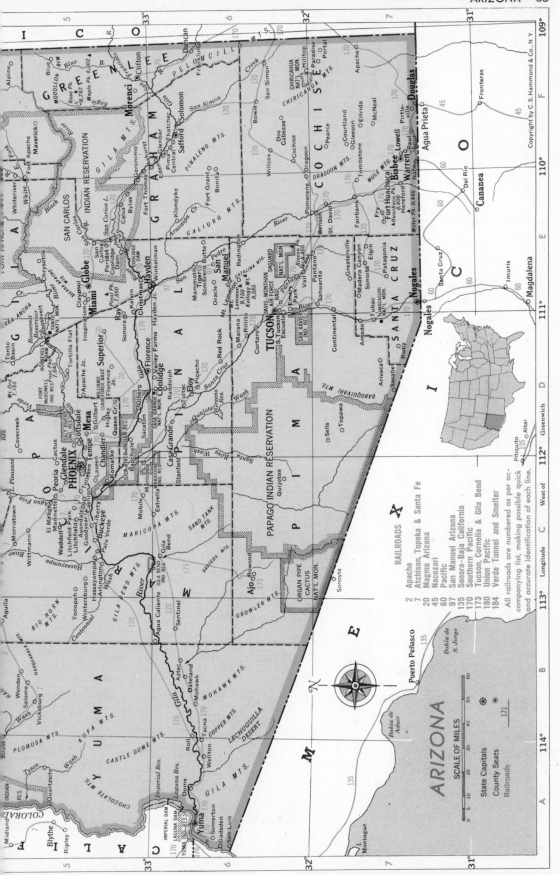

Copyright by C. S. Hammond & Co., N. Y.

ARIZONA

SCALE OF MILES

0 5 10 20   30   40   50   60

State Capitals ⊛

County Seats ◉

Railroads —— 171

RAILROADS

2	Apache
7	Atchison, Topeka & Santa Fe
20	Magma Arizona
45	Nacozari
60	Pacific
97	San Manuel Arizona
135	Sonora-Baja California
170	Southern Pacific
173	Tucson, Cornelia & Gila Bend
180	Union Pacific
184	Verde Tunnel and Smelter

All railroads are numbered as per accompanying list, making possible quick and accurate identification of each line.

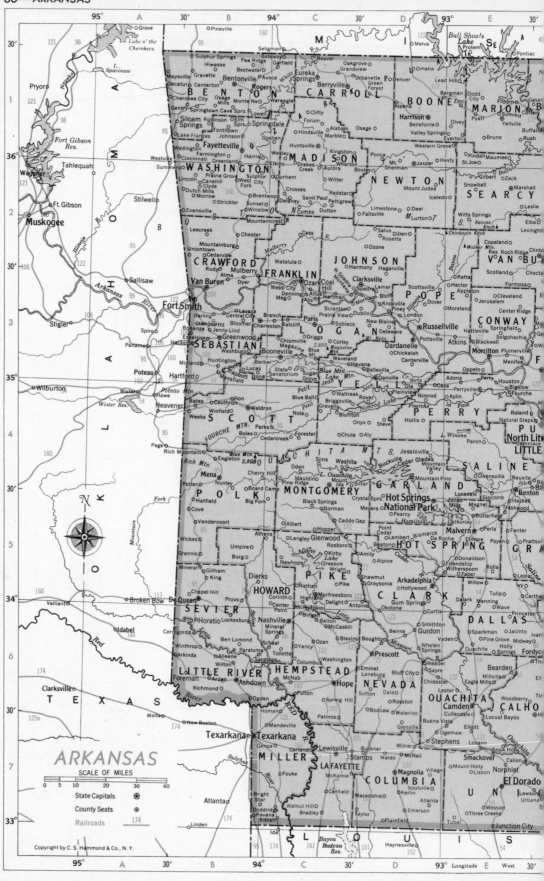

ARKANSAS

SCALE OF MILES

0 5 10 20 30 40

⊛ State Capitals

◉ County Seats

Railroads   174

Copyright by C. S. Hammond & Co., N. Y.

All railroads are numbered as per accompanying list, making possible quick and accurate identification of each line.

RAILROADS

2	Arkansas
5	Arkansas & Louisiana Missouri
7	Arkansas & Ozarks
9	Ashley, Drew & Northern
10	Augusta
11	Bauxite & Northern
54	Chicago, Rock Island and Pacific
56	Dardanelle & Russellville
56a	Delta Valley & Southern
57	De Queen and Eastern
58	Doniphan, Kensett & Searcy
59	El Dorado and Wesson
62	Fordyce and Princeton
62	Fort Smith, Subiaco & Rock Island
66	Graysonia, Nashville & Ashdown
80	Helena & Northwestern
87	Illinois Central
95	Kansas City Southern
98	Kansas, Oklahoma & Gulf
101	Louisiana & Arkansas
102	Louisiana and North West
104	Louisiana & Pine Bluff
105	Louisville & Nashville
106	Midland Valley
121	Missouri-Kansas-Texas
122	Missouri Pacific
125	Murfreesboro and Nashville
125a	Nashville, Chattanooga & St. Louis
125b	Paris and Mt. Pleasant
127	Prescott and Northwestern
128	Reader
160	St. Louis-San Francisco
161	St. Louis Southwestern
168	Southern
171	Texas, Oklahoma & Eastern
174	Texas and Pacific
176	Warren & Ouachita Valley
177	Warren & Saline River

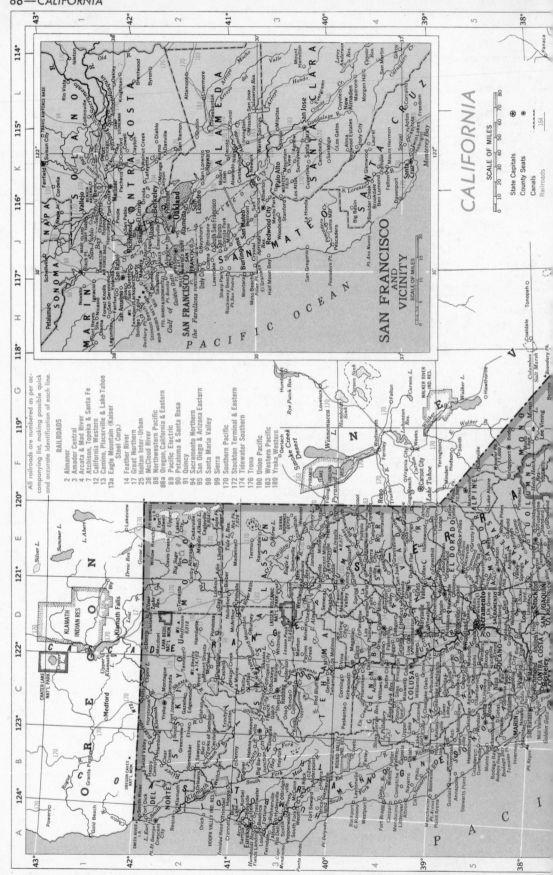

CALIFORNIA

SCALE OF MILES

State Capitals
County Seats
Canals
Railroads

SAN FRANCISCO AND VICINITY

SCALE OF MILES

PACIFIC OCEAN

RAILROADS

All railroads are numbered as per accompanying list, making possible quick and accurate identification of each line.

1 Almanor
2 Amador Central
3 Arcata & Mad River
7 Atchison, Topeka & Santa Fe
12 California Western
13 Camino, Placerville & Lake Tahoe
13a Eagle Mountain (Kaiser Steel Corp.)
14 Feather River
17 Great Northern
25 Holton Inter-Urban
38 McCloud River
88 Northwestern Pacific
88a Oregon, California & Eastern
89 Pacific Electric
90 Petaluma & Santa Rosa
91 Quincy
94 Sacramento Northern
95 San Diego & Arizona Eastern
98 Santa Maria Valley
99 Sierra
170 Southern Pacific
172 Stockton Terminal & Eastern
174 Tidewater Southern
176 Trona
180 Union Pacific
183 Western Pacific
189 Yreka Western

OREGON
NEVADA
PACIFIC OCEAN

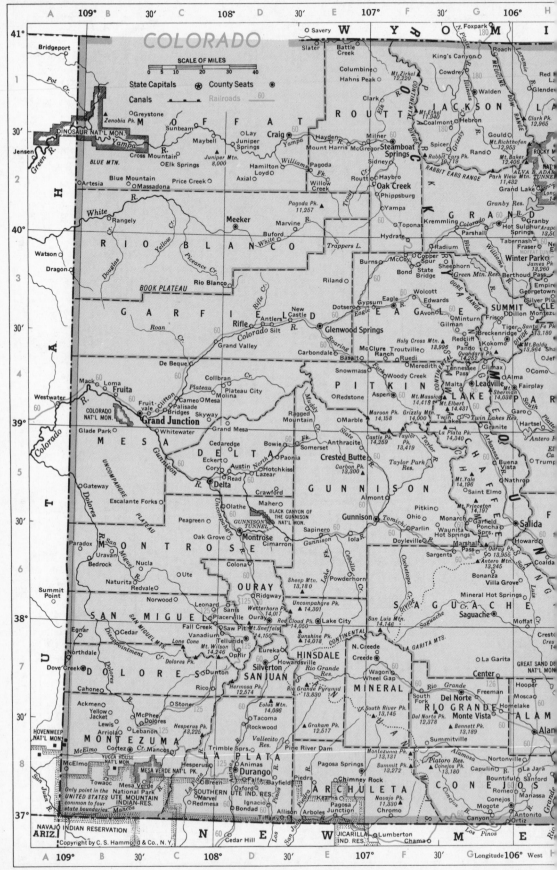

COLORADO

SCALE OF MILES

State Capitals ⊛   County Seats ⊙

Canals ├─┼─┤   Railroads 60

RAILROADS

7 Atchison, Topeka & Santa Fe

45 Chicago, Burlington & Quincy
54 Chicago, Rock Island & Pacific

54a Colorado
55 Colorado & South-Eastern

56 Colorado & Southern
57 Colorado & Wyoming

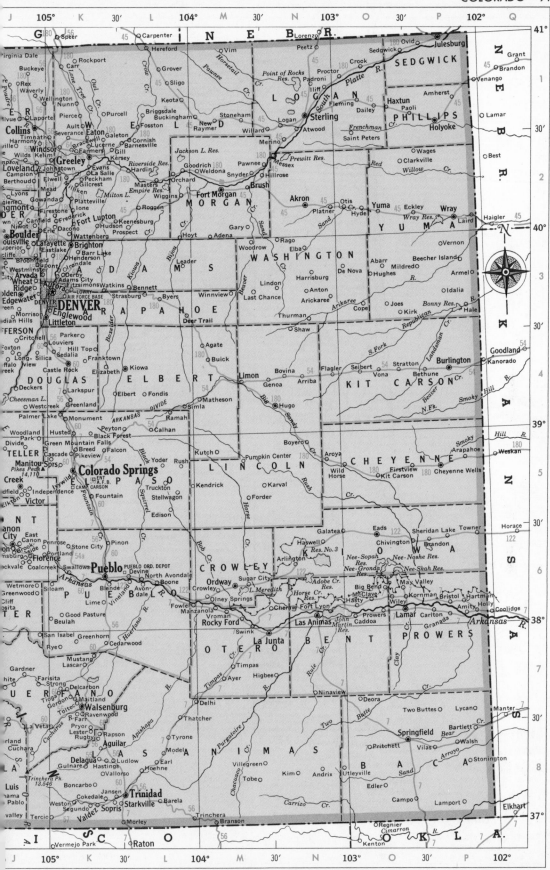

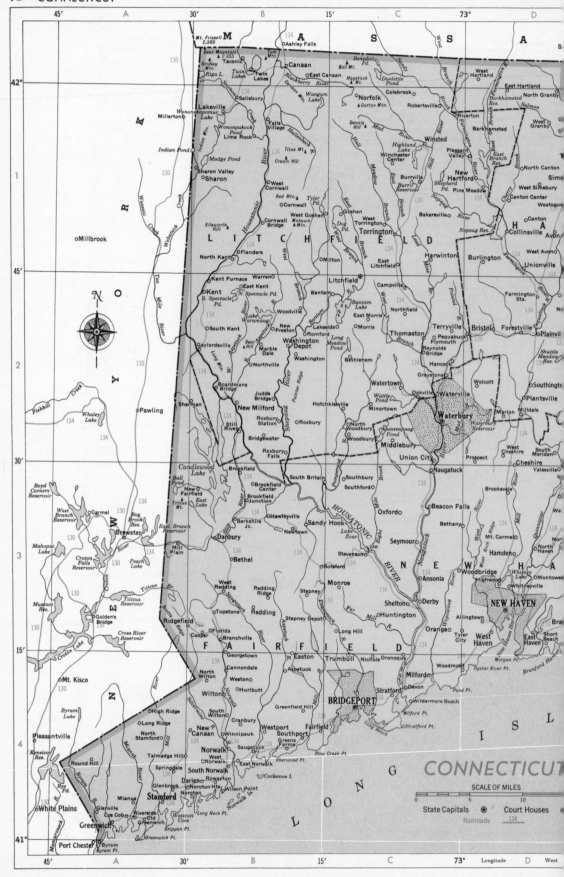

CONNECTICUT

SCALE OF MILES

0   5   10

State Capitals ⊛   Court Houses ●

Railroads   134

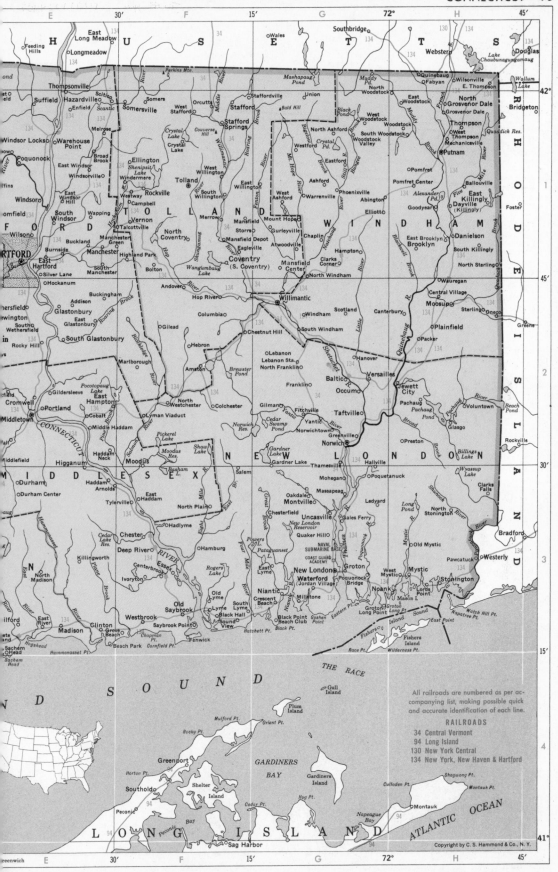

All railroads are numbered as per accompanying list, making possible quick and accurate identification of each line.

RAILROADS
34 Central Vermont
94 Long Island
130 New York Central
134 New York, New Haven & Hartford

Copyright by C. S. Hammond & Co., N. Y.

FLORIDA

SCALE OF MILES

State Capitals ⊛
County Seats ◉
Canals ————
Railroads ═164═

All railroads are numbered as per accompanying list, making possible quick and accurate identification of each line.

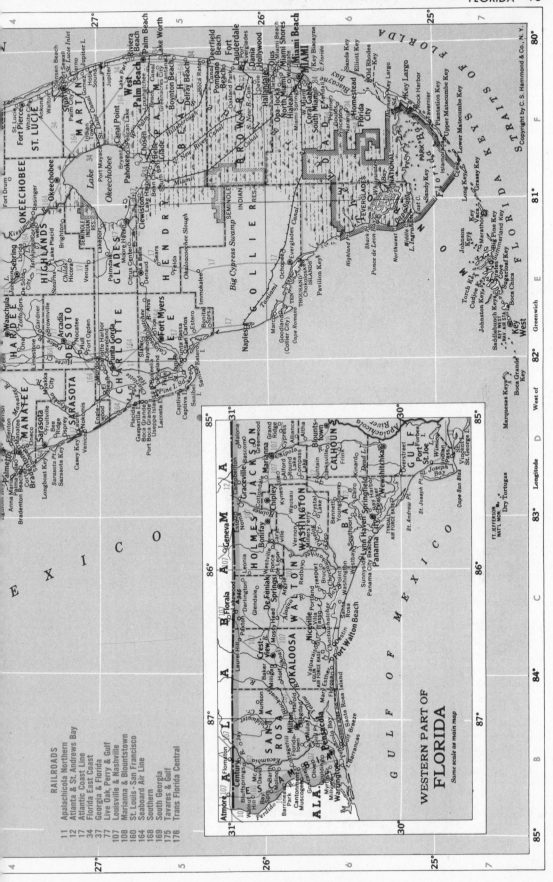

FLORIDA

WESTERN PART OF
FLORIDA
Same scale as main map

RAILROADS

11	Apalachicola Northern
12	Atlanta & St. Andrews Bay
17	Atlantic Coast Line
34	Florida East Coast
37	Georgia & Florida
77	Live Oak, Perry & Gulf
107	Louisville & Nashville
108	Marianna & Blountstown
160	St. Louis-San Francisco
164	Seaboard Air Line
168	Southern
169	South Georgia
175	Tavares & Gulf
176	Trans Florida Central

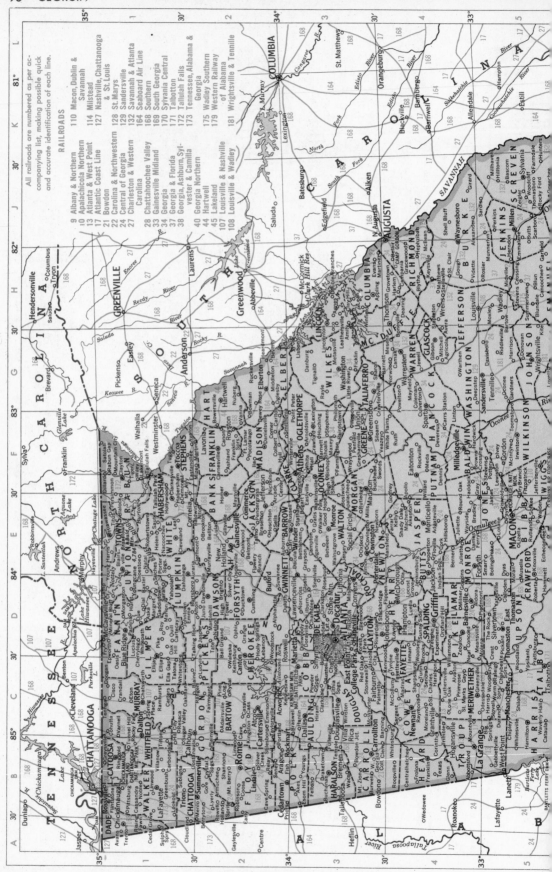

All railroads are numbered as per accompanying list, making possible quick and accurate identification of each line.

RAILROADS

9 Albany & Northern	110 Macon, Dublin & Savannah
10 Apalachicola Northern	114 Milstead
13 Atlanta & West Point	127 Nashville, Chattanooga & St. Louis
17 Atlantic Coast Line	
21 Bowdon	128 St Marys
23 Carolina & Northwestern	129 Sandersville
24 Central of Georgia	132 Savannah & Atlanta
27 Charleston & Western Carolina	164 Seaboard Air Line
	168 Southern
28 Chattahoochee Valley	169 South Georgia
32 Gainesville Midland	170 Sylvania Central
37 Georgia	171 Talbotton
38 Georgia & Florida	172 Tallulah Falls
38 Georgia, Ashburn, Sylvester & Camilla	173 Tennessee, Alabama & Georgia
40 Georgia Northern	175 Wadley Southern
44 Hartwell	179 Western Railway of Alabama
45 Lakeland	
107 Louisville & Nashville	181 Wrightsville & Tennille
108 Louisville & Wadley	

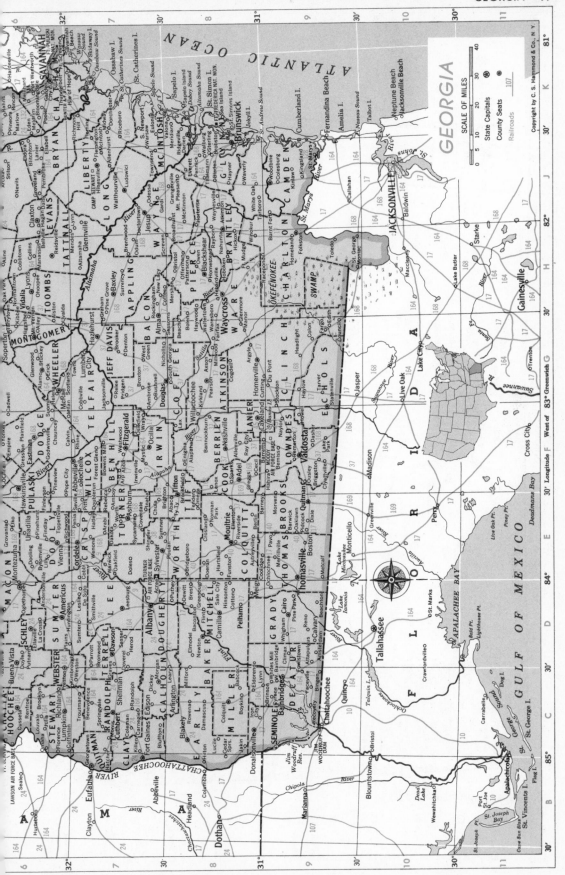

GEORGIA

SCALE OF MILES

State Capitals
County Seats
Railroads

Copyright by C. S. Hammond & Co., N.Y.

ATLANTIC OCEAN

GULF OF MEXICO

F L O R I D A

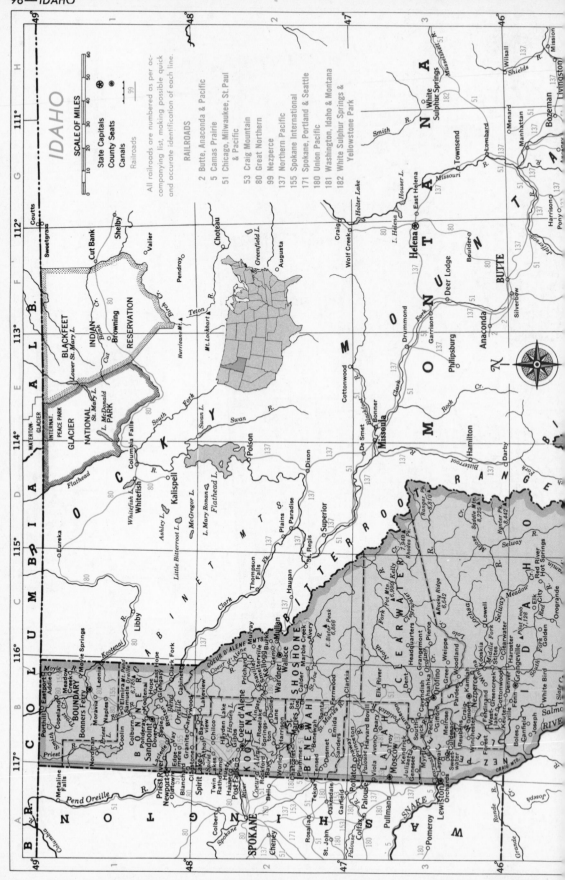

IDAHO

SCALE OF MILES

0   10   20   30   40   50   60

State Capitals ⊛

County Seats ⊙

Canals

Railroads _____ 99

All railroads are numbered as per accompanying list, making possible quick and accurate identification of each line.

RAILROADS

2   Butte, Anaconda & Pacific
5   Camas Prairie
51 Chicago, Milwaukee, St. Paul & Pacific
53 Craig Mountain
80 Great Northern
99 Nezperce
137 Northern Pacific
155 Spokane International
171 Spokane, Portland & Seattle
180 Union Pacific
181 Washington, Idaho & Montana
182 White Sulphur Springs & Yellowstone Park

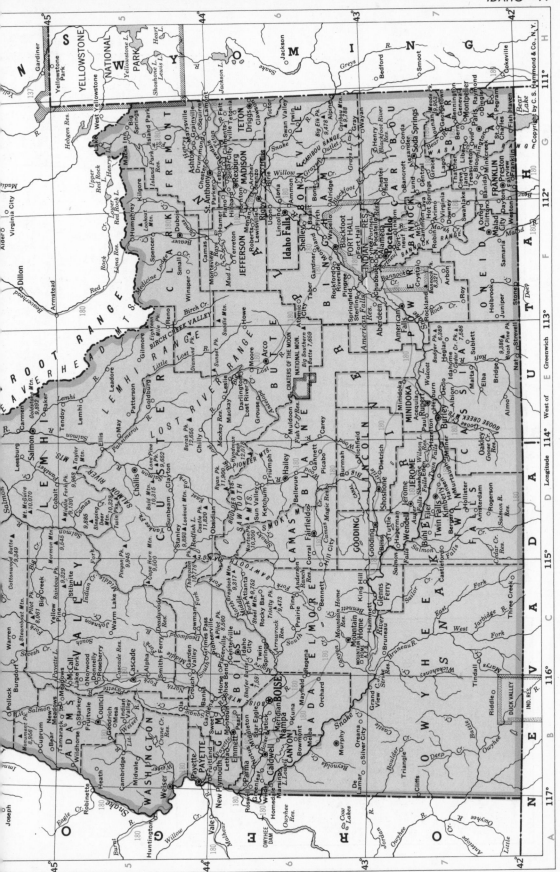

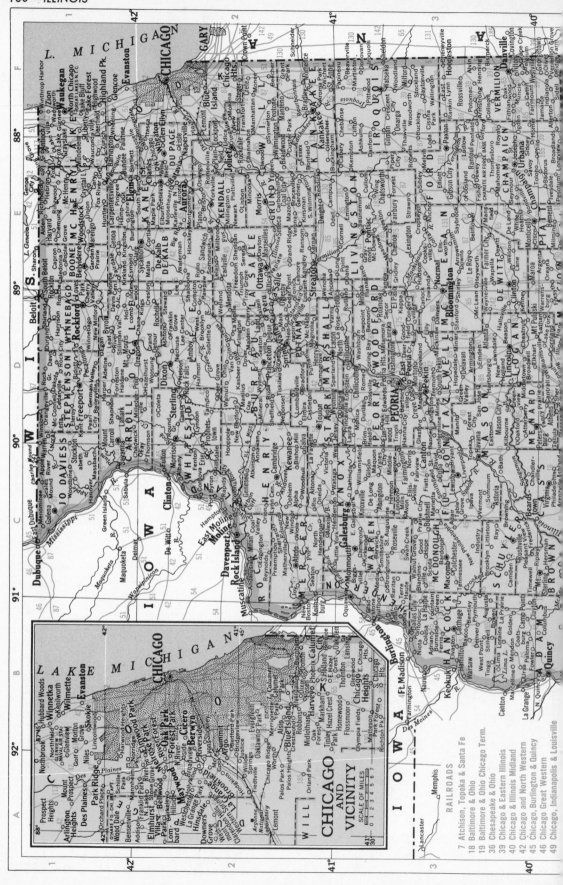

CHICAGO AND VICINITY

SCALE OF MILES
0 1 2 3 4 5 6 7

RAILROADS

7 Atchison, Topeka & Santa Fe
18 Baltimore & Ohio
19 Baltimore & Ohio Chicago Term.
36 Chesapeake & Ohio
39 Chicago & Eastern Illinois
40 Chicago & Illinois Midland
42 Chicago and North Western
45 Chicago, Burlington & Quincy
46 Chicago Great Western
49 Chicago, Indianapolis & Louisville

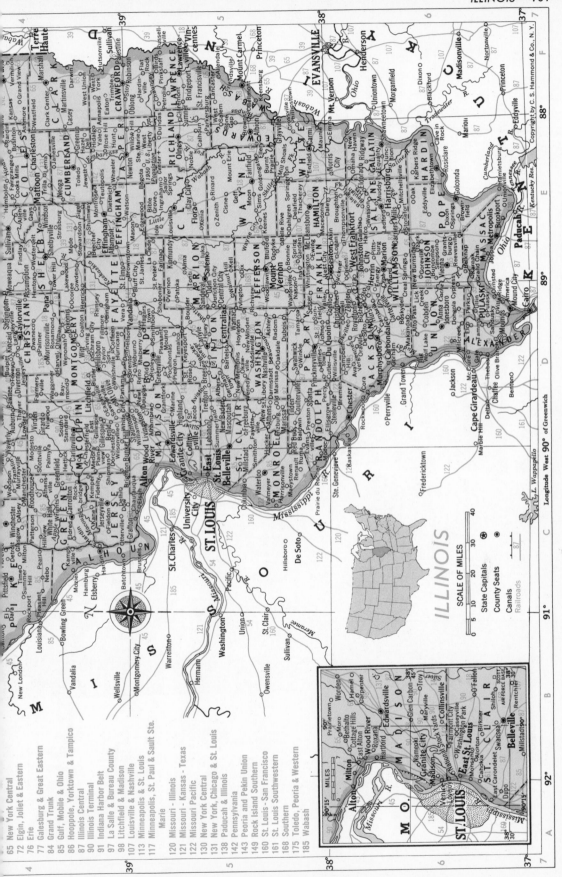

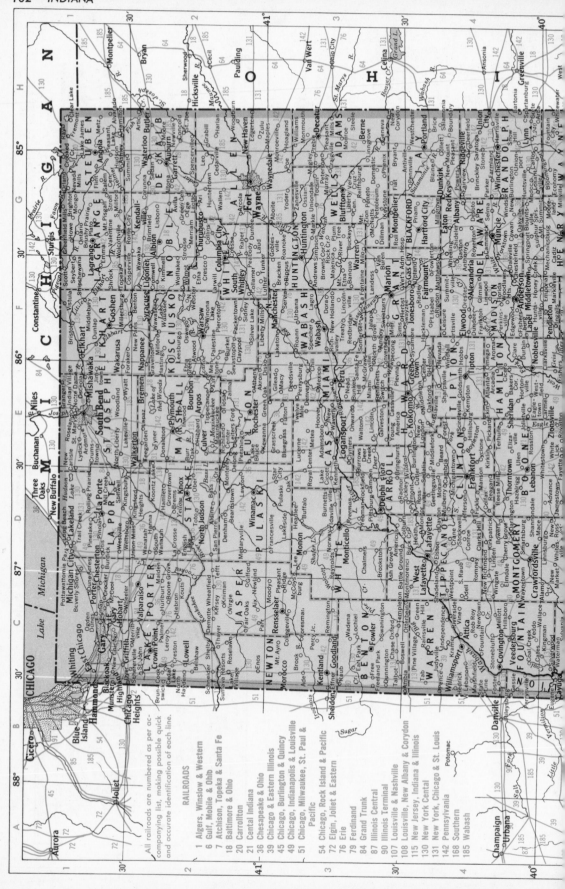

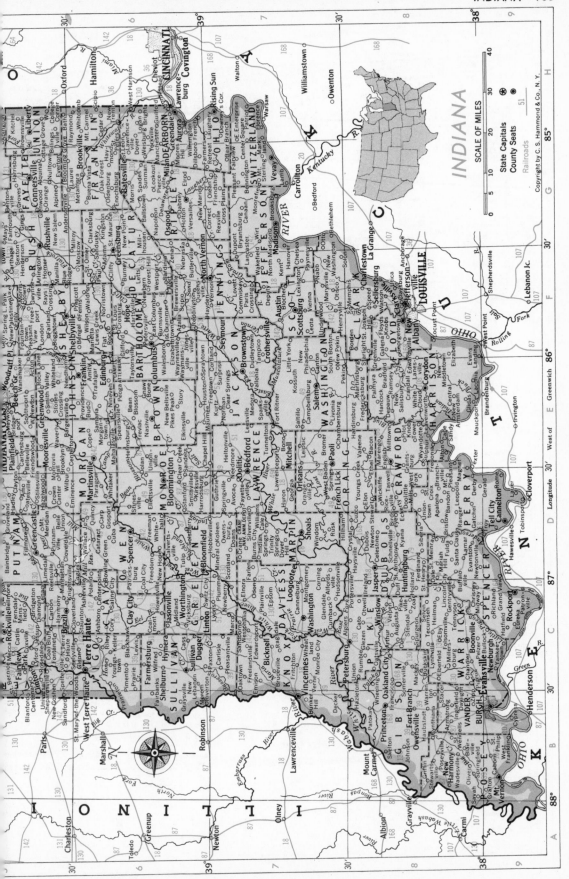

INDIANA

SCALE OF MILES

State Capitals ⊛
County Seats ⊙
Railroads

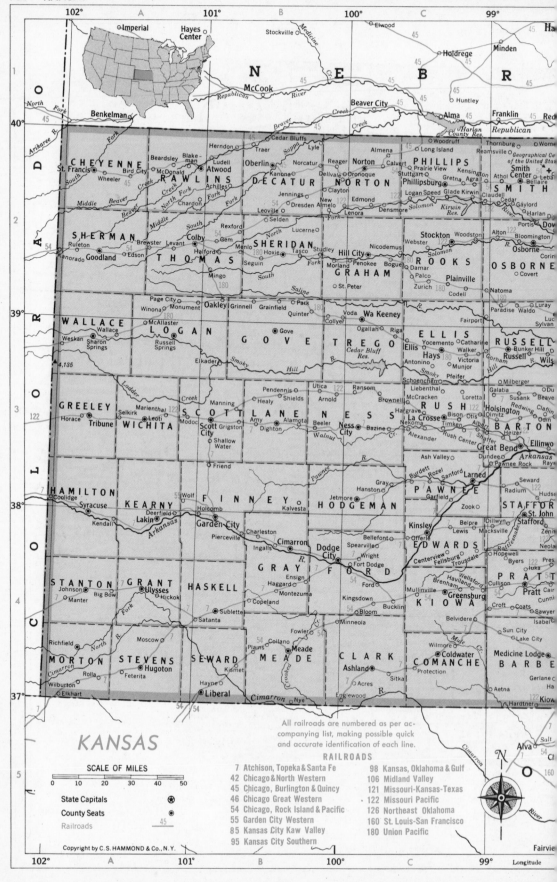

KANSAS

SCALE OF MILES

0 10 20 30 40 50

State Capitals ⊛

County Seats ◎

Railroads 45

All railroads are numbered as per accompanying list, making possible quick and accurate identification of each line.

RAILROADS

7 Atchison, Topeka & Santa Fe
42 Chicago & North Western
45 Chicago, Burlington & Quincy
46 Chicago Great Western
54 Chicago, Rock Island & Pacific
55 Garden City Western
85 Kansas City Kaw Valley
95 Kansas City Southern

98 Kansas, Oklahoma & Gulf
106 Midland Valley
121 Missouri-Kansas-Texas
122 Missouri Pacific
126 Northeast Oklahoma
160 St. Louis-San Francisco
180 Union Pacific

Copyright by C. S. HAMMOND & Co., N.Y.

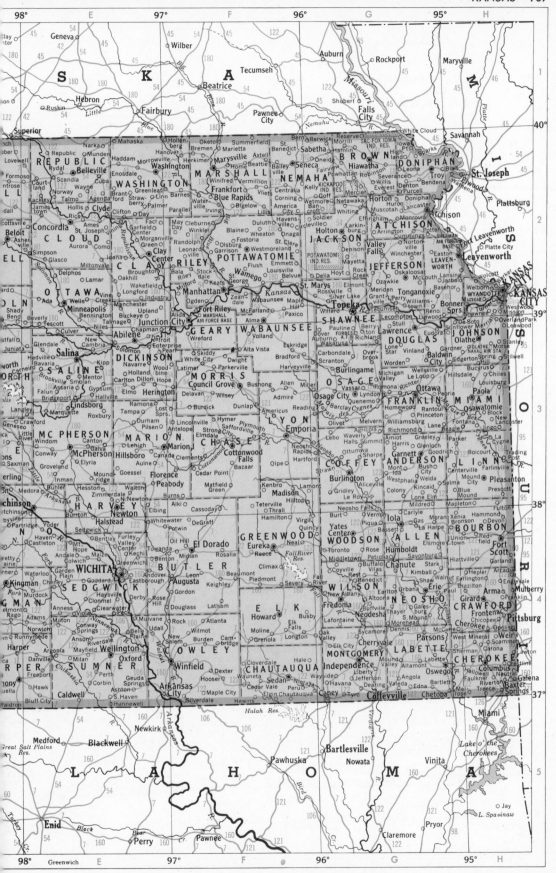

WESTERN PART OF KENTUCKY

Same scale as main map.

LOUISIANA

SCALE OF MILES

State Capitals ⊛   Canals
Parish Seats ⊚   Railroads   107

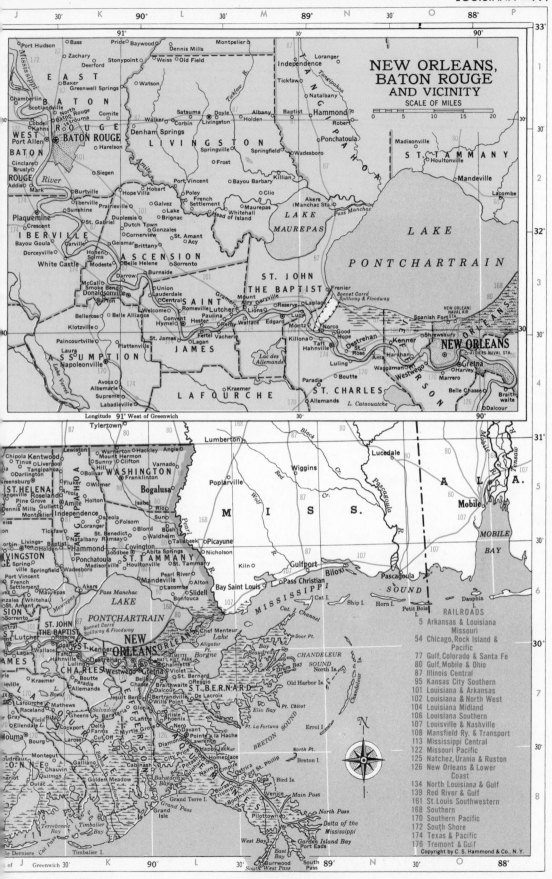

NEW ORLEANS, BATON ROUGE AND VICINITY

SCALE OF MILES

0   5   10   15   20

Longitude 91° West of Greenwich

RAILROADS

5	Arkansas & Louisiana Missouri
54	Chicago, Rock Island & Pacific
77	Gulf, Colorado & Santa Fe
80	Gulf, Mobile & Ohio
87	Illinois Central
95	Kansas City Southern
101	Louisiana & Arkansas
102	Louisiana & North West
104	Louisiana Midland
106	Louisiana Southern
107	Louisville & Nashville
108	Mansfield Ry. & Transport
113	Mississippi Central
122	Missouri Pacific
125	Natchez, Urania & Ruston
126	New Orleans & Lower Coast
134	North Louisiana & Gulf
139	Red River & Gulf
161	St. Louis Southwestern
168	Southern
170	Southern Pacific
172	South Shore
174	Texas & Pacific
176	Tremont & Gulf

Copyright by C. S. Hammond & Co., N. Y.

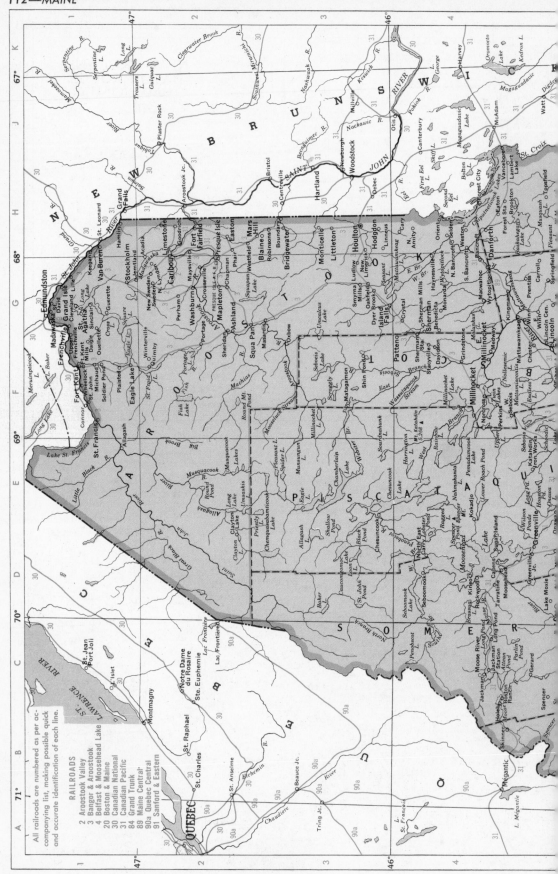

RAILROADS

All railroads are numbered as per accompanying list, making possible quick and accurate identification of each line.

2 Aroostook Valley
3 Bangor & Aroostook
4 Belfast & Moosehead Lake
20 Boston & Maine
30 Canadian National
31 Canadian Pacific
84 Grand Trunk
89 Maine Central
90a Quebec Central
91 Sanford & Eastern

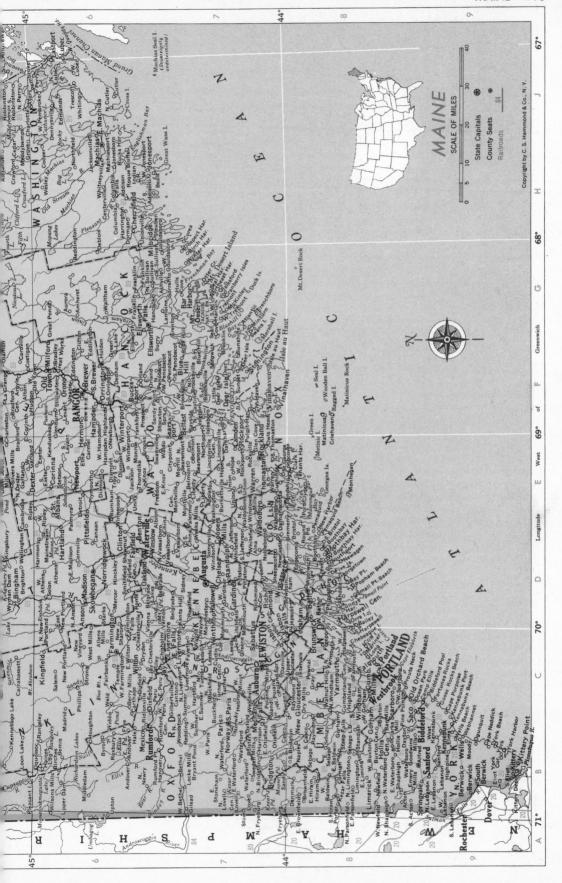

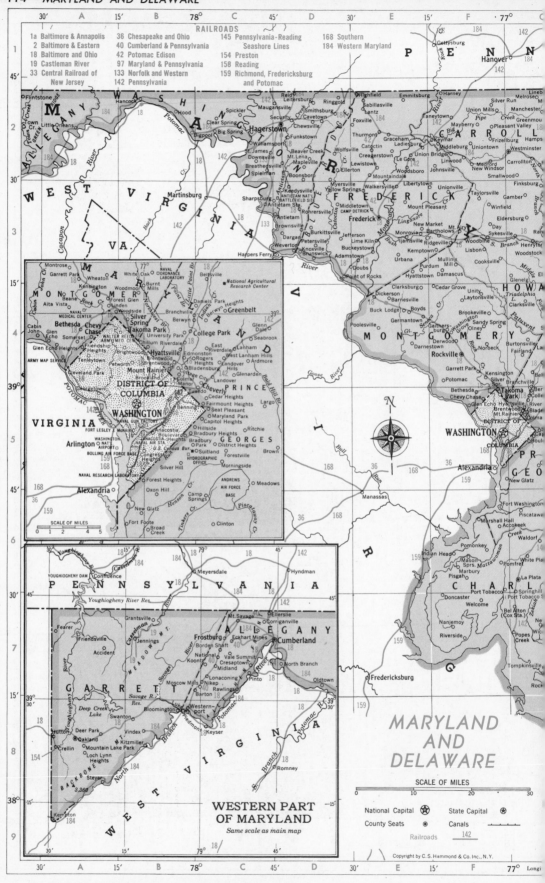

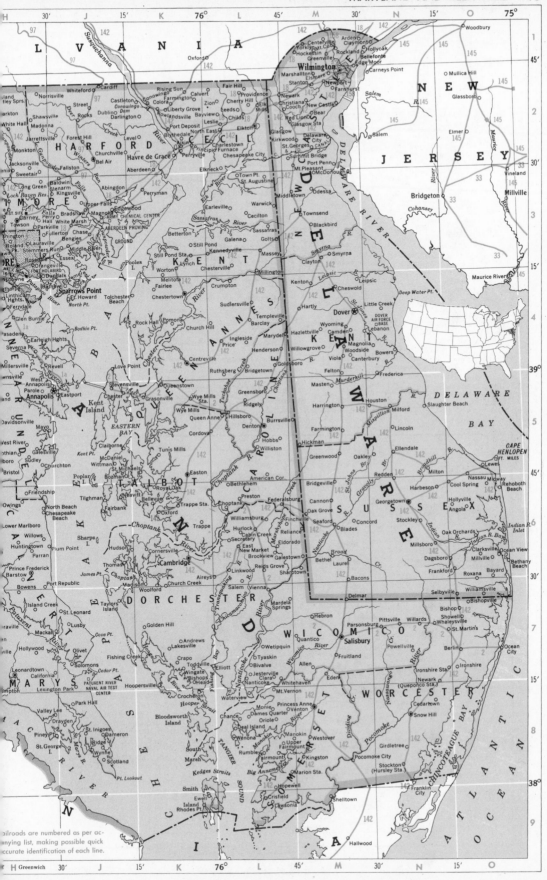

Railroads are numbered as per accompanying list, making possible accurate identification of each line.

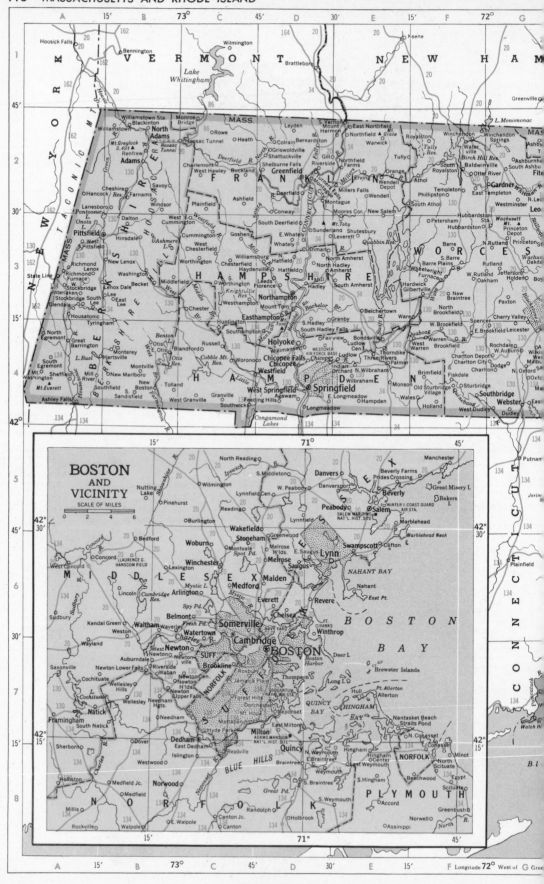

BOSTON
AND
VICINITY

SCALE OF MILES

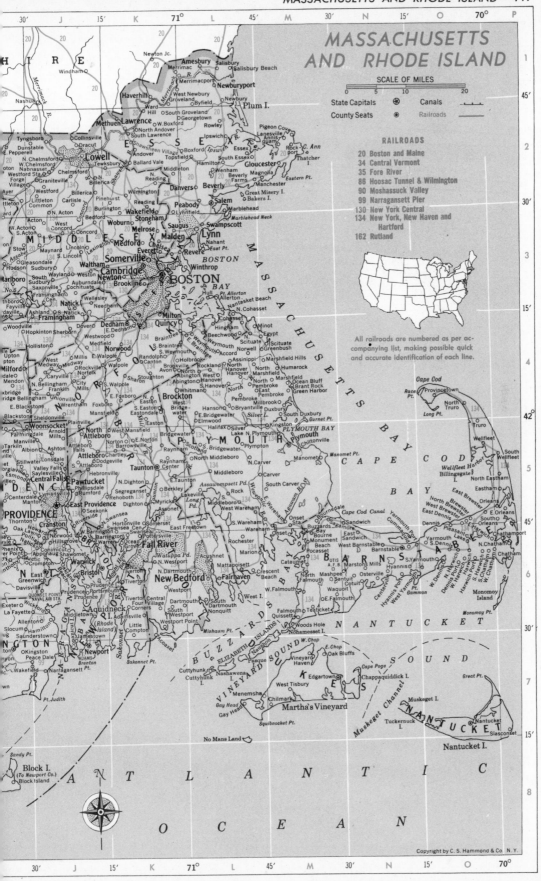

MASSACHUSETTS AND RHODE ISLAND

SCALE OF MILES

0   5   10   20

⊗ State Capitals   ⊢⊣ Canals
◉ County Seats   Railroads

RAILROADS

20 Boston and Maine
34 Central Vermont
35 Fore River
88 Hoosac Tunnel & Wilmington
90 Moshassuck Valley
99 Narragansett Pier
130 New York Central
134 New York, New Haven and
    Hartford
162 Rutland

All railroads are numbered as per accompanying list, making possible quick and accurate identification of each line.

MICHIGAN

SCALE OF MILES

0 10 20 30 40 50

⊕ State Capitals
⊙ County Seats
Canals
Railroads

Same scale as main map

ISLE ROYALE
(NATIONAL PARK)
Same scale as main map
L. SUPERIOR

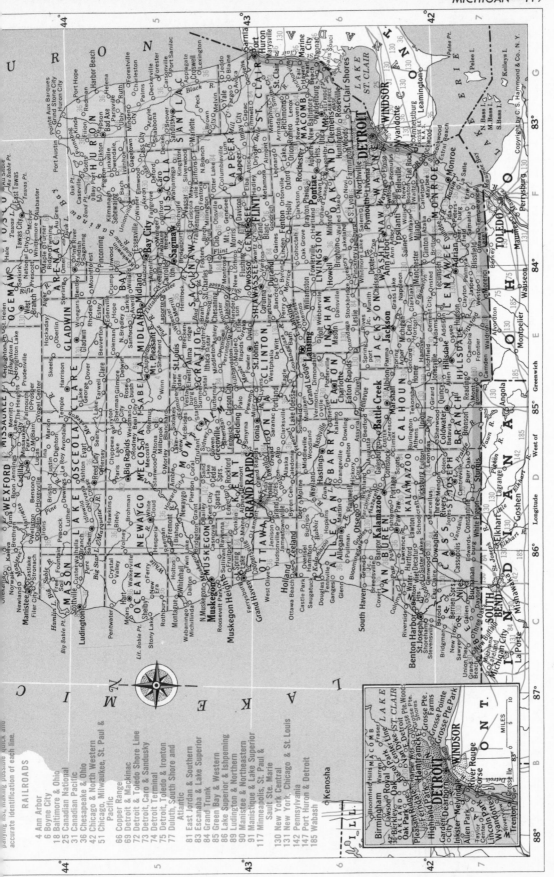

RAILROADS

4 Ann Arbor
6 Boyne City
18 Baltimore & Ohio
25 Canadian National
31 Canadian Pacific
36 Chesapeake & Ohio
42 Chicago & North Western
51 Chicago, Milwaukee, St. Paul & Pacific
66 Copper Range
69 Detroit & Mackinac
72 Detroit & Toledo Shore Line
73 Detroit, Caro & Sandusky
74 Detroit Terminal
75 Detroit, Toledo & Ironton
77 Duluth, South Shore and Atlantic
81 East Jordan & Southern
83 Escanaba & Lake Superior
84 Grand Trunk
85 Green Bay & Western
86 Lake Superior & Ishpeming
89 Ludington & Northern
90 Manistee & Northeastern
91 Manistique & Lake Superior
117 Minneapolis, St. Paul & Sault Ste. Marie
130 New York Central
131 New York, Chicago & St. Louis
142 Pennsylvania
147 Port Huron & Detroit
185 Wabash

NORTHEASTERN
PART OF
MINNESOTA

Same scale as main map

RAILROADS

30 Canadian National	79 Erie Mining Co.
31 Canadian Pacific	80 Great Northern
42 Chicago & North Western	82 Green Bay & Western
45 Chicago, Burlington & Quincy	87 Illinois Central
46 Chicago Great Western	113 Minneapolis & St. Louis
51 Chicago, Milwaukee, St. Paul & Pacific	115 Minneapolis, Northfield & Southern
54 Chicago, Rock Island & Pacific	117 Minneapolis, St. Paul & Sault Ste. Marie
55 Chicago, St. Paul, Minneapolis & Omaha	123 Minneapolis Transfer
57 Duluth & Northeastern	125 Minnesota Western
75 Duluth, Missabe & Iron Range	137 Northern Pacific
77 Duluth, South Shore & Atlantic	145 Reserve Mining Co.

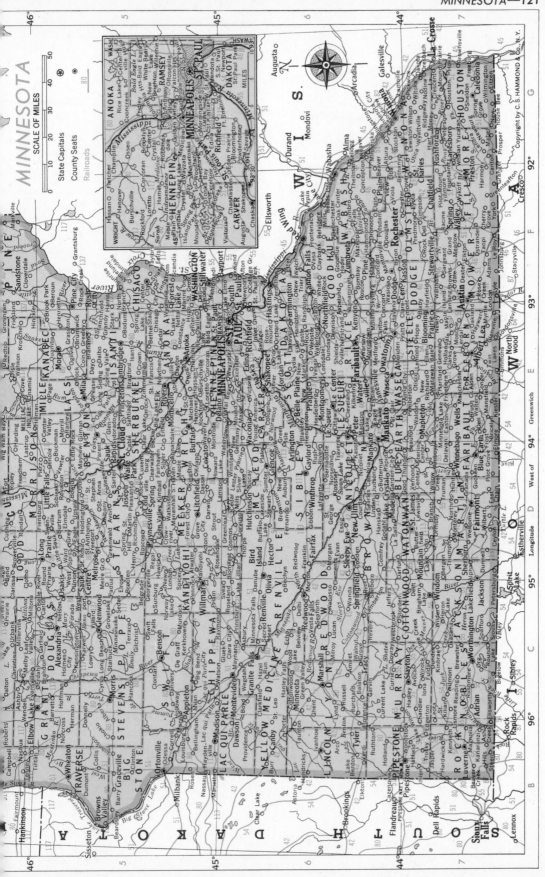

MINNESOTA

SCALE OF MILES

0 10 20 30 40 50

⊕ State Capitals

◉ County Seats

Railroads

Copyright by C. S. HAMMOND & CO., N.Y.

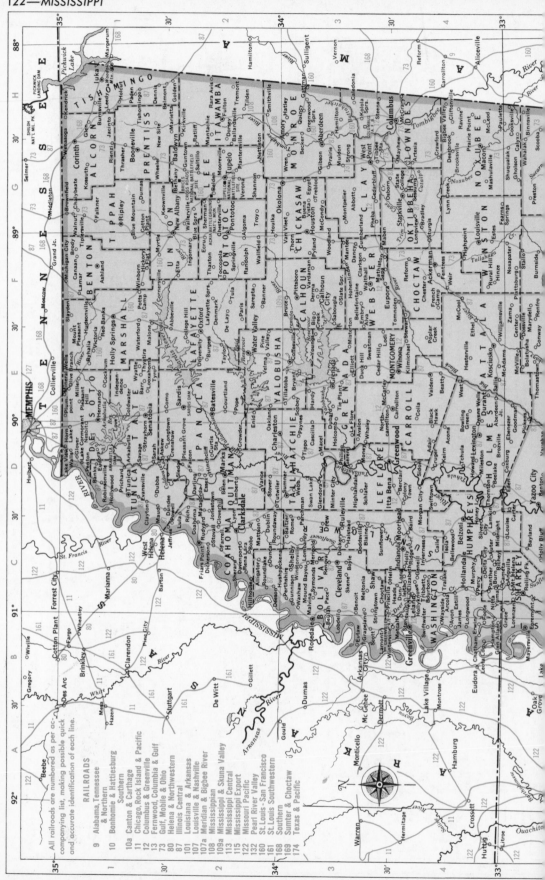

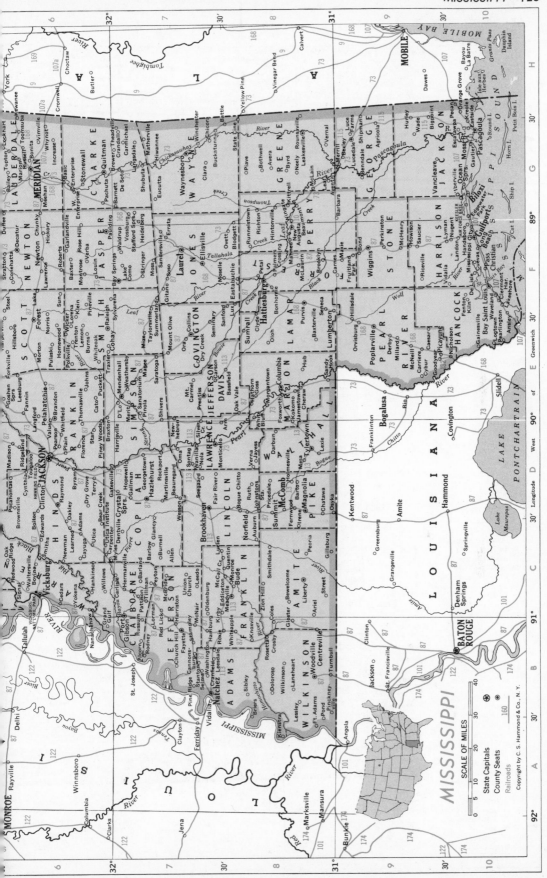

MISSISSIPPI

SCALE OF MILES

State Capitals
County Seats
Railroads

Copyright by C. S. Hammond & Co., N. Y.

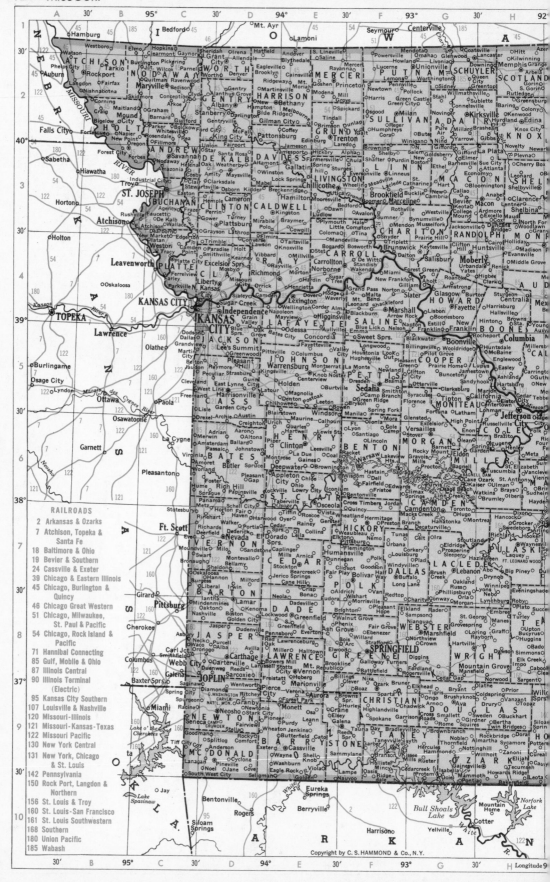

RAILROADS

2 Arkansas & Ozarks
7 Atchison, Topeka &
   Santa Fe
18 Baltimore & Ohio
19 Bevier & Southern
24 Cassville & Exeter
45 Chicago & Eastern Illinois
45 Chicago, Burlington &
   Quincy
46 Chicago Great Western
51 Chicago, Milwaukee,
   St. Paul & Pacific
54 Chicago, Rock Island &
   Pacific
71 Hannibal Connecting
85 Gulf, Mobile & Ohio
87 Illinois Central
90 Illinois Terminal
   (Electric)
95 Kansas City Southern
107 Louisville & Nashville
120 Missouri-Illinois
121 Missouri-Kansas-Texas
122 Missouri Pacific
130 New York Central
131 New York, Chicago
   & St. Louis
142 Pennsylvania
150 Rock Port, Langdon &
   Northern
156 St. Louis & Troy
160 St. Louis-San Francisco
161 St. Louis Southwestern
168 Southern
180 Union Pacific
185 Wabash

Copyright by C. S. HAMMOND & Co., N.Y.

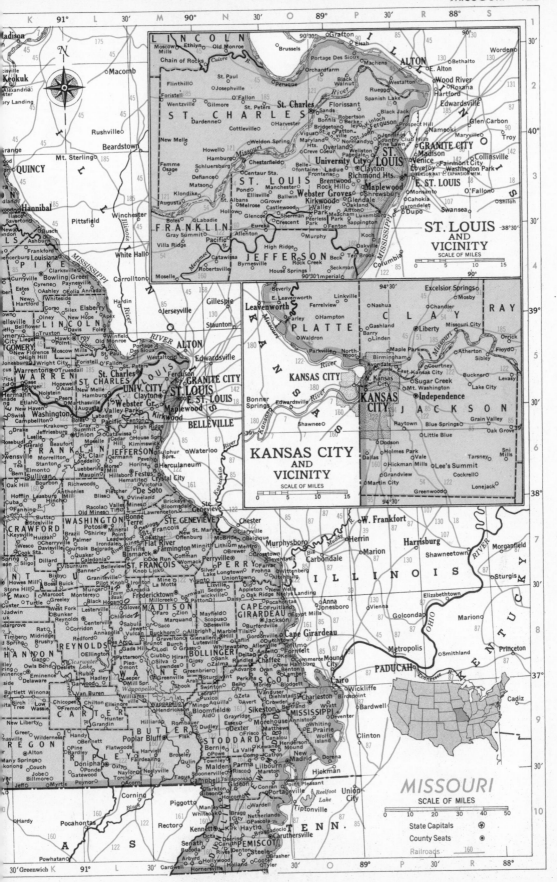

ST. LOUIS AND VICINITY
SCALE OF MILES

KANSAS CITY AND VICINITY
SCALE OF MILES

MISSOURI
SCALE OF MILES

State Capitals
County Seats
Railroads

MONTANA

SCALE OF MILES

0 10 20   40   60   80

⊗ State Capitals
⊙ County Seats
Railroads   137

All railroads are numbered as per accompanying list, making possible quick and accurate identification of each line.

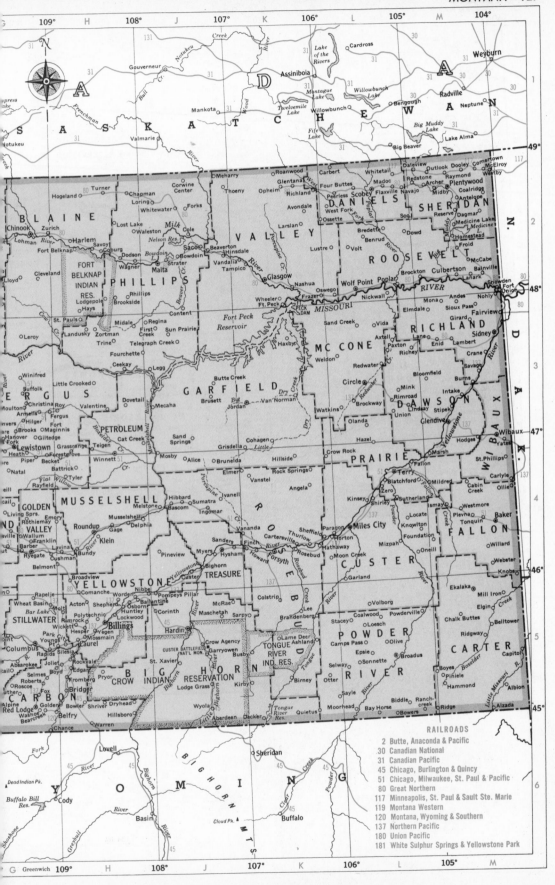

RAILROADS
2 Butte, Anaconda & Pacific
30 Canadian National
31 Canadian Pacific
45 Chicago, Burlington & Quincy
51 Chicago, Milwaukee, St. Paul & Pacific
80 Great Northern
117 Minneapolis, St. Paul & Sault Ste. Marie
119 Montana Western
120 Montana, Wyoming & Southern
137 Northern Pacific
180 Union Pacific
181 White Sulphur Springs & Yellowstone Park

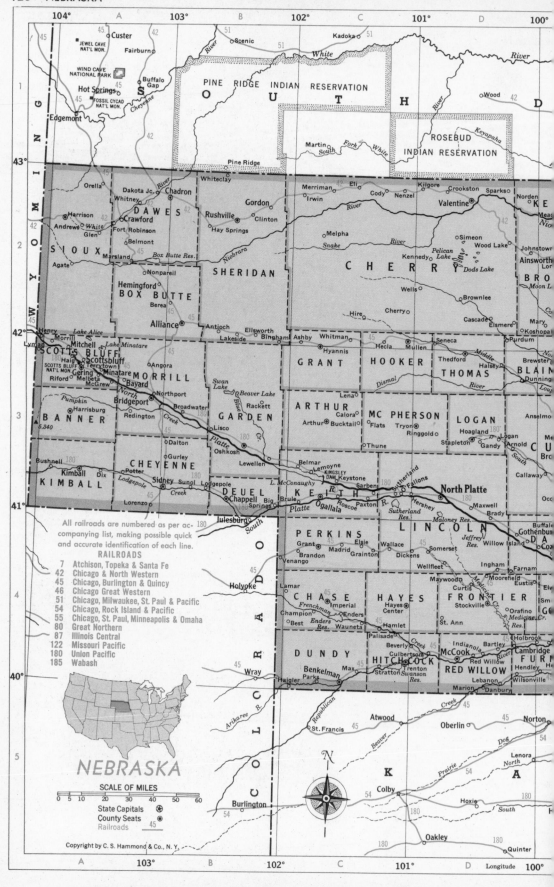

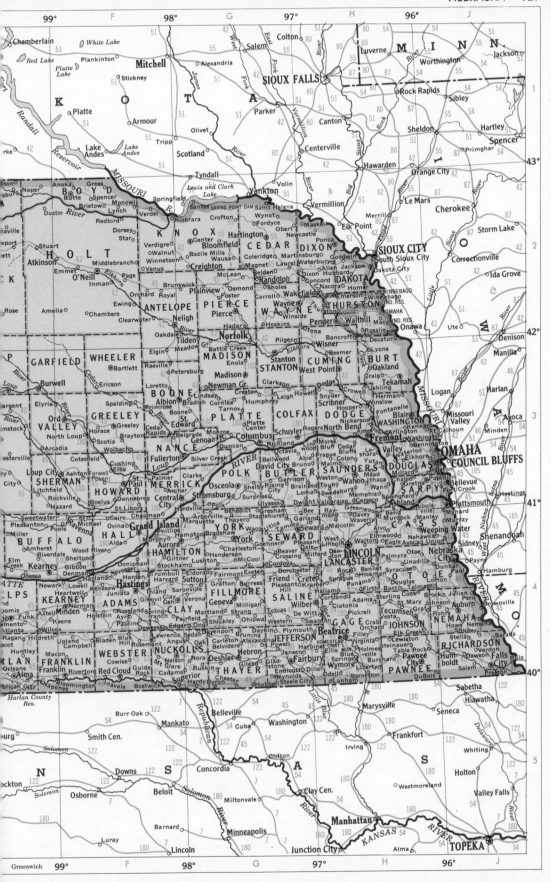

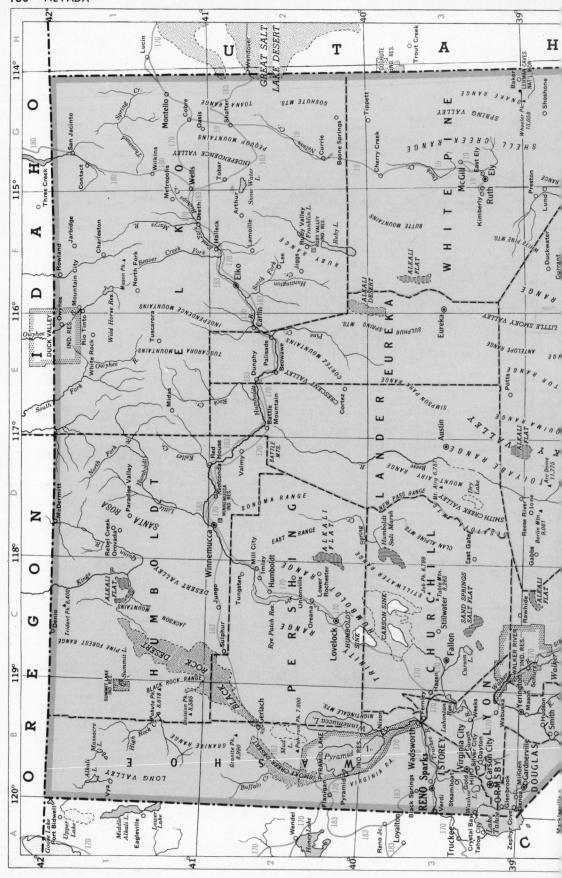

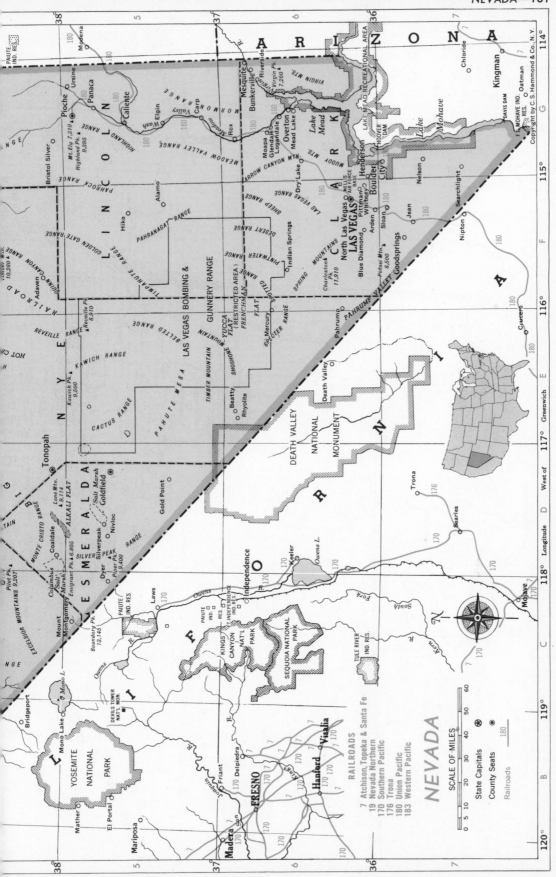

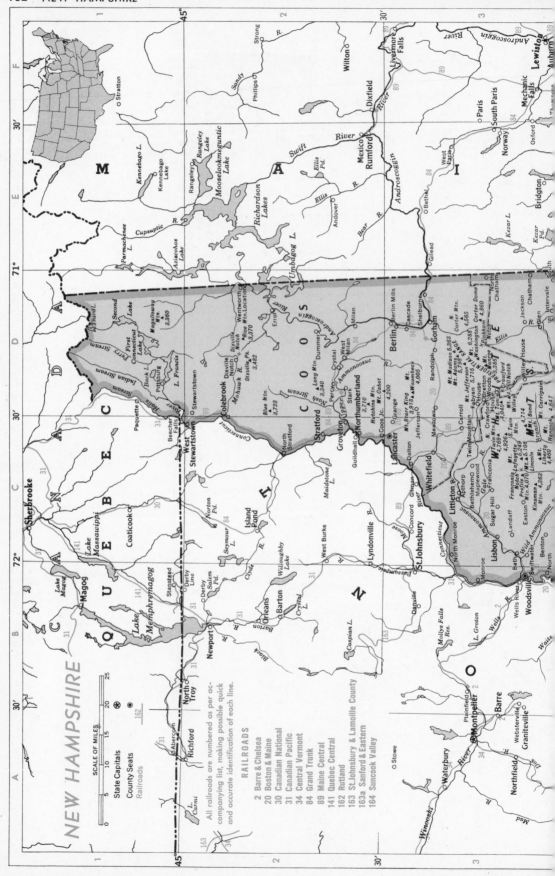

NEW HAMPSHIRE

SCALE OF MILES

0 5 10 15 20 25

State Capitals ⊛
County Seats ⦿
Railroads

RAILROADS

All railroads are numbered as per accompanying list, making possible quick and accurate identification of each line.

2 Barre & Chelsea
20 Boston & Maine
30 Canadian National
31 Canadian Pacific
34 Central Vermont
84 Grand Trunk
89 Maine Central
141 Quebec Central
162 Rutland
163 St.Johnsbury & Lamoille County
163a Sanford & Eastern
164 Suncook Valley

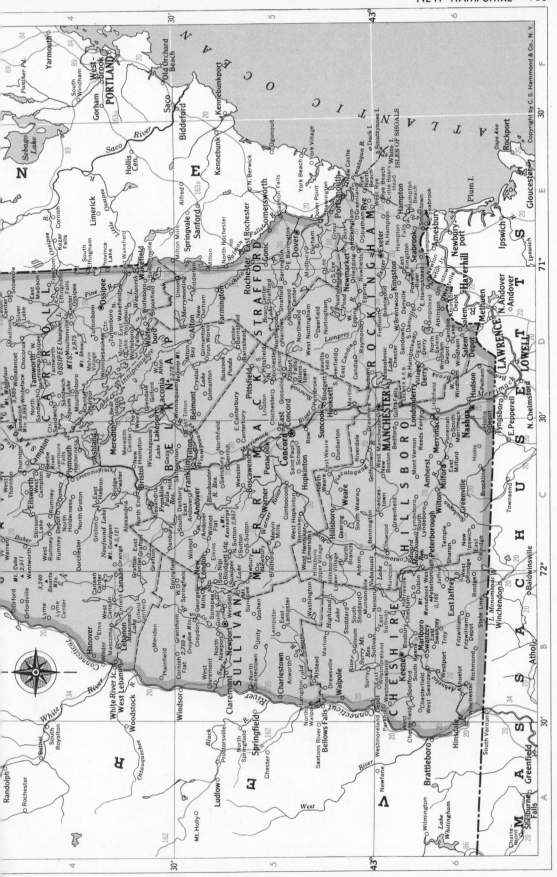

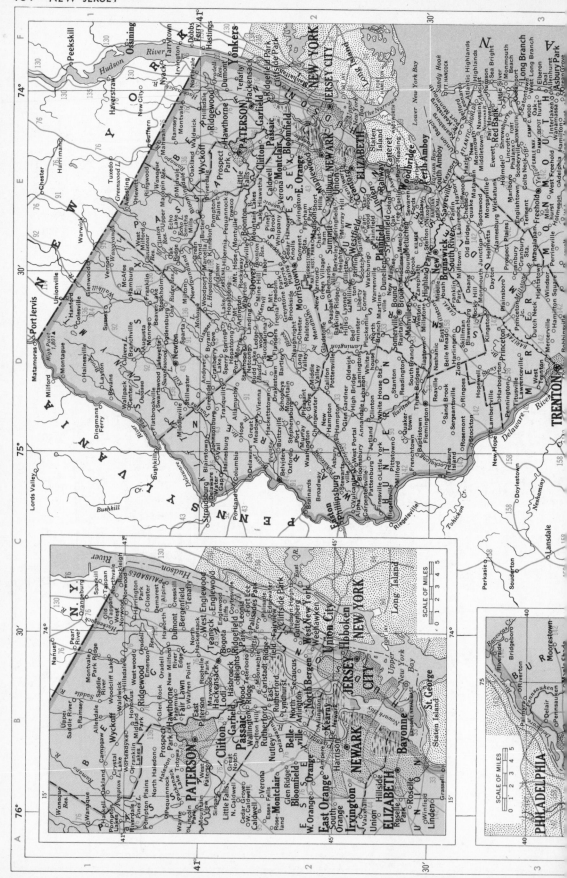

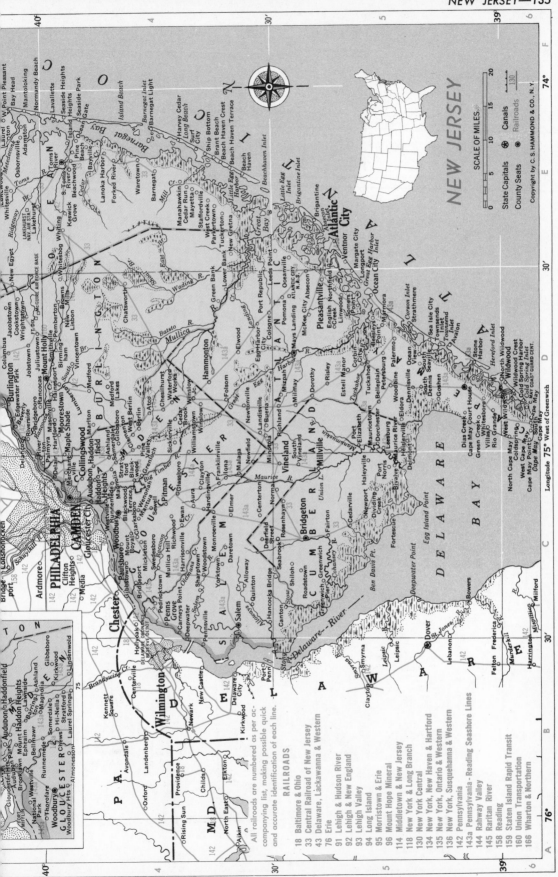

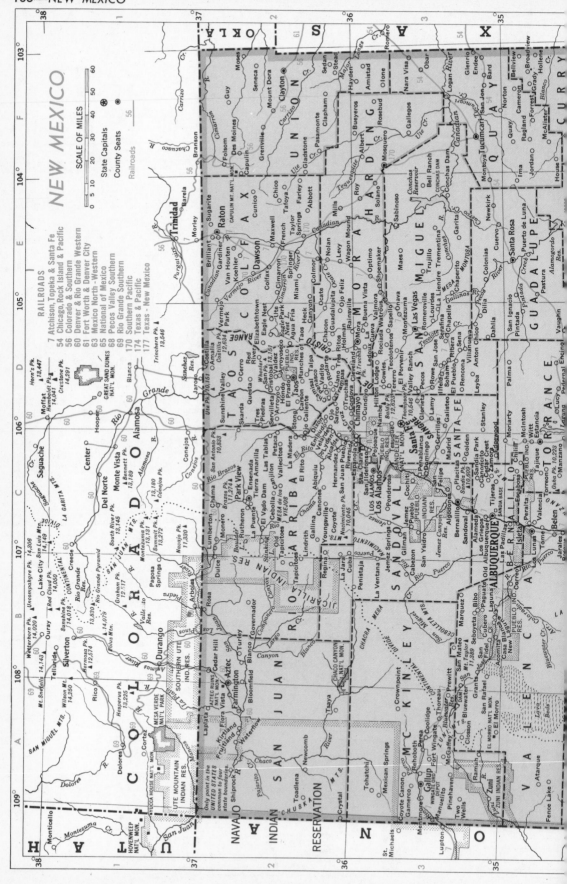

NEW MEXICO

SCALE OF MILES
0 5 10 20 30 40 50 60

◉ State Capitals
⊙ County Seats
Railroads

RAILROADS
7 Atchison, Topeka & Santa Fe
54 Chicago, Rock Island & Pacific
56 Colorado & Southern
60 Denver & Rio Grande Western
61 Fort Worth & Denver City
63 Mexico North - Western
65 National of Mexico
68 Pecos Valley Southern
69 Rio Grande Southern
170 Southern Pacific
174 Texas & Pacific
177 Texas - New Mexico

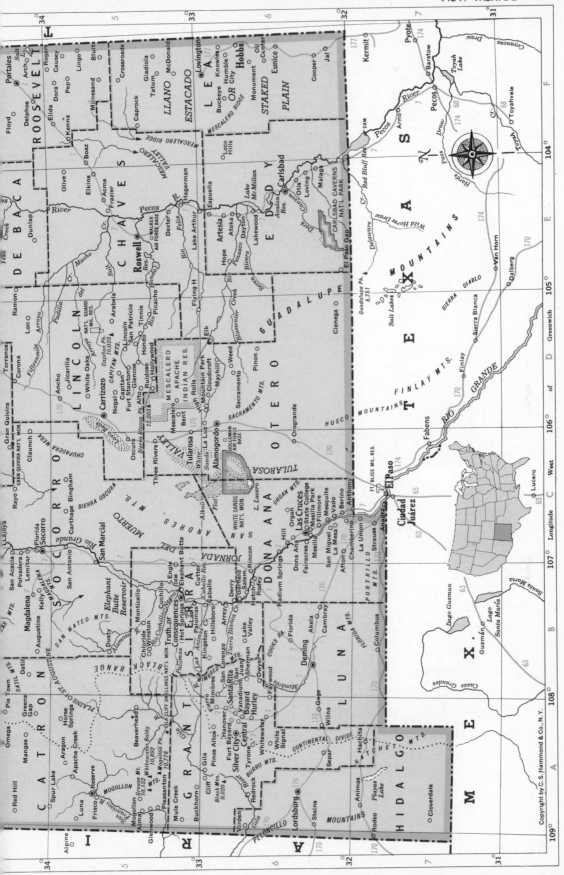

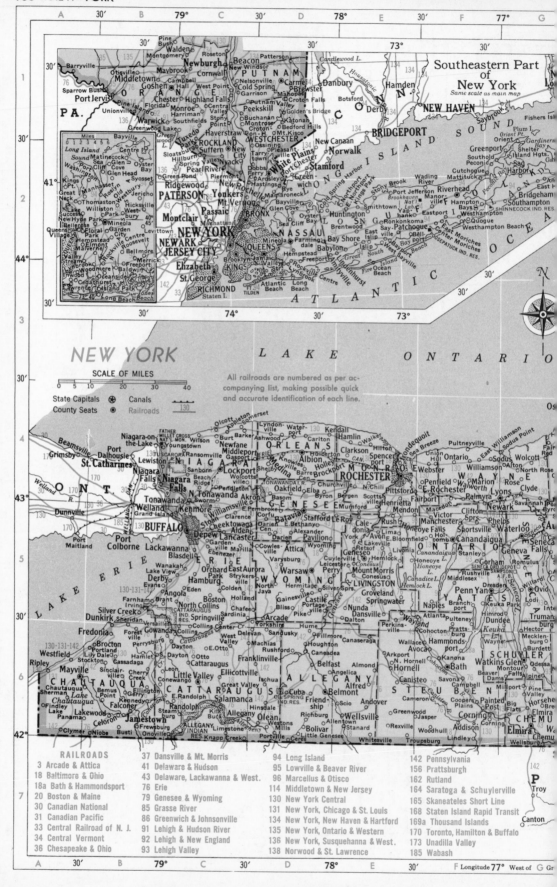

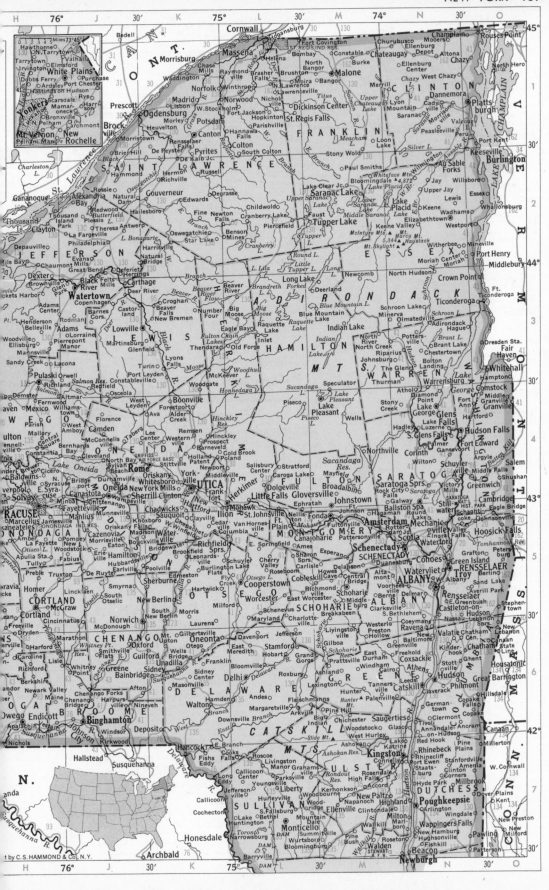

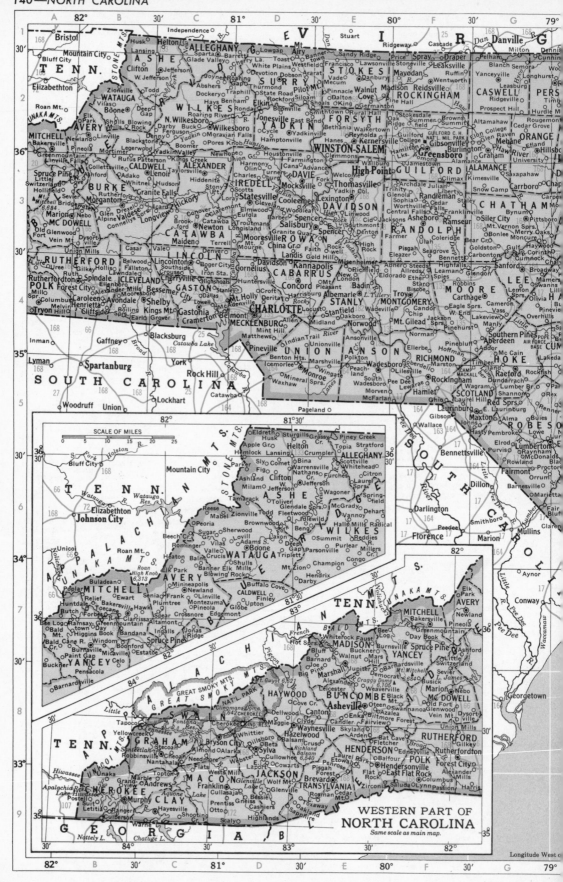

WESTERN PART OF
NORTH CAROLINA
Same scale as main map.

All railroads are numbered as per accompanying list, making possible quick and accurate identification of each line.

RAILROADS
...en & Rockfish
...er
...c & Danville
...c & East Carolina
...c & Western
...c Coast Line
...rt Morehead
...Mountain
...ear
...a & Northwestern
...a Southern

27 Charleston & Western Carolina
28 Cliffside
66 Clinchfield
69 Durham & Southern
71 East Carolina
72 East Tennessee & Western North Carolina
75 Graham County
78 High Point, Thomasville & Denton
81 Laurinburg & Southern

82 Lawndale Ry. & Industrial Co.
107 Louisville & Nashville
133 Norfolk & Western
135 Norfolk Southern
150 Piedmont & Northern
163 Rockingham
164 Seaboard Air Line
168 Southern
172 Tallulah Falls
177 Virginia & Carolina Southern
178 Warrenton
182 Winston-Salem Southbound

NORTH CAROLINA

SCALE OF MILES
0 10 20 30 40 50

State Capitals
County Seats
Canals
Railroads   66

Copyright by C. S. Hammond & Co., N. Y.

NORTH DAKOTA

SCALE OF MILES

| 0 | 10 | 20 | 30 |

State Capitals ⊗
County Seats ◉
Railroads 117

All railroads are numbered as per accompanying list, making possible quick and accurate identification of each line.

RAILROADS

30 Canadian National
31 Canadian Pacific
42 Chicago and North Western
51 Chicago, Milwaukee, St. Paul and Pacific
80 Great Northern
81 Midland Continental
113 Minneapolis & St. Louis
117 Minneapolis, St. Paul & Sault Ste. Marie
137 Northern Pacific

Copyright by C. S. Hammond & Co., N.Y.

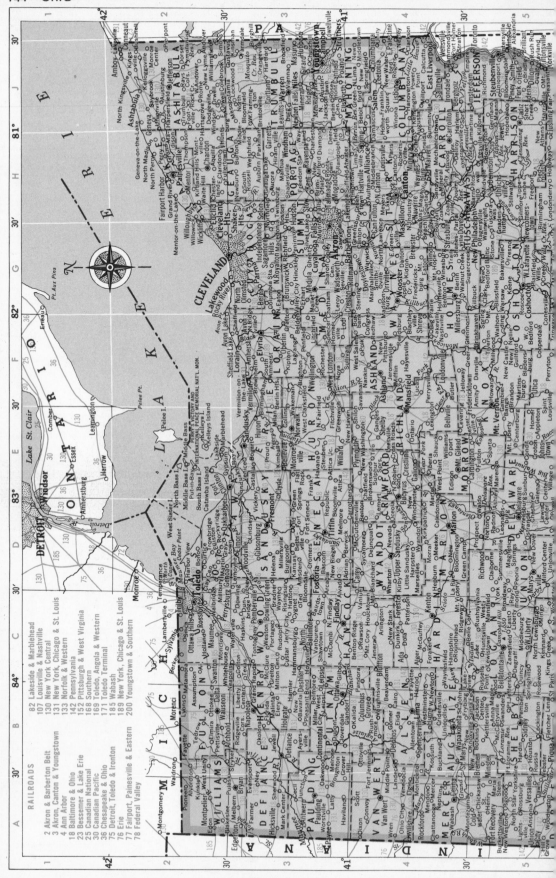

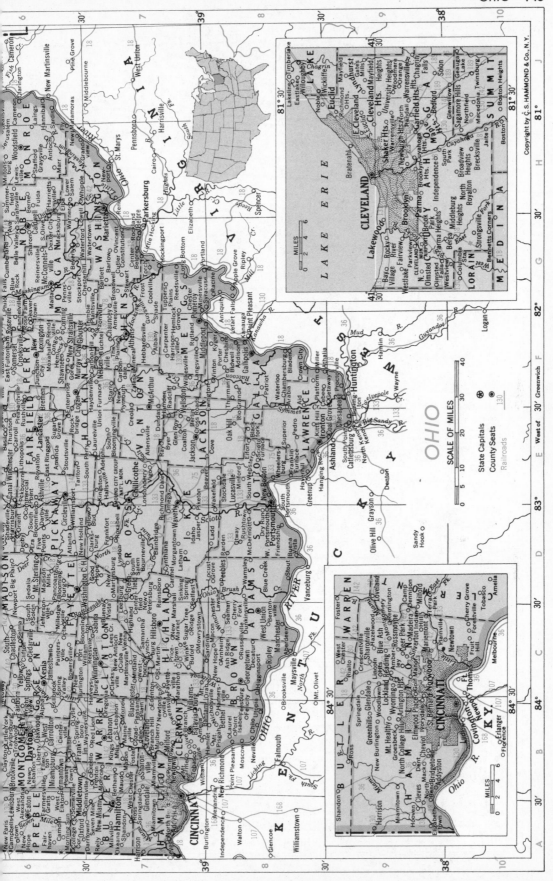

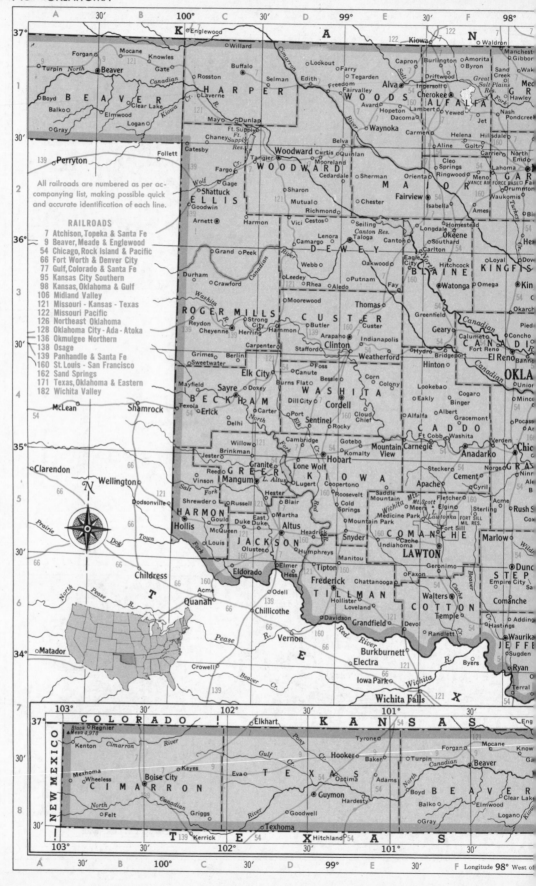

All railroads are numbered as per accompanying list, making possible quick and accurate identification of each line.

RAILROADS
7 Atchison, Topeka & Santa Fe
9 Beaver, Meade & Englewood
54 Chicago, Rock Island & Pacific
66 Fort Worth & Denver City
77 Gulf, Colorado & Santa Fe
95 Kansas City Southern
98 Kansas, Oklahoma & Gulf
106 Midland Valley
121 Missouri - Kansas - Texas
122 Missouri Pacific
126 Northeast Oklahoma
128 Oklahoma City - Ada - Atoka
136 Okmulgee Northern
138 Osage
139 Panhandle & Santa Fe
160 St. Louis - San Francisco
162 Sand Springs
171 Texas, Oklahoma & Eastern
182 Wichita Valley

OKLAHOMA

SCALE OF MILES

0 5 10   20   30   40

State Capitals   ⊛
County Seats   ◉
Railroads   98

Copyright by C. S. Hammond & Co., N. Y.

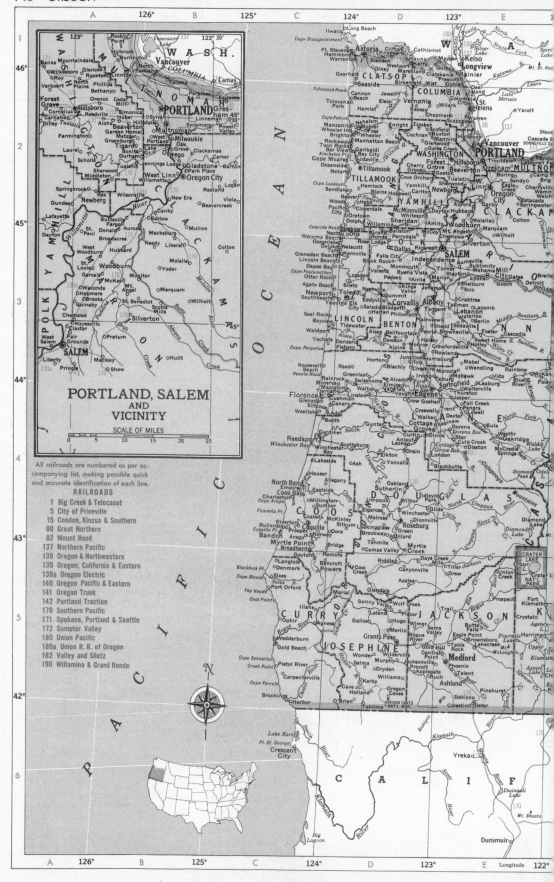

PORTLAND, SALEM
AND
VICINITY

SCALE OF MILES

0   5   10   15   20   25

All railroads are numbered as per accompanying list, making possible quick
and accurate identification of each line.

RAILROADS

1   Big Creek & Telocaset
5   City of Prineville
15 Condon, Kinzua & Southern
80 Great Northern
82 Mount Hood
137 Northern Pacific
138 Oregon & Northwestern
139 Oregon, California & Eastern
139a Oregon Electric
140 Oregon Pacific & Eastern
141 Oregon Trunk
142 Portland Traction
170 Southern Pacific
171 Spokane, Portland & Seattle
172 Sumpter Valley
180 Union Pacific
180a Union R. R. of Oregon
182 Valley and Siletz
190 Willamina & Grand Ronde

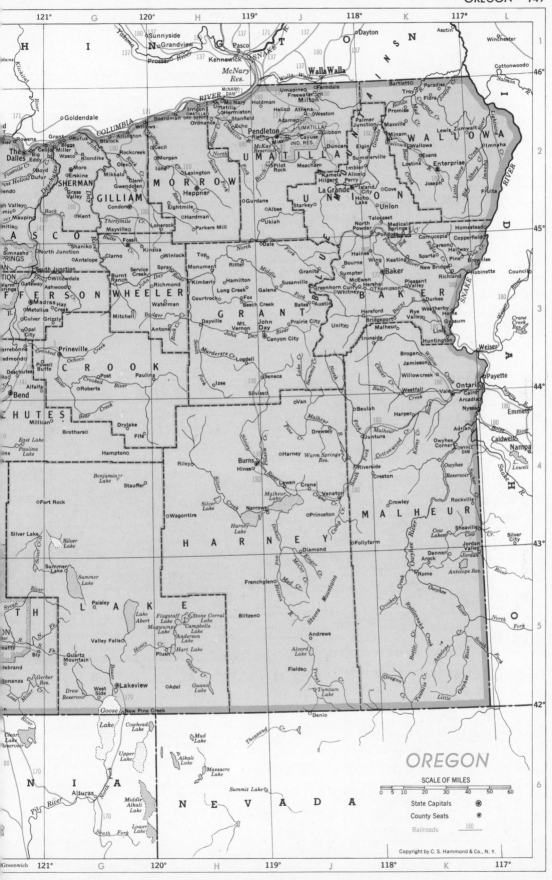

OREGON

SCALE OF MILES

0 5 10   20   30   40   50   60

State Capitals   ⊛

County Seats   ⊙

Railroads   180

Copyright by C. S. Hammond & Co., N. Y.

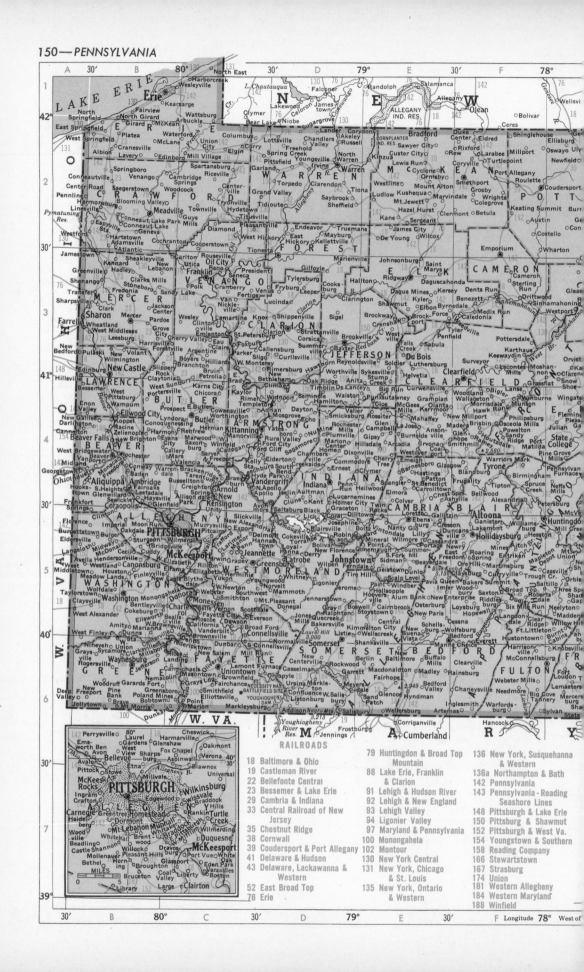

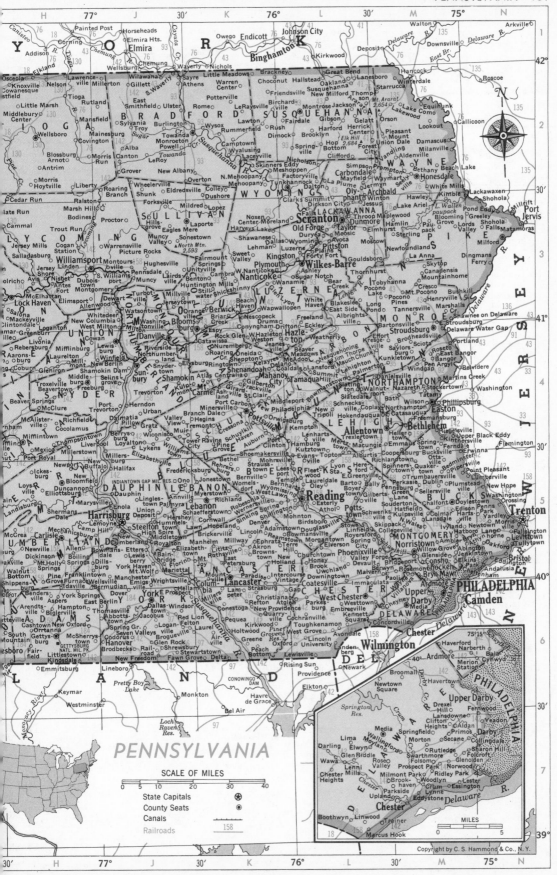

PENNSYLVANIA

SCALE OF MILES

0 5 10   20   30   40

State Capitals ⊛
County Seats ⊙
Canals
Railroads

158

Copyright by C. S. Hammond & Co., N. Y.

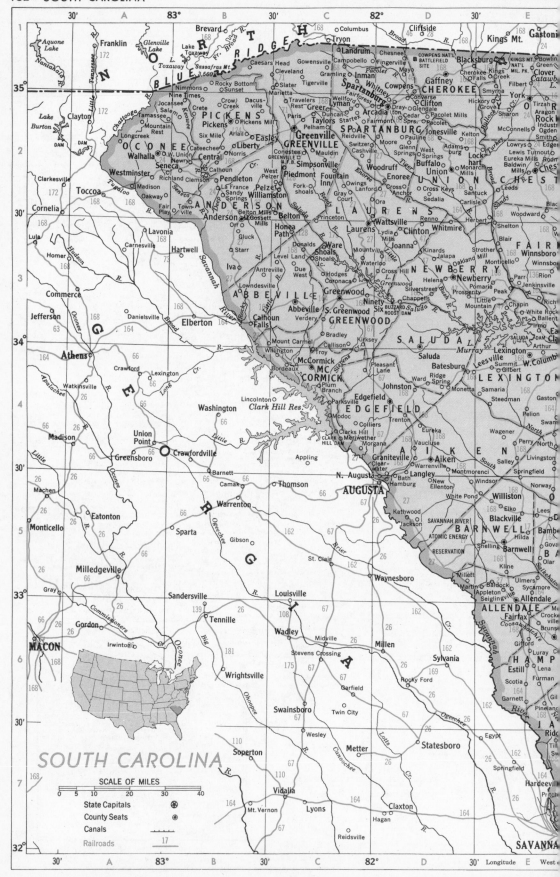

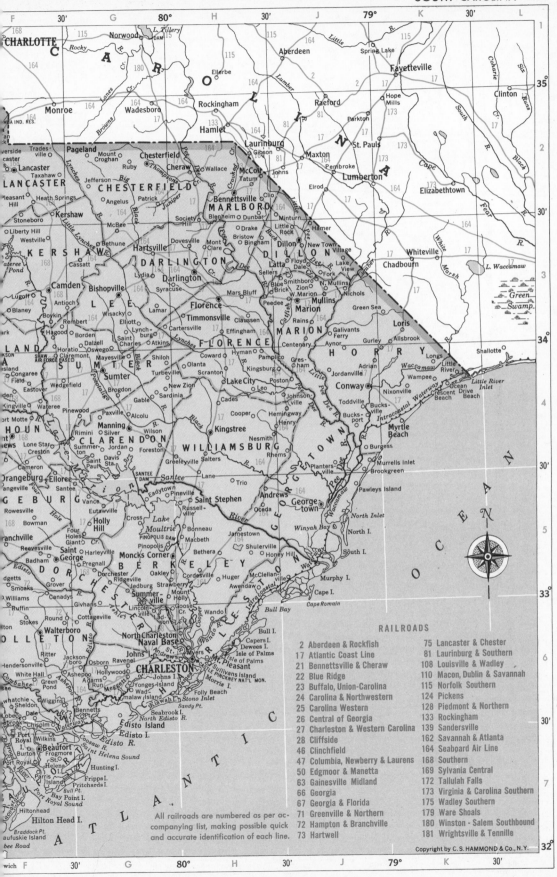

RAILROADS

2	Aberdeen & Rockfish	75	Lancaster & Chester
17	Atlantic Coast Line	81	Laurinburg & Southern
21	Bennettsville & Cheraw	108	Louisville & Wadley
22	Blue Ridge	110	Macon, Dublin & Savannah
23	Buffalo, Union-Carolina	115	Norfolk Southern
24	Carolina & Northwestern	124	Pickens
25	Carolina Western	128	Piedmont & Northern
26	Central of Georgia	133	Rockingham
27	Charleston & Western Carolina	139	Sandersville
28	Cliffside	162	Savannah & Atlanta
46	Clinchfield	164	Seaboard Air Line
47	Columbia, Newberry & Laurens	168	Southern
50	Edgmoor & Manetta	169	Sylvania Central
63	Gainesville Midland	172	Tallulah Falls
66	Georgia	173	Virginia & Carolina Southern
67	Georgia & Florida	175	Wadley Southern
71	Greenville & Northern	179	Ware Shoals
72	Hampton & Branchville	180	Winston - Salem Southbound
73	Hartwell	181	Wrightsville & Tennille

All railroads are numbered as per accompanying list, making possible quick and accurate identification of each line.

Copyright by C. S. HAMMOND & Co., N.Y.

Copyright by C. S. Hammond & Co., N. Y.

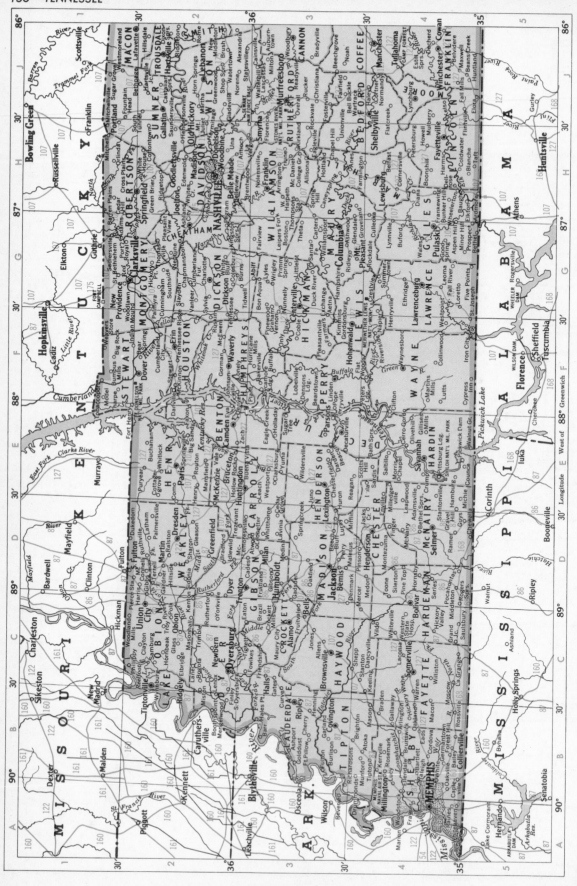

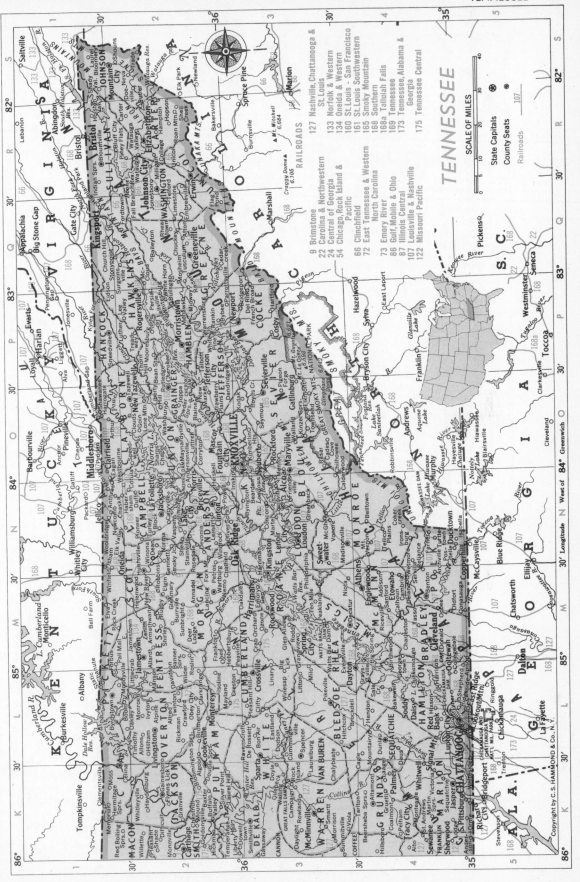

TENNESSEE

SCALE OF MILES

State Capitals ⊛

County Seats ⊙

Railroads

RAILROADS

9	Brimstone
22	Carolina & Northwestern
24	Central of Georgia
54	Chicago, Rock Island & Pacific
66	Clinchfield
72	East Tennessee & Western North Carolina
73	Emory River
86	Gulf, Mobile & Ohio
87	Illinois Central
107	Louisville & Nashville
122	Missouri Pacific
127	Nashville, Chattanooga & St. Louis
133	Norfolk & Western
134	Oneida & Western
160	St. Louis - San Francisco
161	St. Louis Southwestern
165	Smoky Mountain
168	Southern
168a	Tallulah Falls
169	Tennessee
173	Tennessee, Alabama & Georgia
175	Tennessee Central

Copyright by C. S. HAMMOND & Co., N. Y.

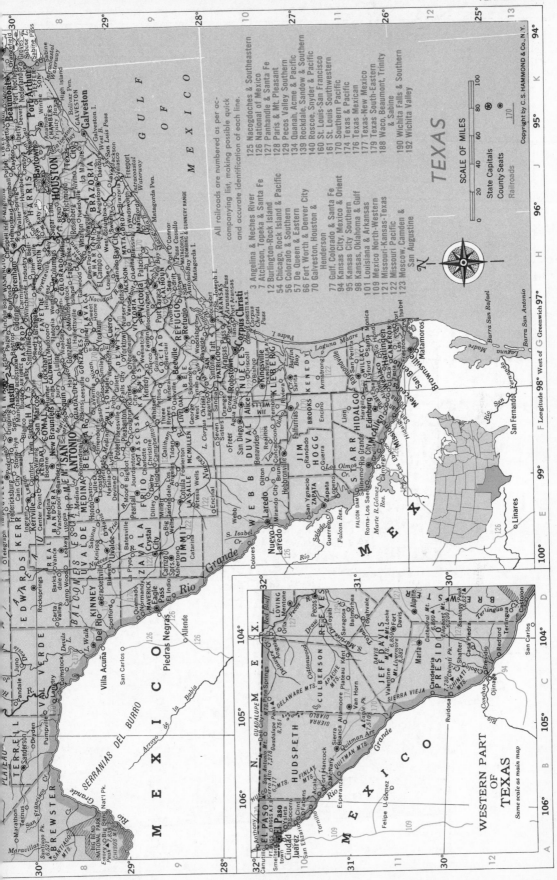

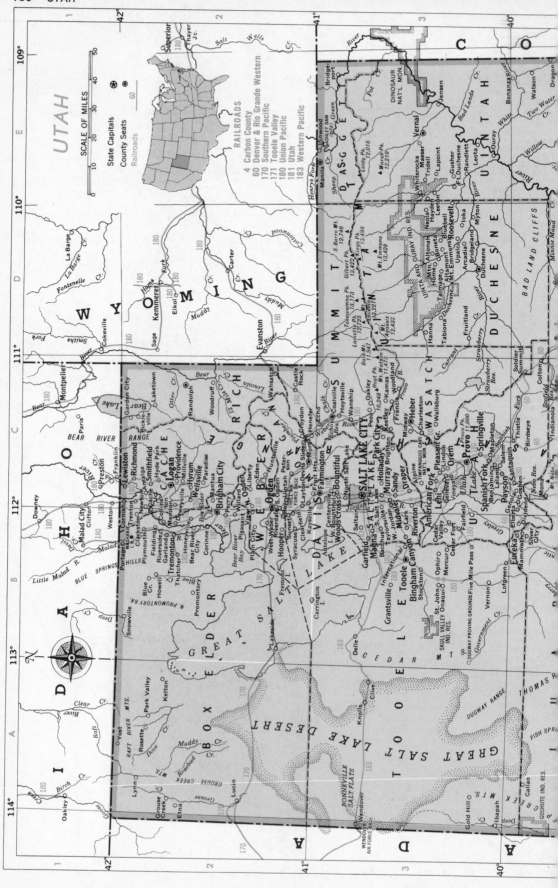

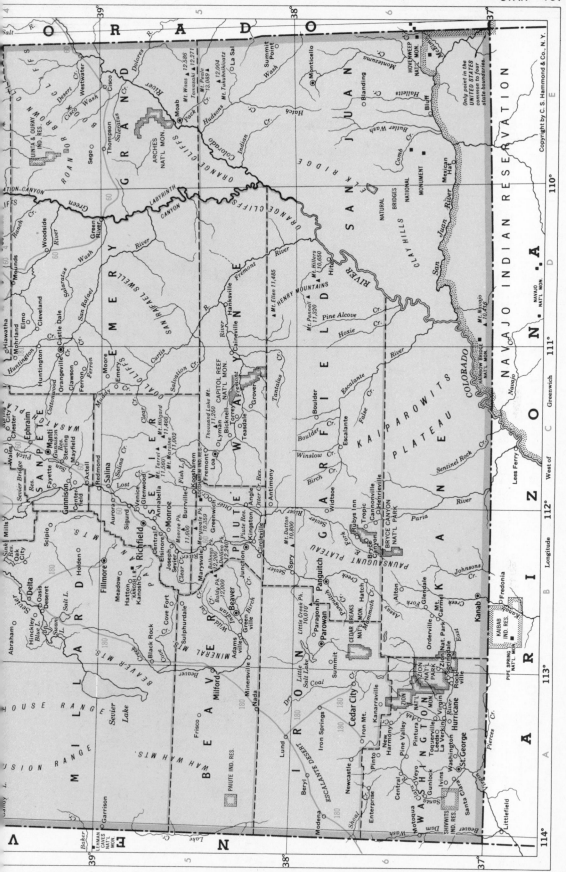

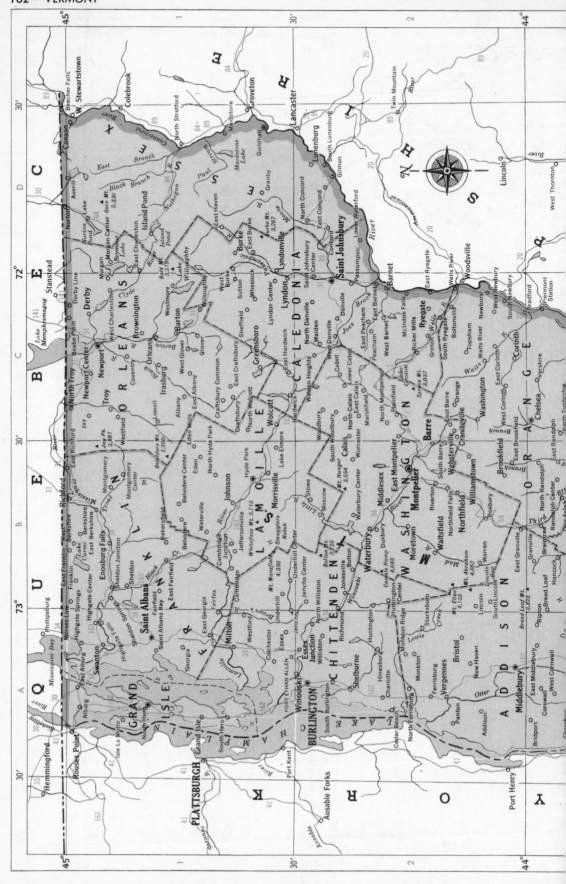

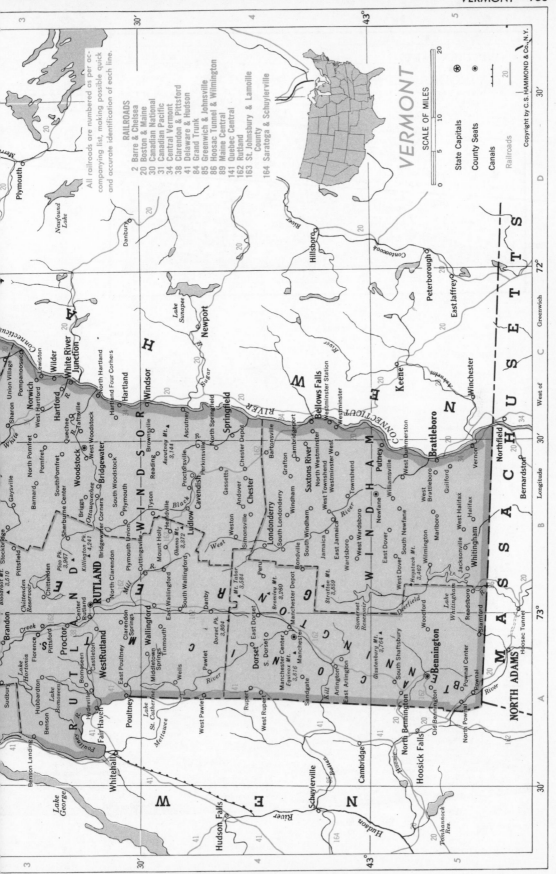

VERMONT

SCALE OF MILES

State Capitals
County Seats
Canals
Railroads

Copyright by C.S. HAMMOND & Co., N.Y.

RAILROADS

2 Barre & Chelsea
20 Boston & Maine
30 Canadian National
31 Canadian Pacific
34 Central Vermont
38 Clarendon & Pittsford
41 Delaware & Hudson
84 Grand Trunk
85 Greenwich & Johnsville
86 Hoosac Tunnel & Wilmington
89 Maine Central
141 Quebec Central
162 Rutland
163 St. Johnsbury & Lamoille County
164 Saratoga & Schuylerville

All railroads are numbered as per accompanying list, making possible quick and accurate identification of each line.

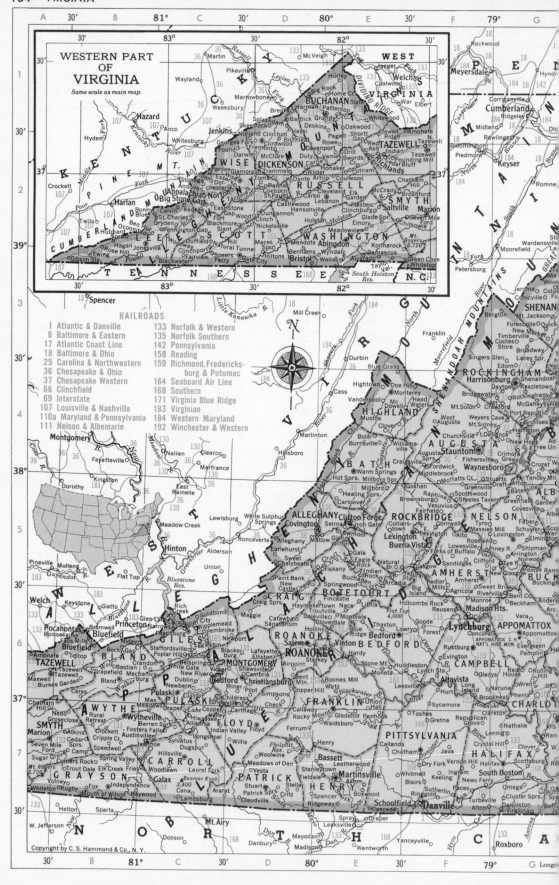

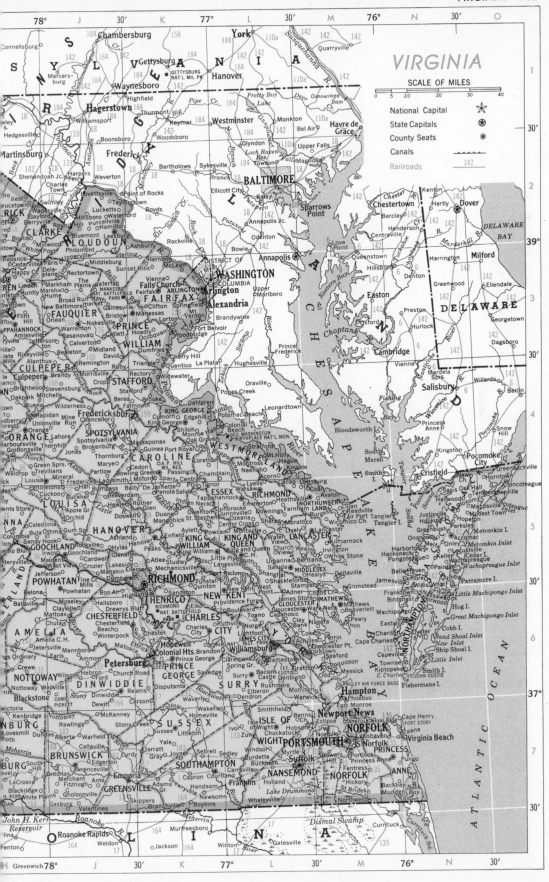

VIRGINIA
SCALE OF MILES
0   5   10   20   30   40

National Capital   ☆
State Capitals   ⊛
County Seats   ◉
Canals   ....
Railroads   142

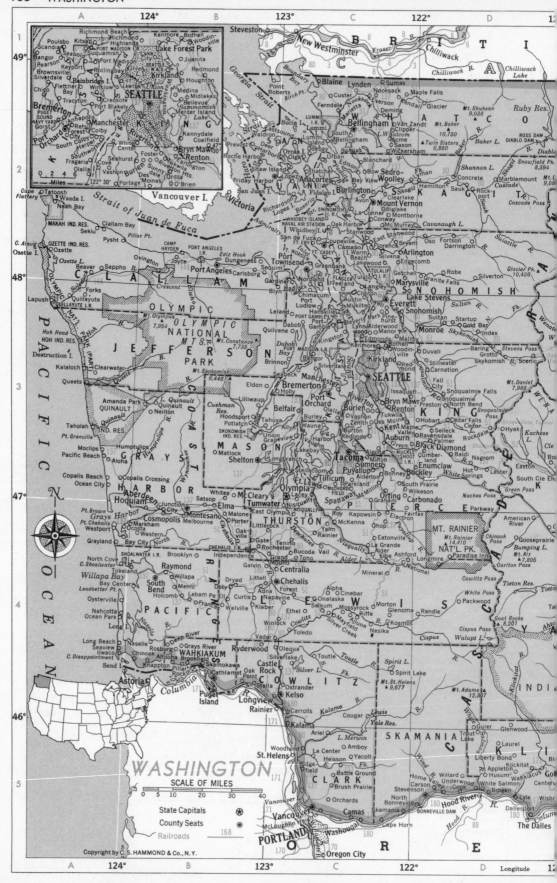

WASHINGTON

SCALE OF MILES

0 5 10 20 30 40

★ State Capitals
◉ County Seats
Railroads

Copyright by C. S. HAMMOND & Co., N.Y.

All railroads are numbered as per accompanying list, making possible quick and accurate identification of each line.

RAILROADS

3 British Columbia Electric	86 Longview, Portland & Northern	145 Port Townsend
5 Camas Prairie	88 Mount Hood	155 Spokane, International
6 Canadian National	137 Northern Pacific	170 Southern Pacific
8 Canadian Pacific	139a Oregon Electric	171 Spokane, Portland & Seattle
51 Chicago, Milwaukee, St. Paul & Pacific	141 Oregon Trunk	180 Union Pacific
52 Cowlitz, Chehalis & Cascade	143 Pacific Coast	181 Walla Walla Valley
80 Great Northern	144 Port Angeles Western	182 Washington, Idaho & Montana
		183 Waterville

All railroads are numbered as per accompanying list, making possible quick and accurate identification of each line.

RAILROADS

18 Baltimore & Ohio	156 Southern
21 Buffalo Creek & Gauley	157 Strouds Creek & Muddlety
23 Campbell's Creek	183 Virginian
36 Chesapeake & Ohio	184 Western Maryland
37 Chesapeake Western	188 West Virginia Northern
40 Cumberland & Pennsylvania	192 Winchester & Western
48 Kanawha Central	193 Winifrede
50 Kelley's Creek & Northwestern	
64 Kelly's Creek	
100 Monongahela	
130 New York Central	
131 New York, Chicago & St. Louis	
133 Norfolk & Western	
142 Pennsylvania	
152 Pittsburgh & West Virginia	
154 Preston	

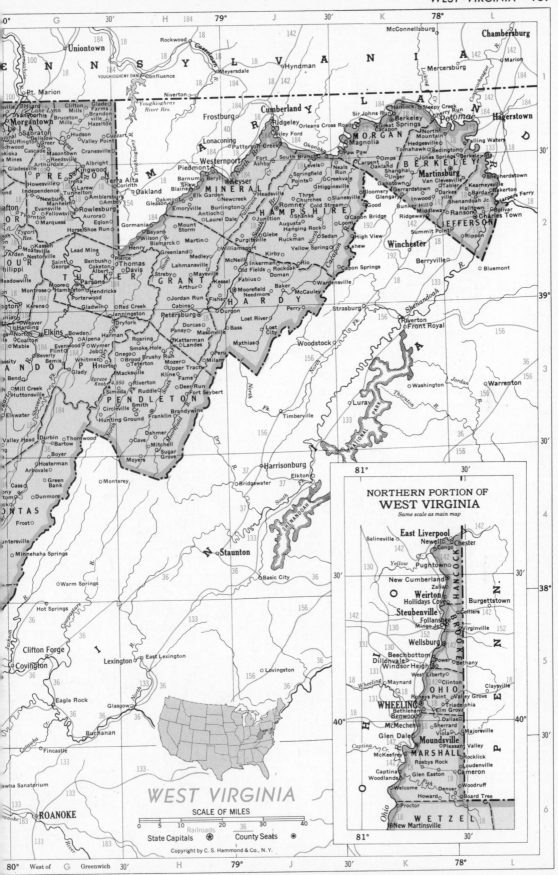

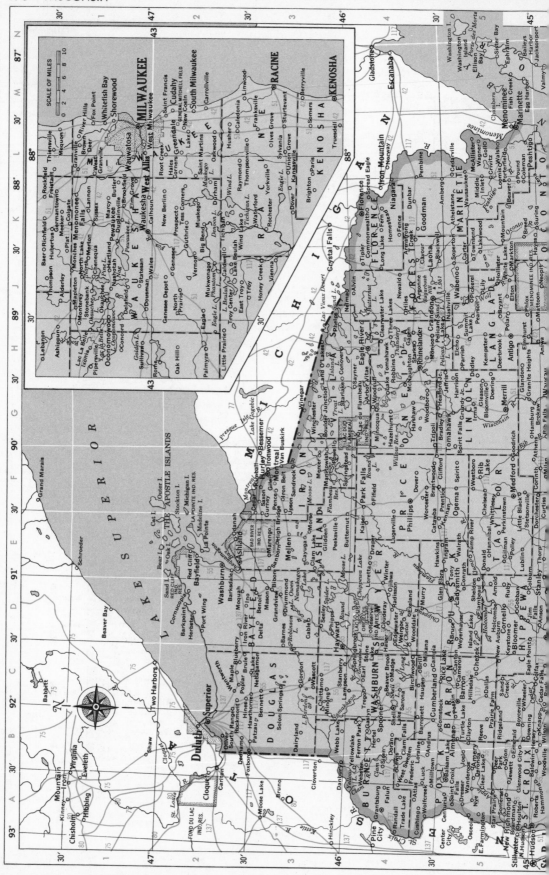

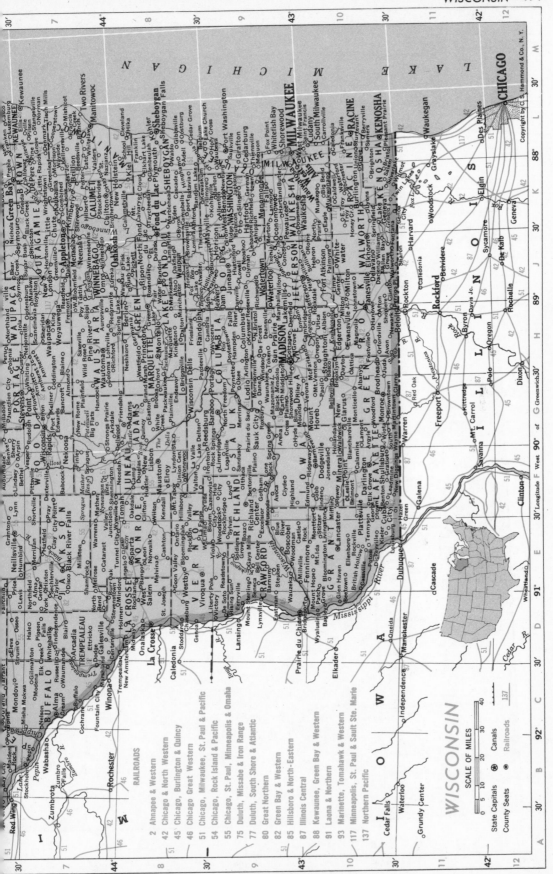

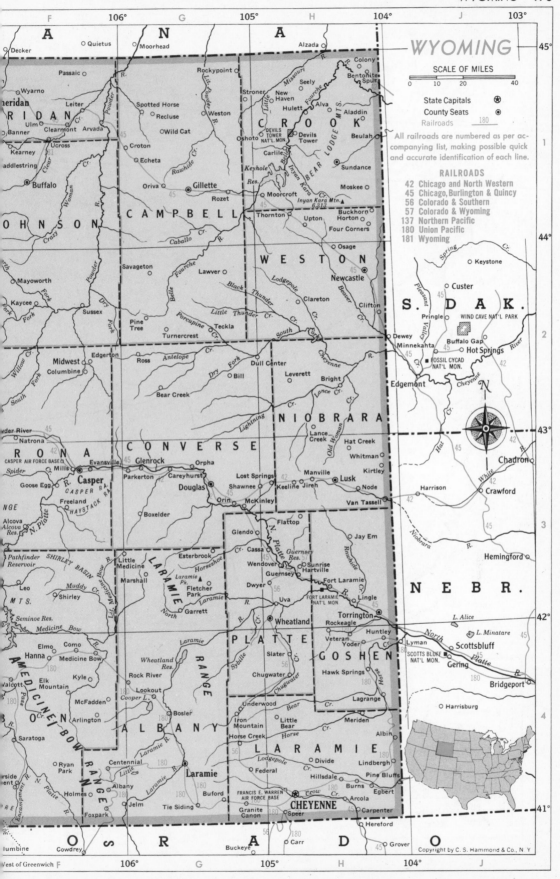

WYOMING—173

WYOMING

SCALE OF MILES

0   10   20   40

⊛ State Capitals
⊚ County Seats
Railroads   180

All railroads are numbered as per accompanying list, making possible quick and accurate identification of each line.

RAILROADS

42 Chicago and North Western
45 Chicago, Burlington & Quincy
56 Colorado & Southern
57 Colorado & Wyoming
137 Northern Pacific
180 Union Pacific
181 Wyoming

Copyright by C. S. Hammond & Co., N Y

West of Greenwich

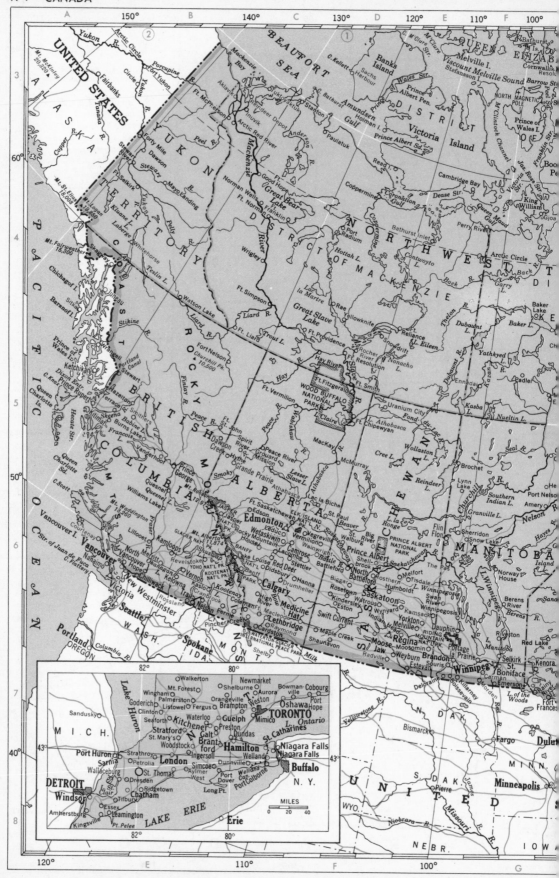

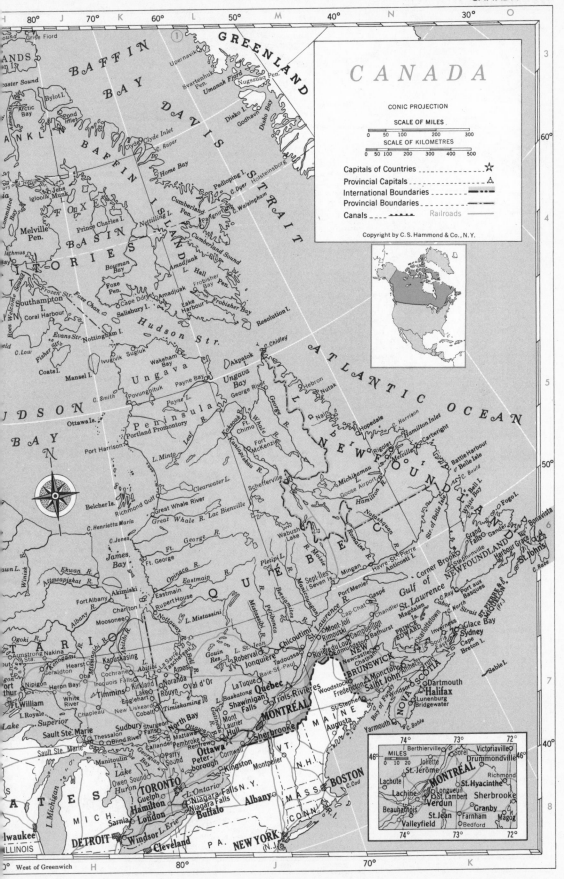

80° 70° 60° 50° 40° 30°

GREENLAND

Grise Fiord

BAFFIN

Upernavik

Svartenhuk Pen.

Umanak Fjord

Nugssuaq Pen.

BAY

Disko Bay

Godhavn

Disko I.

DAVIS

3

60°

Lancaster Sound

Arctic Bay

Bylot I.

Admiralty In.

Pond Inlet

Clyde Clyde Inlet

C. Raper

Home Bay

Holsteinsborg

BAFFIN

STRAIT

4

Igloolik

Jens Munk I.

FOX

Prince Charles I.

Nettilling L.

Cumberland Pen.

Pangnirtung

C. Dyer

C. Walsingham

Melville Pen.

BASIN

ISLAND

Cumberland Sound

TERRITORIES

Amadjuak

L. Hall

Amadjuak L.

Frobisher Bay Pen.

Frobisher Bay

Bowman Bay

Foxe Pen.

Cape Dorset

Isthmus

Southampton I.

Frozen Str. Foxe Chan.

Nottingham I.

Salisbury I.

Lake Harbour

Resolution I.

Coral Harbour

Fisher Str.

Evans Str.

Hudson Str.

C. Chidley

ATLANTIC OCEAN

C. Low

Coats I.

Mansel I.

Wakeham Bay

Akpatok I.

Hebron

Nutak

5

50°

C. Smith

Povungnituk

Ungava

Payne Bay

Ungava Bay

George River

Nain

Hopedale

C. Harrison

Ottawa Is.

Peninsula

Payne L.

Koksoak R.

Ft. Chimo

Fort McKenzie

Kaniapiskau R.

Whale R.

Rigolet

Melville

Hamilton Inlet

Cartwright

Port Harrison

Portland Promontory

Leaf R.

L. Minto

Schefferville

L. Michikamau

Goose Airport

Battle Harbour

Belle Isle

C. Bauld

Clearwater L.

Hamilton R.

Bell I.

White Bay

6

Belcher Is.

Richmond Gulf

Great Whale River

Great Whale R. Lac Bienville

Wabush Lake

Str. of Belle Isle

Grand Falls

Fogo I.

Bonavista

C. Henrietta Maria

George R.

Romaine R.

Harbour Grace

St. John's

C. Jones

Ft. McKenzie

Eastmain

Opinaca R.

Natashquan R.

Stephenville

NEWFOUNDLAND

C. Race

James Bay

Ft. George

Pletipi L.

R.

Moisie

Mingan

Havre-St. Pierre

Anticosti I.

Corner Brook

Gander

Ekwan R.

Nottaway R.

Eastmain

Rupert House

QUEBEC

Bersimis R.

Sept-Iles Seven Is.

Port Menier

Gulf

St. Lawrence

of

St. George's

Port aux Basques

Attawapiskat R.

Akimiski I.

L. Mistassini

Manicouagan R.

Cabot Str.

North Sydney

St. PIERRE & MIQUELON (Fr.)

Winisk

Fort Albany

Charlton I.

Mistassibi R.

Lawrence

Cap-Chat

St. Lawrence

C. Ray

Glace Bay

Ogoki R.

Albany

Moosonee

Abitibi R.

Gouin Res.

L. St. Jean

Mont-Joli

Rimouski

Gaspé

Chandler

Magdalen

Charlottetown

Inverness

Sydney

C. North

Cape Breton I.

Armstrong Nakina

Kenogami

Kapuskasing

Abitibi L.

Tascherau

Roberval

Jonquiere

Tadoussac

Rivière du Loup

Edmundston

Campbellton

Bathurst

PRINCE EDWARD ISLAND

Souris

Ottawa Is.

Sable I.

Nipigon

Heron Bay

Hearst

Geraldton

Oba

Cochrane

Iroquois Falls

Amos

Noranda

La Tuque

Shawinigan Falls

Baie-St-Paul

Quebec

Trois-Rivières

Woodstock

Newcastle

Chatham

NEW

Moncton

Amherst

NOVA

Dartmouth

Ft. William

I. Royale

White River

Chapleau

Timmins

Kirkland Lake

Rouyn

Oval d'Or

Baskatong Res.

Mont Laurier

MONTRÉAL

Hull

Fredericton

BRUNSWICK

Saint John

Windsor

SCOTIA

Halifax

7

40°

Port Arthur

L. Superior

Nipigon

Sudbury

Sturgeon Falls

North Bay

New Liskeard

Cobalt

L. Timiskaming

Englehart

Sherbrooke

MAINE

St. Stephen

Bay of Fundy

Lunenburg

Bridgewater

Sault Ste. Marie

Thessalon

Blind River

Callander

Mattawa

Pembroke

Renfrew

Ottawa

Cornwall

Augusta

Yarmouth

C. Sable

Sault Ste. Marie

Manitoulin I.

Georgian Bay

Parry Sound

Peterborough

Kingston

Montpelier

VT.

N.H.

BOSTON

C. Cod

Milwaukee

Owen Sound

L. Huron

Barrie

L. Ontario

Niagara Falls N.Y.

Albany

MASS.

ILLINOIS

MICH.

TORONTO

Guelph

Hamilton

Niagara Falls

Buffalo

CONN.

R.I.

8

Port

DETROIT

Sarnia

London

Windsor L. Erie

Cleveland

PA.

NEW YORK

N.J.

80° 70°

West of Greenwich H J K

CANADA

CONIC PROJECTION

SCALE OF MILES

0 50 100 200 300

SCALE OF KILOMETRES

0 50 100 200 300 400 500

Capitals of Countries ⋆

Provincial Capitals △

International Boundaries

Provincial Boundaries

Canals   Railroads

Copyright by C. S. Hammond & Co., N.Y.

74° 73° 72°

MILES

0 10 20

Berthierville

Sorel

Victoriaville

46°

Joliette

St-Jérôme

Lachute

St. Lambert

Lachine

MONTRÉAL

Longueuil

Verdun

Beauharnois

St. Jean

Valleyfield

Bedford

Farnham

Drummondville

Richmond

St. Hyacinthe

Sherbrooke

Granby

Magog

74° 73° 72°

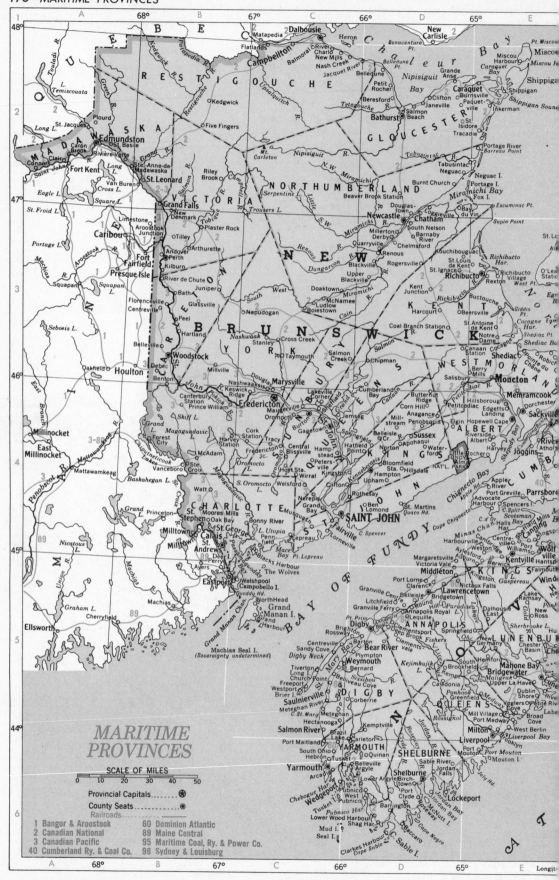

MARITIME
PROVINCES

SCALE OF MILES

0 10 20 30 40 50

Provincial Capitals........⊛
County Seats............⊙
Railroads................

1 Bangor & Aroostook	60 Dominion Atlantic
2 Canadian National	89 Maine Central
3 Canadian Pacific	95 Maritime Coal, Ry. & Power Co.
40 Cumberland Ry. & Coal Co.	98 Sydney & Louisburg

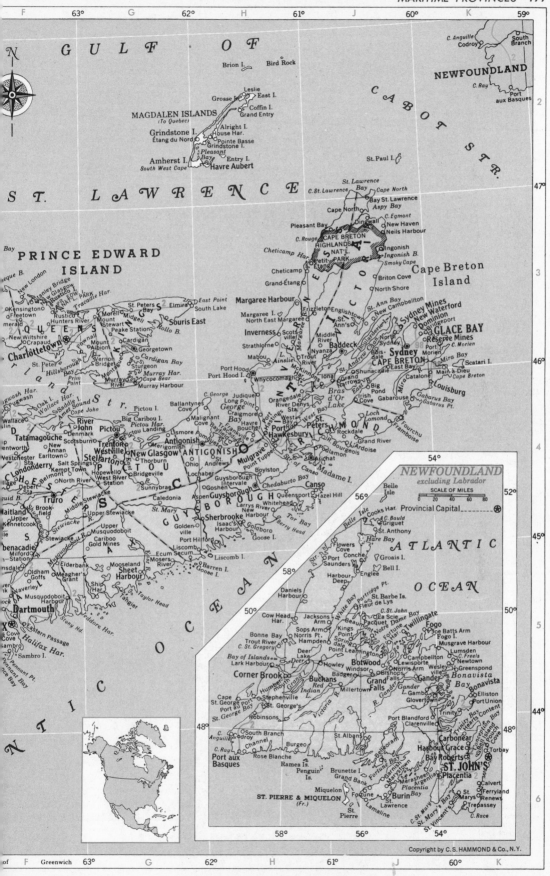

GULF · OF

N

Brion I. Bird Rock

Leslie
Grosse Î. East I.
Coffin I.
Grand Entry
MAGDALEN ISLANDS
(To Quebec)
Alright I.
Grindstone I. House Har.
Étang du Nord Pointe Basse
Grindstone I.
Pleasant
Amherst I. Bay Entry I.
South West Cape Havre Aubert

St. Paul I.

NEWFOUNDLAND

C. Anguille
Codroy South Branch

C. Ray Port
aux Basques

CABOT STR.

ST. LAWRENCE

Bay

St. Lawrence
Bay
C. St. Lawrence Cape North
Bay St. Lawrence
Aspy Bay
Cape North
Pleasant Bay C. Egmont Dingwall New Haven
Neils Harbour
C. Rouge CAPE BRETON
Cheticamp Har. HIGHLANDS Ingonish
Petit- NAT'L Ingonish B.
Étang PARK Smoky Cape
Cheticamp Briton Cove
Grand-Étang North Shore

Cape Breton
Island

PRINCE EDWARD
ISLAND

Bay
que B.
New London
Stanley Bridge Frizzleton Englishtown
Glasgow Rustico St. Ann Bay New Waterford
Brackley New Campbellton New Waterford
Kensington Hunters River East Point Sydney Mines Dominion
merald St. Peters South Lake Margaree I. Scotts- Dominion
New Wiltshire Bay Elmira North East Margaree North GLACE BAY
Crapaud Morell Souris East Inverness ville Sydney Reserve Mines
QUEENS Mount Strathlorne Middle North C. Morien
Charlottetown Stewart Rollo B. Mabou Nyanza Baddeck Sydney Port
Wednesboro Cardigan Georgetown Trout St. Andrew Morien
St. Peter Vernon KINGS Cardigan Bay River CAPE BRETON Mira Bay
Hillsborough Bridge Sturgeon Ainslie East Bay Scatari I.
Prim Montague Cape Bear Port Hood McKinnon Main-à-Dieu
Point Murray River Port Hood I. Shunacadie Grand C. Breton
Murray Har. Whycocomagh Narrows Big
Murray Harbour C. George Judique Iona Pond Louisburg
Wallace Har. Pictou I. Long Point Orangedale East Irish
Pugwash Ballantynes George River Denys Bras Cove Gabarus Bay
Oak I. Cove Bay Sta. d'Or Gabarus Pt.
Saddle I. Big Caribou I. Malignant Havre West Lake Loch
Wallace Cape John Cove Frankville Boucher Lomond
River Pictou Har. Lismore Hastings West Bay St. Touchie
John Pictou Landing Pomquet Frankville Peters Framboise
Denmark Merigomish Port- Hawkesbury RICHMOND Grand River
Tatamagouche Scotsburn Ohio land Rockdale Ardoise
New Trenton ANTIGONISH Point Tupper L'Ardoise
Annan Westville PICTOU St. Andrews Louisdale Madame I.
Salt Springs Stellarton Thorburn Boylston of Richmond
Londonderry Kempt Town New Glasgow Bridgeville Lochaber Canso Hazel Hill
Belmont Hopewell West River Guysborough Canso
North River Station Intervale Chedabucto Bay
Debert Sunnybrae Goshen Queensport Hazel Hill
Truro Caledonia GUYSBOROUGH Larrys River Whitehaven
Brook- Middle Stewiacke St. Mary Sherbrooke Harbour Tor Bay
field Upper Stewiacke Golden- Isaac's Berry Head
Maitland Stewiacke ville Harbour
Upper Stewiacke Port Hilford Goose I.
Kennetcook Upper Musquodoboit Liscomb
benacadie Cariboo Ecum Secum Liscomb I.
Milford Gold Mines Mosers Barren I.
Station Elderbank River Goose I.
sdale Oldham Mooseland Sheet
Naverley Meagher's Harbour
Grant Ship Har.
Musquodoboit Goffs Tangier
Harbour Taylor Head
Dartmouth Fiddore Har.
Eastern Passage
Cove Halifax Har.
Sambro Pennant Pt.
Sambro I. Bay
rence Bay

ATLANTIC

OCEAN

N

GREENWICH

NEWFOUNDLAND
excluding Labrador
SCALE OF MILES
0 20 40 60 80
⊛ Provincial Capital _____

Belle
Isle
Belle Isle Cooks Har.
C. Bauld
Griguet
St. Anthony
Hare Bay
Flowers Conche
Cove Groais I.
Port Bell I.
Saunders
Harbour
Deep
Daniels
Harbour Partridge Pt.
White Bay Fleur de Lys
Cow Head Jacksons C. St. John
Arm La Scie
Sops Arm Beaumont Pacquet Notre Dame Bay
Bonne Bay Kings Spring- Fortune Twillingate Fogo
Norris Pt. Point dale Har. Joe Batts Arm
Trout River Hampden Point Leamington Musgrave Harbour
C. St. Gregory Deer Lewisporte Lumsden
Lake Howley Botwood Norris Arm C. Freels
Bay of Islands Badger Windsor Bishops Newtown
Lark Harbour Red Falls Greenspond
Corner Brook Buchans Indian Grand Wesley- Bonavista
Stephenville Millertown Falls Gander ville Bay
Cape Victoria L. Gambo Glovertown Elliston
St. George port Robinsons Port Union
Port au Port Blandford Bonavista
St. George (Bay) St. George's Clarenville Trinity
South Branch St. Albans Trinity Bay Content
C. Codroy Hearts Cove
Anguille Channel Burgeo Bellisle Torbay
Port aux Rose Blanche Bay Carbonear
Basques Ramea Is. Harbour Grace
C. Ray Penguin Brunette I. Bay Roberts
Is. Grand Bank Garnish Placentia ST. JOHN'S
Miquelon Fortune Marystown Placentia Placentia Calvert
ST. PIERRE & MIQUELON Burin Bay Ferryland
(Fr.) Lamaline St. Lawrence Renews
St. St. Mary's Bay Trepassey
Pierre St. Vincent's C. Race

ATLANTIC

OCEAN

GASPÉ PENINSULA
MILES
0 5 10   20   30   40

QUEBEC

SCALE OF MILES
0 5 10   20   30   40

National Capital .... ⊕
Provincial Capital .... ⊛
County Seats .... ⊚
International
Boundaries ....

Provincial
Boundaries ....
County Boundaries ......
Railroads ....

1 Alma and Jonquières
1a Canada & Gulf Terminal
2 Canadian National

3 Canadian Pacific
3a Central Vermont
5 Montreal and Southern Counties

7 Napierville Junction
9 New York Central
10 Quebec Central

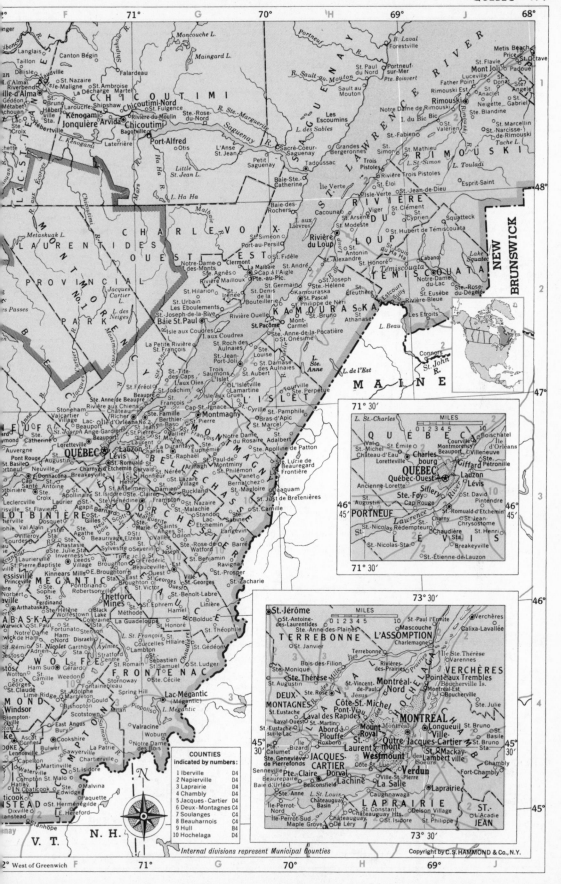

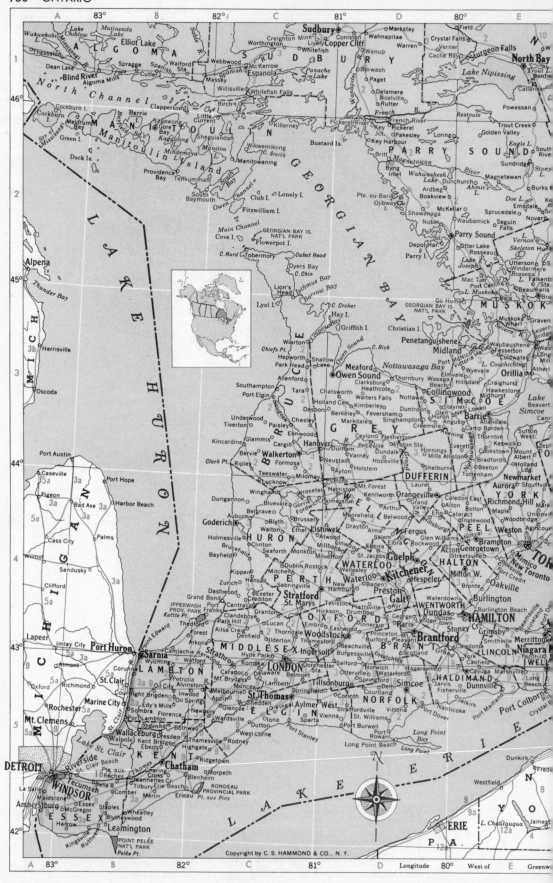

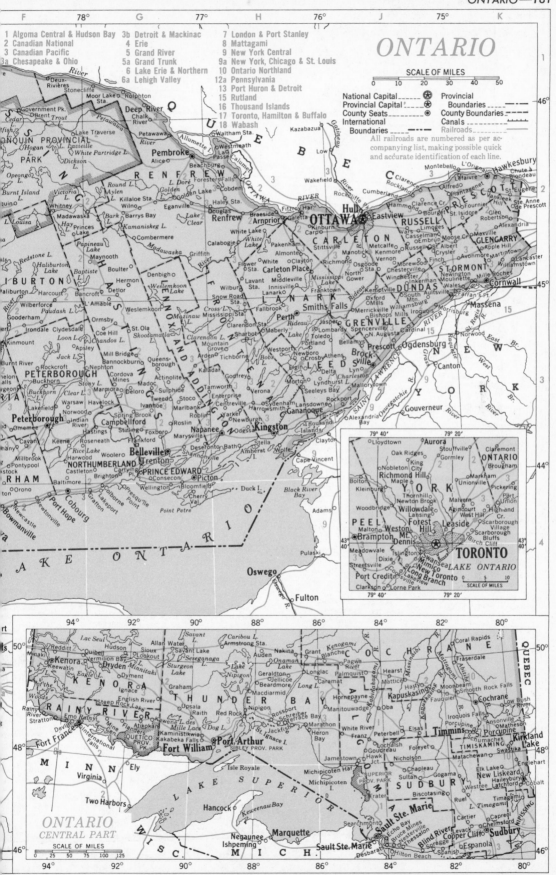

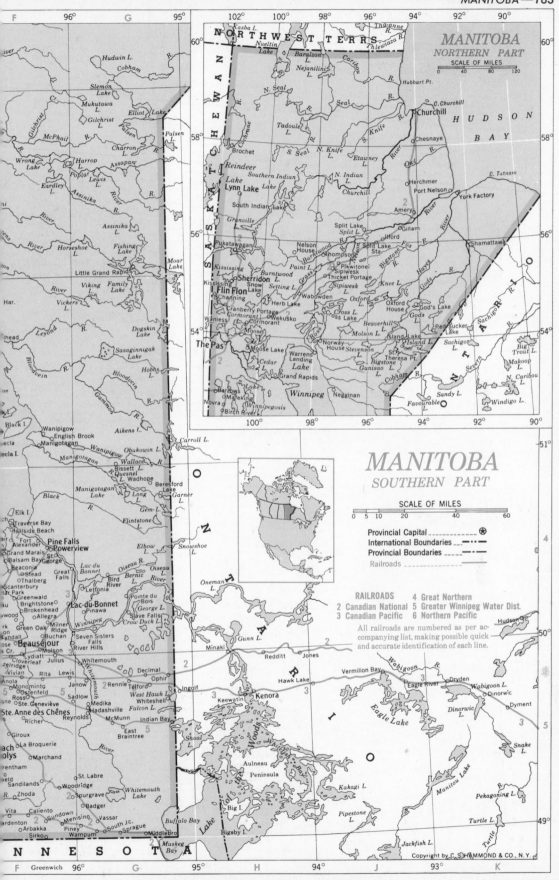

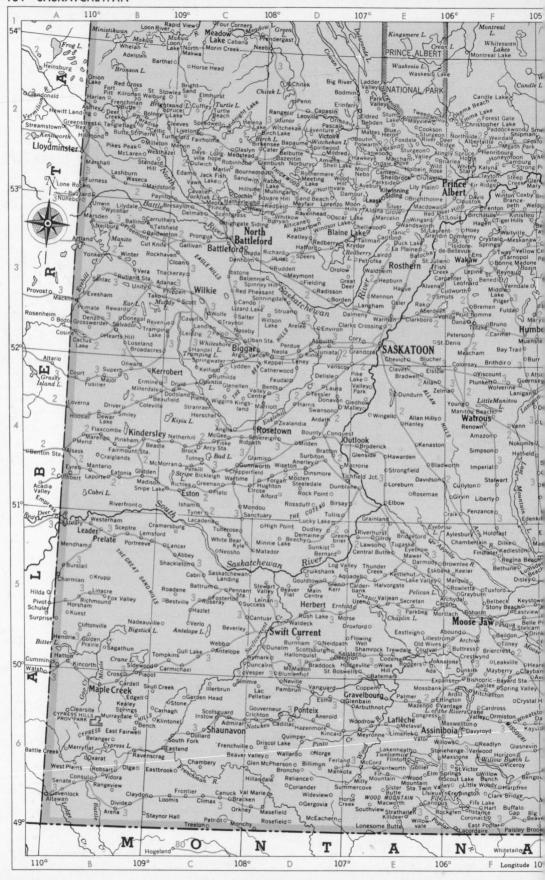

SASKATCHEWAN

SCALE OF MILES

0 5 10   20   40   60

Provincial Capital ⊛
International Boundaries ▬ ▬ ▬
Provincial Boundaries ▬ ▬ ▬
Railroads

RAILROADS

2 Canadian National   80 Great Northern
3 Canadian Pacific   117 Minneapolis, St. Paul
                          & Sault Ste. Marie

All railroads are numbered as per accompanying list, making possible quick and accurate identification of each line.

SASKATCHEWAN
NORTHERN PART

0   20   40   60   80 100
MILES

N. W. TERR'S.

Copyright by C. S. HAMMOND & CO., N.Y.

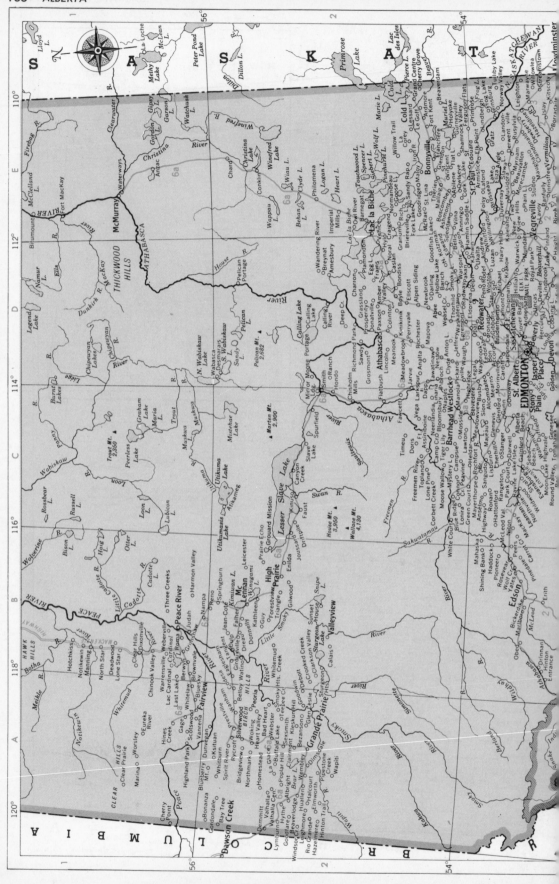

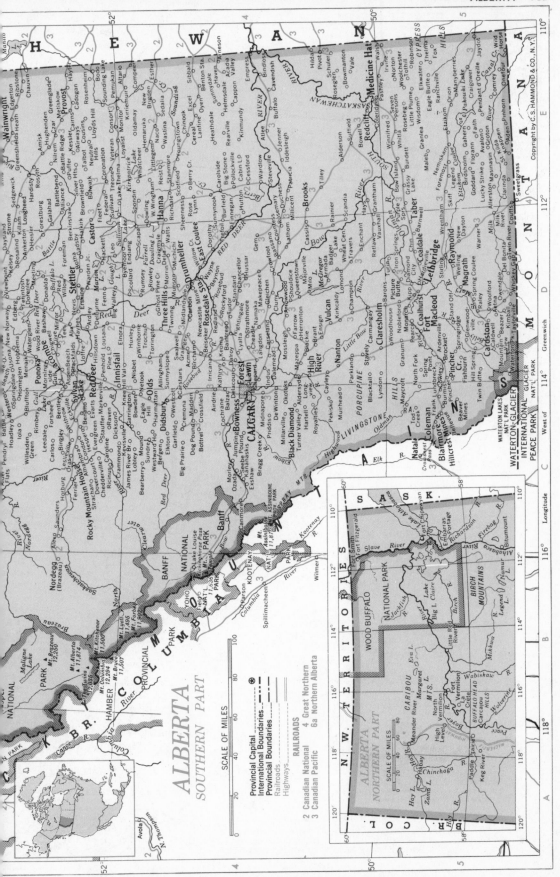

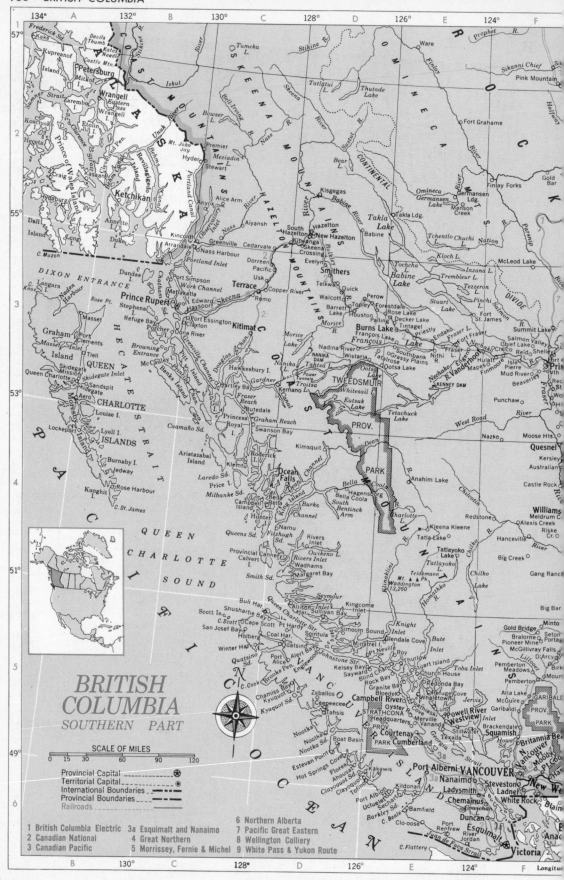

BRITISH
COLUMBIA
SOUTHERN PART

SCALE OF MILES

Provincial Capital .... ⊕
Territorial Capital .... ◉
International Boundaries ___ _ ___
Provincial Boundaries ___ ___ ___
Railroads ....

1 British Columbia Electric   3a Esquimalt and Nanaimo   6 Northern Alberta
2 Canadian National   4 Great Northern   7 Pacific Great Eastern
3 Canadian Pacific   5 Morrissey, Fernie & Michel 8 Wellington Colliery
                                                           9 White Pass & Yukon Route

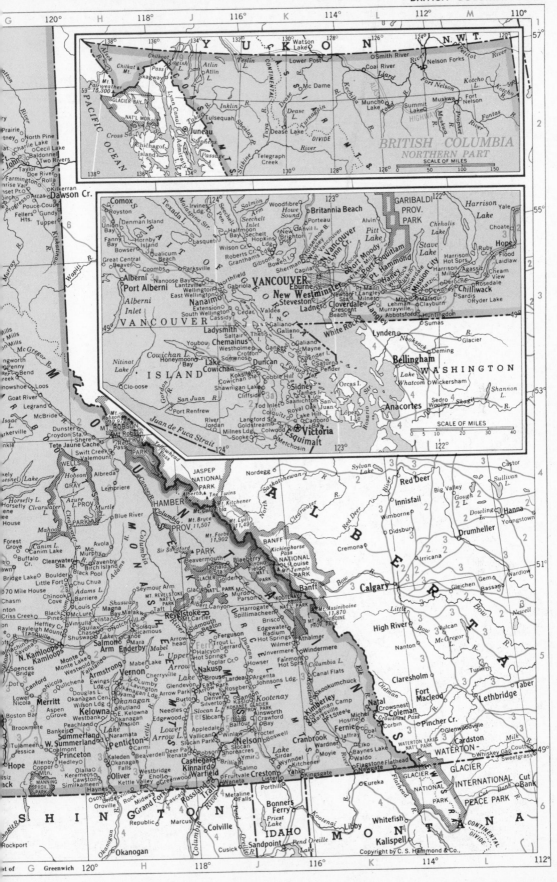

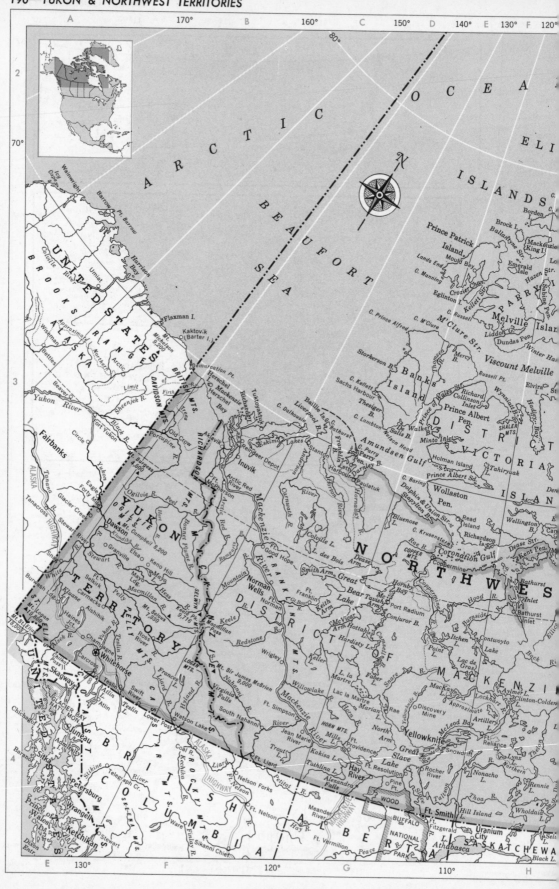

YUKON AND NORTHWEST TERRITORIES

SCALE OF MILES

0 50 100 200 300

Territorial Capitals............ ⊛	Provincial & Territorial Boundaries _ . _ . _
Administrative Center (N. W. Terr.) ◉	District Boundaries _ _ _ _
International Boundaries........	Railroads _____
	Highways _____

1 Alaska   8 White Pass & Yukon

All railroads are numbered as per accompanying list, making possible quick and accurate identification of each line.

GREENLAND

(Denmark)

Baffin Bay

Davis Strait

Baffin Island

Hudson Strait

Hudson Bay

TERRITORIES

DISTRICT OF KEEWATIN

QUEBEC

MANITOBA

LINCOLN SEA

Ungava Bay

Ungava Peninsula

All islands in Hudson and James Bays lie within the District of Keewatin.

Copyright by C. S. HAMMOND & Co., N.Y.

Longitude West K of Greenwich

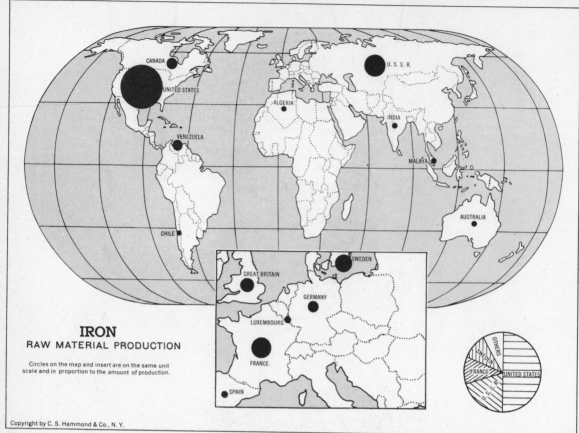

IRON
RAW MATERIAL PRODUCTION

Circles on the map and insert are on the same unit
scale and in proportion to the amount of production.

Copyright by C. S. Hammond & Co., N. Y.

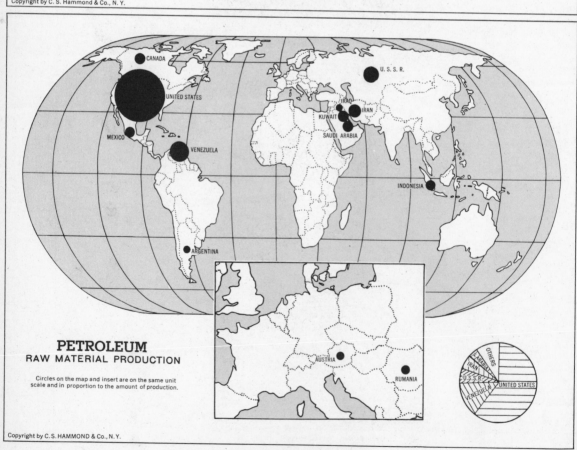

PETROLEUM
RAW MATERIAL PRODUCTION

Circles on the map and insert are on the same unit
scale and in proportion to the amount of production.

Copyright by C.S. HAMMOND & Co., N.Y.

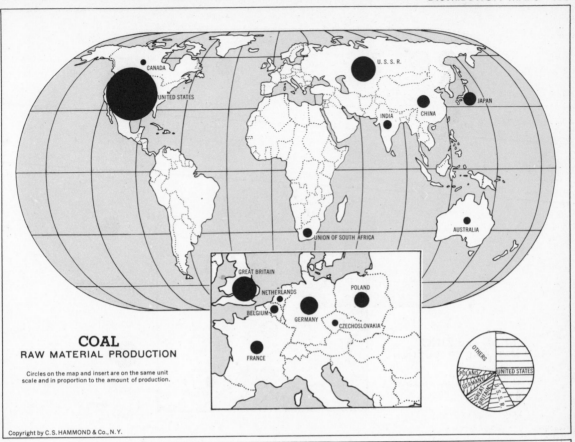

COAL
RAW MATERIAL PRODUCTION

Circles on the map and insert are on the same unit
scale and in proportion to the amount of production.

Copyright by C. S. HAMMOND & Co., N.Y.

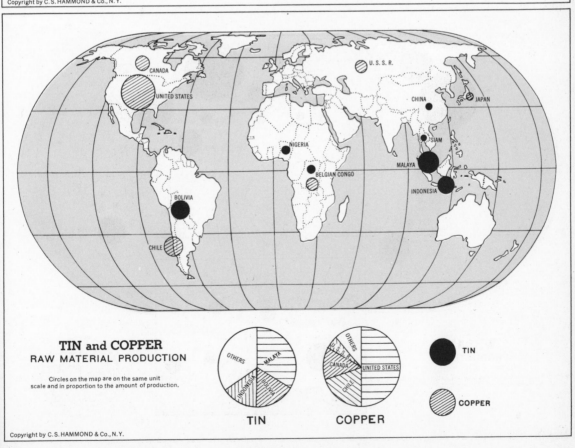

TIN and COPPER
RAW MATERIAL PRODUCTION

Circles on the map are on the same unit
scale and in proportion to the amount of production.

Copyright by C. S. HAMMOND & Co., N.Y.

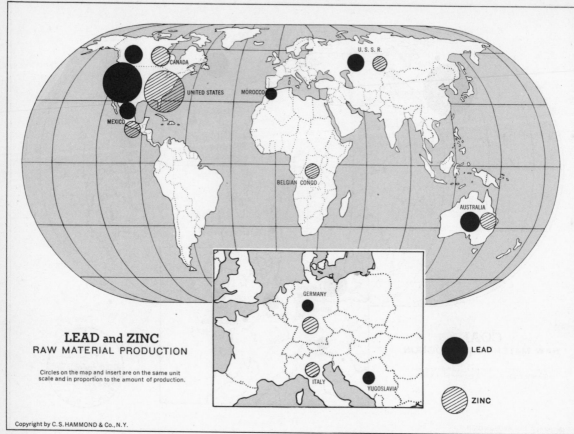

LEAD and ZINC
RAW MATERIAL PRODUCTION

Circles on the map and insert are on the same unit scale and in proportion to the amount of production.

LEAD

ZINC

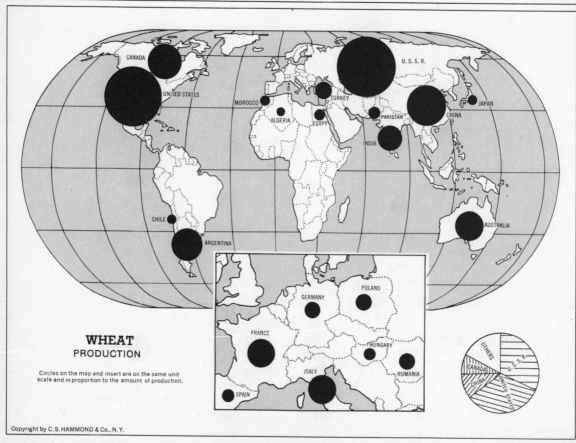

WHEAT
PRODUCTION

Circles on the map and insert are on the same unit scale and in proportion to the amount of production.

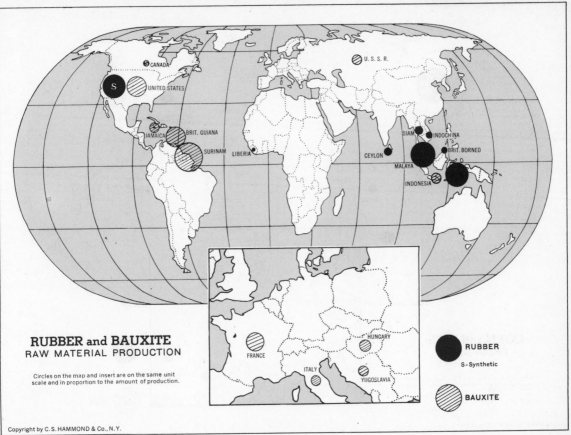

RUBBER and BAUXITE
RAW MATERIAL PRODUCTION

Circles on the map and insert are on the same unit scale and in proportion to the amount of production.

RUBBER
S-Synthetic

BAUXITE

Copyright by C. S. HAMMOND & Co., N.Y.

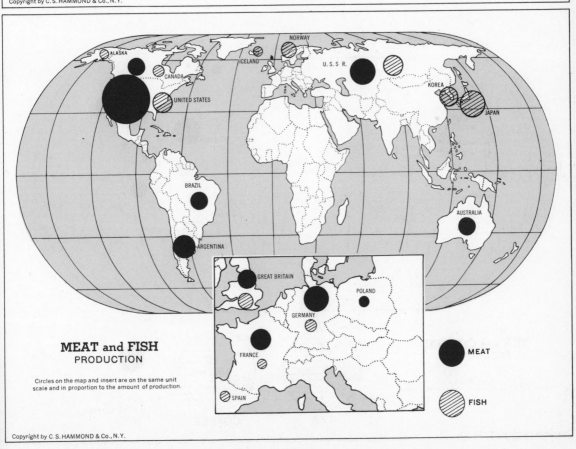

MEAT and FISH
PRODUCTION

Circles on the map and insert are on the same unit scale and in proportion to the amount of production.

MEAT

FISH

Copyright by C. S. HAMMOND & Co., N.Y.

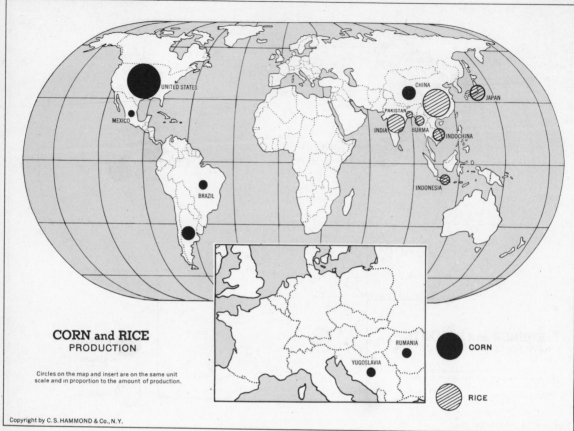

CORN and RICE
PRODUCTION

Circles on the map and insert are on the same unit
scale and in proportion to the amount of production.

CORN

RICE

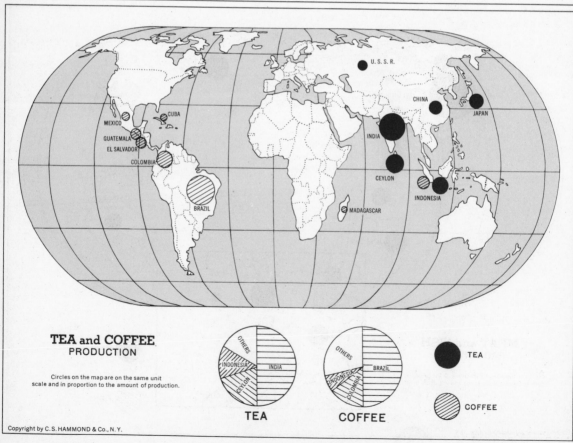

TEA and COFFEE
PRODUCTION

Circles on the map are on the same unit
scale and in proportion to the amount of production.

TEA

COFFEE

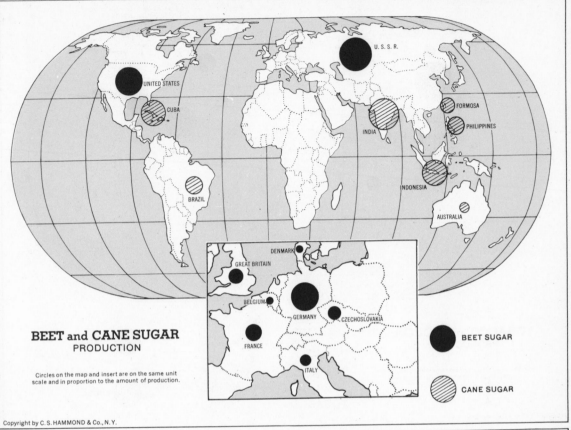

BEET and CANE SUGAR
PRODUCTION

Circles on the map and insert are on the same unit
scale and in proportion to the amount of production.

BEET SUGAR

CANE SUGAR

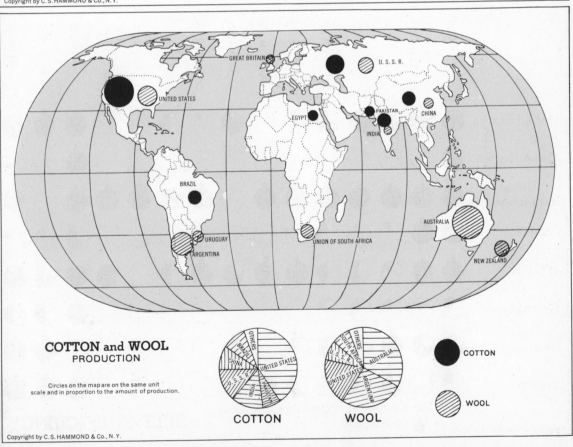

COTTON and WOOL
PRODUCTION

Circles on the map are on the same unit
scale and in proportion to the amount of production.

COTTON

WOOL

COTTON

WOOL

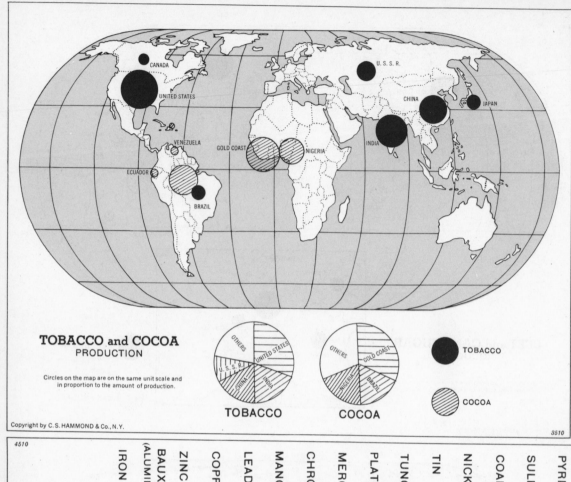

TOBACCO and COCOA
PRODUCTION

Circles on the map are on the same unit scale and
in proportion to the amount of production.

TOBACCO

COCOA

● TOBACCO

▨ COCOA

Copyright by C.S. HAMMOND & Co., N.Y.

3510

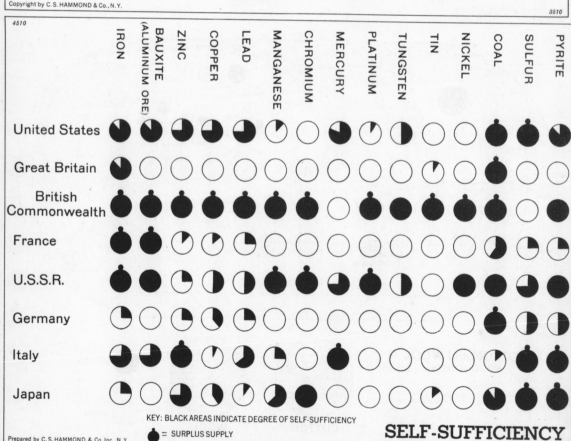

4510

	IRON	BAUXITE (ALUMINUM ORE)	ZINC	COPPER	LEAD	MANGANESE	CHROMIUM	MERCURY	PLATINUM	TUNGSTEN	TIN	NICKEL	COAL	SULFUR	PYRITE
United States															
Great Britain															
British Commonwealth															
France															
U.S.S.R.															
Germany															
Italy															
Japan															

KEY: BLACK AREAS INDICATE DEGREE OF SELF-SUFFICIENCY

● = SURPLUS SUPPLY

SELF-SUFFICIENCY

Prepared by C.S. HAMMOND & Co. Inc., N.Y.

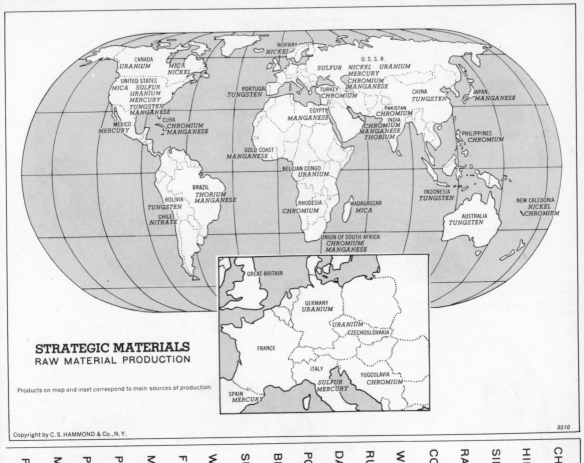

STRATEGIC MATERIALS
RAW MATERIAL PRODUCTION

Products on map and inset correspond to main sources of production.

Copyright by C.S. HAMMOND & Co., N.Y.

8510

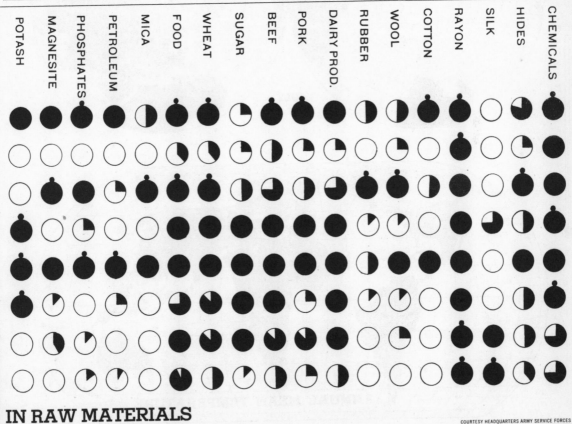

IN RAW MATERIALS

TEMPERATURE
after Napier Shaw

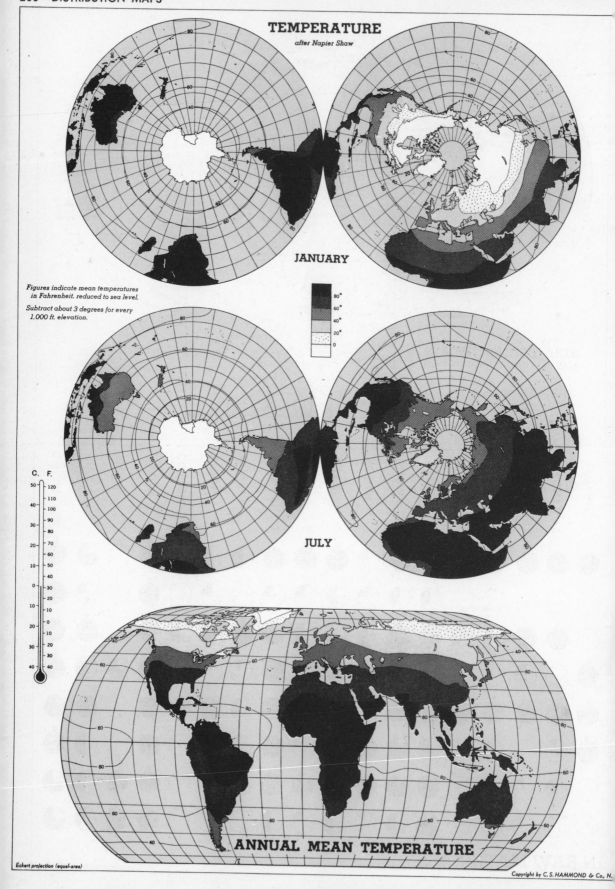

Figures indicate mean temperatures in Fahrenheit, reduced to sea level.

Subtract about 3 degrees for every 1,000 ft. elevation.

JANUARY

JULY

ANNUAL MEAN TEMPERATURE

Eckert projection (equal-area)

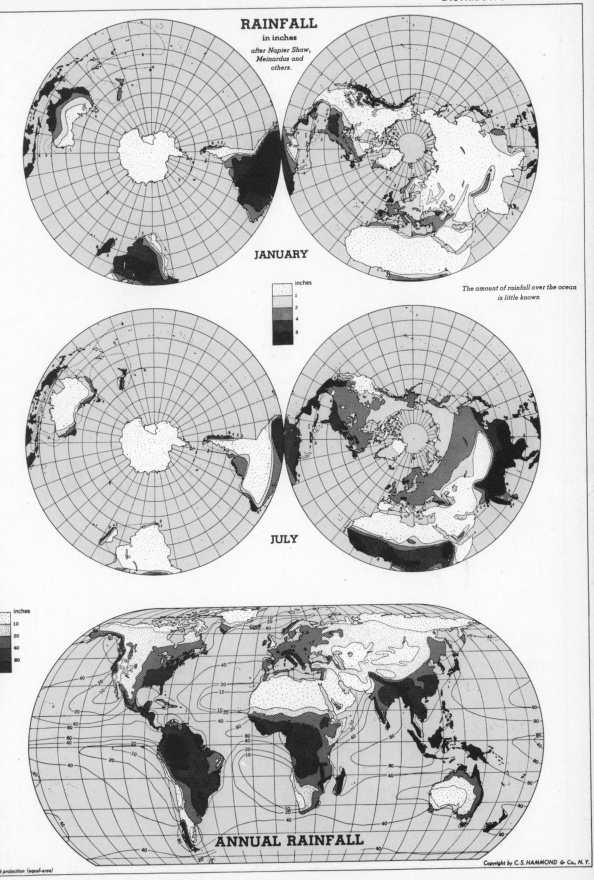

RAINFALL
in inches
*after Napier Shaw,
Meinardus and
others.*

JANURY

inches
1
2
4
8

*The amount of rainfall over the ocean
is little known*

JULY

inches
10
20
40
80

ANNUAL RAINFALL

ckert projection (equal-area)

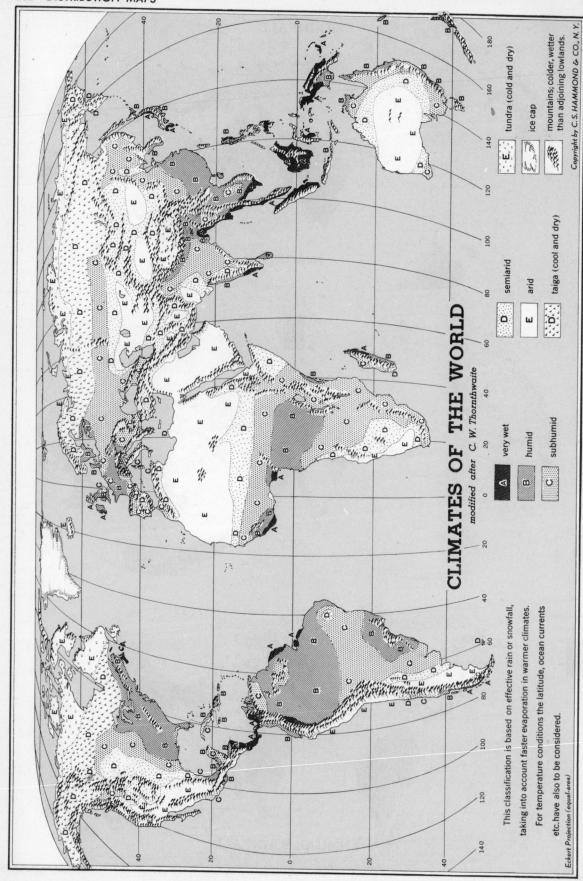

CLIMATES OF THE WORLD

modified after C. W. Thornthwaite

This classification is based on effective rain or snowfall, taking into account faster evaporation in warmer climates.

For temperature conditions the latitude, ocean currents etc. have also to be considered.

Eckert Projection (equal-area)

	very wet		semiarid		tundra (cold and dry)
	humid		arid		ice cap
	subhumid		taiga (cool and dry)		mountains; colder, wetter than adjoining lowlands.

Copyright by C. S. HAMMOND & CO., N. Y.

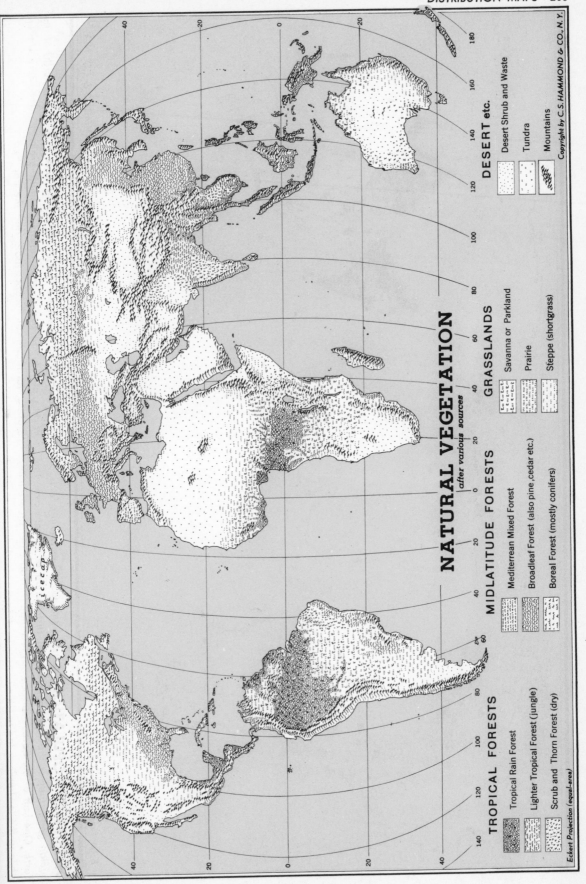

NATURAL VEGETATION
after various sources

TROPICAL FORESTS

- Tropical Rain Forest
- Lighter Tropical Forest (jungle)
- Scrub and Thorn Forest (dry)

MIDLATITUDE FORESTS

- Mediterranean Mixed Forest
- Broadleaf Forest (also pine, cedar etc.)
- Boreal Forest (mostly conifers)

GRASSLANDS

- Savanna or Parkland
- Prairie
- Steppe (shortgrass)

DESERT etc.

- Desert Shrub and Waste
- Tundra
- Mountains

Copyright by C.S. HAMMOND & CO., N.Y.

Eckert Projection (equal-area)

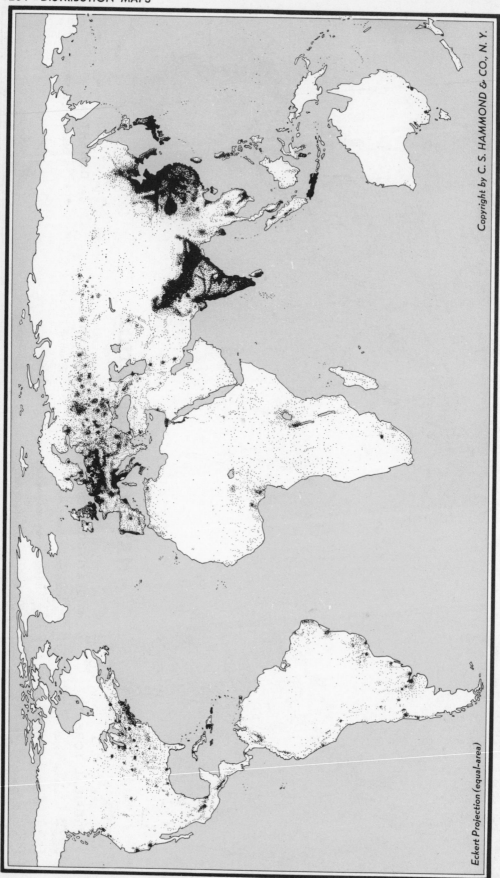

Eckert Projection (equal-area)

Copyright by C. S. HAMMOND & CO., N. Y.

DENSITY OF POPULATION. One of the most outstanding facts of human geography is the extremely uneven distribution of people over the Earth. One-half of the Earth's surface has less than 3 people per square mile, while in the lowlands of India, China, Java and Japan rural density reaches the incredible congestion of 2000-3000 per square mile. Three-fourths of the Earth's population live in four relatively small areas; Northeastern United States, North-Central Europe, India and the Far East.

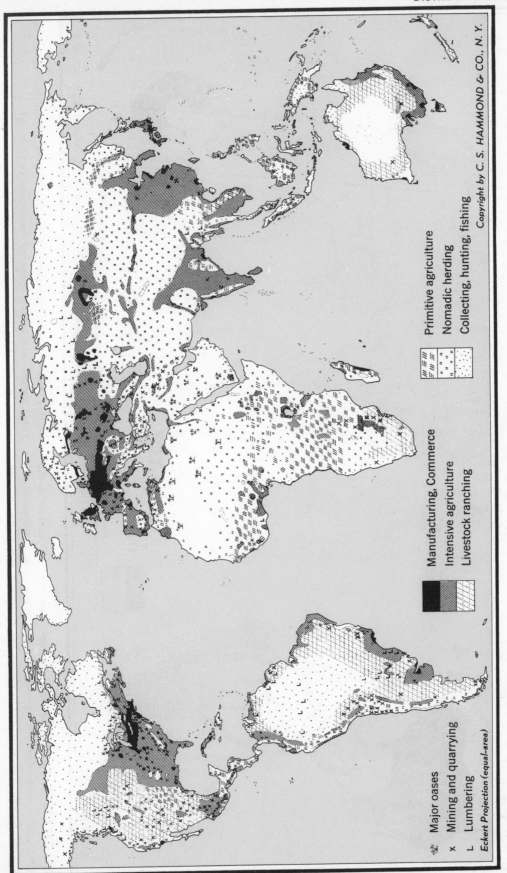

Major oases
x Mining and quarrying
L Lumbering

Eckert Projection (equal-area)

Manufacturing, Commerce
Intensive agriculture
Livestock ranching

Primitive agriculture
Nomadic herding
Collecting, hunting, fishing

Copyright by C. S. HAMMOND & CO., N. Y.

OCCUPATIONS. Correlation with the density of population shows that the most densely populated areas fall into the regions of manufacturing and intensive farming. All other economies require considerable space. The most sparsely inhabited areas are those of collecting, hunting and fishing. Areas with practically no habitation are left blank.

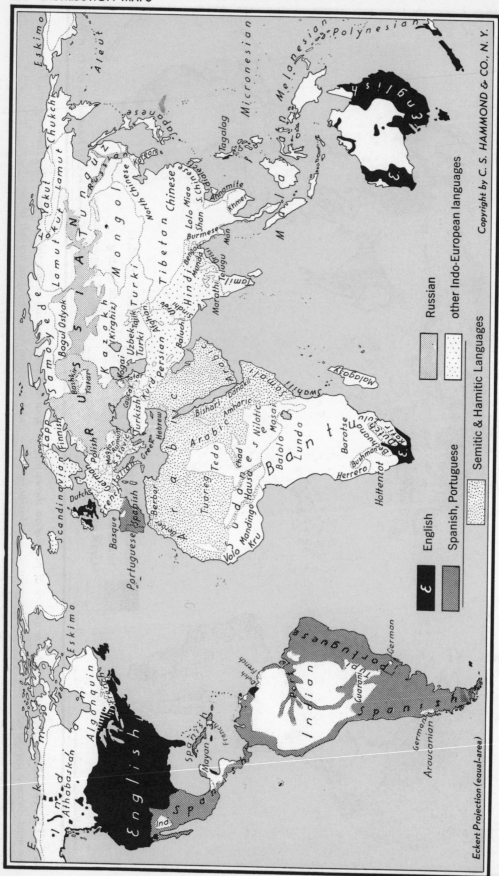

Eckert Projection (equal-area)

LANGUAGES. Several hundred different languages are spoken in the World, and in many places two or more languages are spoken, sometimes by the same people. The map above shows the dominant languages in each locality. English, French, Spanish, Russian, Arabic and Swahili are spoken by many people as a second language for commerce or travel.

Copyright by C. S. HAMMOND & CO., N. Y.

Legend:
- English
- Spanish, Portuguese
- Russian
- other Indo-European languages
- Semitic & Hamitic Languages

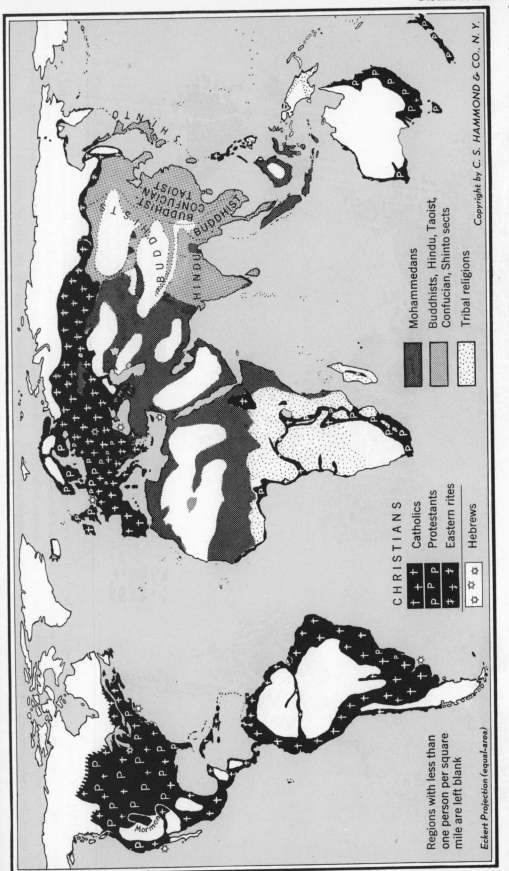

CHRISTIANS

	Catholics
+ + +	Protestants
P P P	Eastern rites
+ + +	

☆ ☆ ☆ Hebrews

Mohammedans

Buddhists, Hindu, Taoist,
Confucian, Shinto sects

Tribal religions

Regions with less than
one person per square
mile are left blank

Eckert Projection (equal-area)

Copyright by C. S. HAMMOND & CO., N. Y.

RELIGIONS. Most people of the Earth belong to four major religions: Christians, Mohammedans, Brahmans, Buddhists and derivatives. The Eastern rites of the Christians include the Greek Orthodox, Greek Catholic, Armenian, Syrian, Coptic and more minor churches. The lamaism of Tibet and Mongolia differs a great deal from Buddhism in Burma and Thailand. In the religion of China the teachings of Buddha, Confucius and Tao are mixed, while in Shinto a great deal of ancestor and emperor worship is added. About 11 million Hebrews live scattered over the globe, chiefly in cities and in the state of Israel.

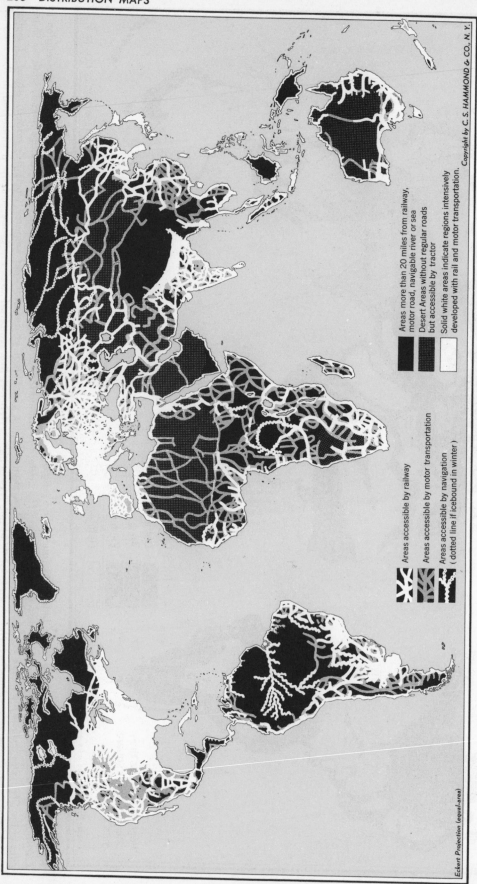

Eckert Projection (equal-area)

Areas accessible by railway

Areas accessible by motor transportation

Areas accessible by navigation (dotted line if icebound in winter)

Areas more than 20 miles from railway, motor road, navigable river or sea

Desert Areas without regular roads but accessible by tractor

Solid white areas indicate regions intensively developed with rail and motor transportation.

Copyright by C. S. HAMMOND & CO., N. Y.

ACCESSIBILITY. Many regions in the world are far from railways, roads, navigable rivers or the seas. Their economic development is retarded because their products can be brought to the world's markets only at great expense. Such areas are in the tundra (alpine), the boreal forest and in the equatorial rain forest regions. Desert areas, if not too mountainous, can be crossed by tractors. The largest inaccessible area is in Tibet, on account of high mountains, the alpine climate and isolationist attitude of the people. Airplane transportation will help to bring inaccessible areas into the orbit of civilization.

ILLUSTRATED
GEOGRAPHY
OF
THE WORLD

Introduction

The headline events of the last half-century have made the average American acutely curious of the vast world beyond the national borders of the American homeland. Constant repetition has tended to make this thought a cliche, yet it is one of the most significant truths of our time. This new national concern for the external world and its problems is one of the hopeful signs pointing to a better future for mankind.

One of the main roads to a better knowledge of this fascinating planet is a thorough indoctrination in the golden lore of geography. This science is not a narrow and limited scholarly discipline but a universal department of knowledge drawing on the sum total of man's explorations in the field of thought. The very pervasiveness of earth science makes it intriguing reading for the average non-specialist. At the same time that it entertains, it also builds a permanent edifice of information for the general reader. As more individuals discover this golden key to understanding the tumultuous happenings of the day, our collective actions in the field of enlightened citizenship will gain immeasurably in effectiveness.

CONTENTS

Canadian National Railroads

Ragged peaks and stoney crags form the watercourse for Emperor Falls in British Columbia.

NORTH AMERICA — Lying across the wide expanse of the Atlantic Ocean, was a new World waiting discovery and recognition. Europe was completely unaware of its existence for many centuries. Its discovery was destined to change the whole course of history and affect the fortunes of men and nations the world over. More than that, its discovery ushered in a whole new era of civilization, and marked the first faltering step towards the exploration and charting of all lands and waters of the world.

No discovery, before or since, has added more to man's opportunities and the wealth of the world; or played a more important part in shaping a world's destiny. Yet, its discoverer died in ignorance of his epoch-making contribution to the world. It remained for those who followed to prove the existence of a New World.

Landing on one of the Bahamas, how was Columbus to know that his quest for a new route to the East Indies had led him to an island outpost of two fabulous empires?... now but a bare few hours by air travel from the sister continents of North and South America. In his wildest dreams Columbus could not have conceived of a land extending virtually from the North Pole to the South Pole, for a distance of some nine thousand miles.

We can imagine Balboa's thrill twenty-one years later, when he fought his way across the rocky Ithmus of Panama to gaze upon the Pacific. But, how was he to know that this narrow ribbon of tapering land joined two vast domains? That, from where he stood, an unbroken expanse of land reached northward for forty-five hundred miles, and actually spread out into a gigantic fan three thousand miles wide? Also, that, to the south a similar, though lesser triangle of land, reached thousands of miles below the equator to the icy waters of the Antarctic?

Today these are historical incidents of common knowledge, thanks to the intrepid discoverers, explorers and map-makers. We take their hard won glories for granted, and even forget the adventure and romance that has gone into the making of our geographical maps.

We must be constantly reminded that, of all the continents of the world, North America is the most favored for natural wealth, climate and position on the earth. Being situated between the two largest oceans has protected the people of North America from enemy invasion, and also enabled them to develop an extensive commerce. The millions of square miles of fertile soil and untold mineral wealth has provided a standard of living unknown elsewhere in the world. Hence, composed of peoples from all over the world, its inhabitants have enjoyed peace and plenty, without fear of their independent ways of life being encroached upon, or destroyed by jealous and covetous neighbors. We can be assured that such a fortunate people will not easily relinquish what they have come to hold so dear.

The principal geographical features of North America are its two mountain ranges and the intervening central plains. The high and rugged mountains to the westward extend from the tip of Alaska to the base of the Isthmus of Panama, or from the northern to the southern extremity of the continent. These mountain ranges include the Coastal system that hugs the Pacific Coast, and the Rocky Mountains that branch out eastward and southward across the United States to become, in Mexico and Central America, the Sierra Madres. The Cascade Mountains, which farther south become the Sierra Nevada, are separate ranges that work inland from the coastal mountains. These diverging mountain chains in the east and west, form the bulwark for a number of high plateaus that lie between. The land adjoining the Cascade Mountains is the Columbia Plateau, while farther south lies the Colorado Plateau. In between is the arid region of the Great Basin. The Great Salt Lake is all that remains to reveal that this vast area was once a geologic lake.

In the east, extending from the Gulf of Saint Lawrence to the Gulf of Mexico is the Appalachian Range. These mountains are older and less rugged than the Rockies. Time has worn them down and rounded their peaks. On the side toward the Atlantic Ocean, they merge with the Piedmont Plateau, which slopes off into a coastal plain.

The great central plains that slope towards the center, and lie between the Rocky Mountain and Appalachian Highlands describe a giant "V" which extends from the Arctic Ocean to the Gulf of Mexico.

More varieties of climate prevail in North America than in any other land in the world. The greater part of the continent, however, enjoys a temperate and invigorating climate. The inhabitants of the far north must adjust themselves to the rigors of Arctic weather, Mexico endures sub-tropical temperatures, and Central America a tropical heat. Even from the east to west there is a wide variety of climate due to difference in altitude, and other conditions not affected by latitude.

To an airman soaring above the shifting panorama of North America, the realization must come that this is indeed a rich land of fertile soils, spreading forests, rolling plains, inland lakes, and mighty rivers. There is hardly an area of any size on the entire continent but contains, on the surface or beneath it, a species of natural wealth. On the western coast, the great Pacific Ocean, generally a protective barrier, separating

North Carolina News Bureau

The American South contains unusually picturesque mountain scenery.

most of North America from the shores of Asia, offers little promise of isolation at its far northwest corner. While eight thousand miles separate the peoples of China from the United States, Russia and Alaska almost meet at the Bering Strait, which is only fifty-seven miles wide.

ALASKA—Purchased from Russia in 1867 for a pittance proved to be the most valued of U.S. possessions and was to be the 49th state. The Senate voted June 30, 1958 for Alaskan statehood. Although partially in the Arctic Circle, it is by no means the frozen and inhospitable land its latitude would suggest. Alaska has a wide area of equable climate. Along its mountainous and island-fringed coast, the warm Japanese Current keeps the temperature at all times above zero. This rises in the summer to a seasonal heat of 80°. These sections endure drenching rain, caused by the condensation of warm winds striking the snow-capped peaks of the mountains. In the center of Alaska is a broad upland where grasses, flowers and mosses grow.

The Yukon River, rising in Canada, swings across Alaska for fifteen hundred miles, twelve hundred of which are navigable. Although frozen for two-thirds of the year, this river is a main artery of travel. Dog sled teams replace the large steamers during the months when it is ice-bound. A half million acres of land is cultivated in the Yukon Valley, and even though the growing season is short, the Arctic days provide long hours of sunshine.

First known as "Seward's Folly," Alaska justified its purchase within a few short years and has proved a veritable storehouse of treasure. Each year it produces more than twice its purchase price, in minerals alone.

The popular conception of the Arctic does, however, exist in the northern regions. Here the ground thaws only a few inches at the surface during the summer. Except for a few Eskimo and reindeer, there is comparatively no life or vegetation able to survive the rigors of the frigid climate.

While at one time Alaska was a remote and unexplored country, today with ever increasing population and extensive building and improvement of roads, development is steadily expanding.

The Aleutian islands are strung out in a broad arc off the tip of Alaska for a thousand miles and separate the Bering Sea from the North Pacific. Numbering about one hundred and fifty islands, they are the tops of submerged mountains. Included in the purchase of Alaska, they have great strategic value as air bases and weather observing stations for the United States.

CANADA—The three thousand mile boundary between the United States and Canada is convincing proof that two great nations may live side by side in peace and harmony. For over a hundred years this boundary line —the longest in the world—has been free from fortification of any kind by either nation. In a world that has been repeatedly torn by war during the past century here is lasting evidence that national progress, pride and ambition can exist without adjoining countries being tempted to encroach on the other's domain.

Canada is the largest domain of the British Commonwealth. It extends from the icy waters of the Arctic to the borders of the United States, and from east to west its greatest distance is 3,700 miles. Its area is greater than that of the United States and nearly as large as the continent of Europe.

Canada is a vast diversified land of fertile plains, of mountains and rivers, and countless lakes. Over 6 per cent of the total is water area, affording ready power for her ever increasing industrial development. Like the United States it can be roughly divided into three sections; the eastern highlands, a great level central plain, and mountain ranges extending from the Rockies to the Pacific.

In the east the Appalachian region is a beautiful land of hilly or mountainous terrain with very heavily forested sections and fertile farm lands. Just west of the highlands lies the St. Lawrence Valley including the Ontario peninsula, the hub of Canada's industry. In this area, rich in minerals, forests, water power and fertile land, is the highest concentration of population. Moderate climate combined with valuable accessible resources have made this section of the greatest economic importance. Northwest of the Valley is the Canadian Shield, an area characterized by low hills, countless lakes connected by streams and rapids. Here is Canada's greatest store of resources, minerals, forests, furs and water power. In the interior Plains is the great wheat belt. In the west, parallel to the Pacific, is the magnificent mountain country formed by the Cordilleran Mountain System. In addition to minerals and valuable forests, this area, in the fertile valleys, produces much of Canada's fruit and vegetable crops.

Although primarily an agricultural country, Canada has developed rapidly in recent years as an industrial country. Lumbering is of great importance, which is to be expected, for the forests of Canada are among the largest in the world. Furs have been an important source of wealth since the early days of the Hudson's Bay Company, and the fishing grounds of Canada are the largest and most productive on earth. Wheat is the principal crop of the prairie provinces, and Canada is one of the biggest producers and exporters of this grain.

The provinces in the southern sections of Canada enjoy much the same climate as exists in the Great Lakes regions of the United States. The southern parts of Ontario and Quebec have less severe winters, but the northern sections of these provinces have very severe winters, with short, hot summers. The prairies experience great extremes in temperature, while moderate rainfall in this region favors wheat production.

About half of the population is of British origin and one quarter is French. The remaining fourth is principally Russian, German, Austrian and Scandinavian. Some hundred thousand Indians live mostly on reservations.

UNITED STATES—In a little over one hundred and fifty years the United States of America has written an amazing chapter in history. In that brief period a wilderness has been tamed, and a powerful nation has arisen to take its place among the foremost countries of the world. A land populated by every race, creed and color, and a haven of refuge for the oppressed, its phenomenal growth has never been equalled. Far removed from the traditions and hampering fetters of the Old World, it has charted a new course in government. Its freedom loving people have devoted their energies to developing the riches that Nature has so lavishly supplied.

The United States has reached its present position of greatness because of a number of reasons. It is blessed with a climate that cannot be surpassed elsewhere in the world, and is rich in mineral wealth beyond that of any other country. With a coastline on three sides well supplied with harbors, it is ideally situated for trade with the rest of the world. Its rivers and lakes are navigable and give easy access into the interior of the country. The variety of climate and the fertility of the soil make a great diversity of crops possible.

Climate has made the people of the United States energetic, and Nature has endowed the land with more than enough to meet their needs. This country's way of life has provided the incentive for continually bettering the standards of living of its people. All this has brought continued economic, cultural and scientific progress.

The United States is the greatest manufacturing nation in the world, with half the

Gendreau

An attraction for all visitors to Mexico is Xochimilco's floating gardens.

population depending upon industry for a living. It has the finest systems of transportation and communication, including the great majority of the automobiles in the world. More than half the coal, and a quarter of the iron in the world, as well as large deposits of almost all important minerals are found here.

The three principal geographical features are a continuation of those in Canada. They are the eastern highlands, comprising the Appalachian Range, the broad central plains, and the Rockies and Coastal ranges in the Far West.

A closer study of the geography of the United States does much to explain the growth of the nation. For example, the stony soil of New England discouraged farming and caused the early settlers to turn to manufacturing and commerce. The swift streams furnished water power and the jagged coastline provided bays for harboring the ships from Europe. Farther south, the coastal plains widen out into broad stretches of fertile land, and the rivers are short and deep. This led to the development of the large plantations in the deep South, where the climate is favorable to crops that require long hot summers. Here the coastal plain includes half of Georgia, all of Florida, and extends along the Gulf of Mexico. It reaches into the interior as far north as southern Illinois.

The lake and prairie region of the upper Mississippi Valley is one of the most fertile in the world, and is linked by waterways with the East and South through the Great Lakes and the Mississippi River system. . The Great Plains region, depending upon the nature of the topsoil and the amount of rainfall, is either grain or grazing country, with valuable deposits of oil in Texas and Oklahoma.

The great size of the country and the seemingly endless store of natural wealth, both above and below the surface of the earth, have been responsible for great waste in the past. Fortunately, strict conservation measures are now in force to protect the resources of the earth for future generations and to assure them an equal place in this "Land of Opportunity".

MEXICO—Beyond the southern border of the United States and across the Rio Grande, where North America begins to taper sharply to a point, lies Latin America. It is difficult to conceive of the contrast to be found beyond this man-made boundary with the rest of the continent. It is another world, with a totally different culture, another language, and traditions and customs which set it apart from its northern neighbors.

About one-fourth the area of the United States, Mexico swings south for about eleven hundred miles, ending in the narrow hook of the peninsula of Yucatan.

While half of Mexico lies in the torrid zone, its climate is determined more by elevation than latitude. Along the coast the weather is hot and humid, with luxuriant tropical vegetation. As the land rises the climate changes to temperate and the mountain peaks are snow-clad. Two mountain chains, that are a continuation of those in the United States, converge and meet at the southern tip, leaving a flat tableland between. The average altitude of this plateau is about 6,500 feet. Mexico's highest concentration of population is here where the fertile land, ideal climate and favorable rainfall afford excellent conditions for agricultural crops. Although industrial development has increased rapidly in recent years

and most of Mexico's wealth is derived from her mines and petroleum, the great majority of the people are still employed in agricultural pursuits. Except for the coastal plain bordering the Gulf of Mexico, mountains and plateaus occupy the greater part of Mexico. Lying in both the temperate and torrid zones allows the country to produce a greater variety of crops than is possible in most other countries.

Mexico is a beautiful and picturesque country with ancient ruins of pyramids and temples still standing as mute evidence of a flourishing civilization that existed before the coming of the Spanish invaders in the early fifteenth century.

CENTRAL AMERICA—As North America decreases in size from a land of magnificent distance to a slender neck of land where the Isthmus of Panama joins South America, the sizes of its nations shrink to even greater extent. In Central America a string of six small countries, Guatemala, Honduras, El Salvador, Nicaragua, Costa Rica and Panama, is confined to an area less than that of the State of Texas. Their total population does not equal that of New York City.

The Cordilleras, a continuation of the mountain chains starting far north in Alaska, extend the entire length of the land. Many of the peaks are volcanic and frequent eruptions occur. These mountains have formed many high and fertile plateaus which provide fine pasturage for livestock and rich soil for a diversity of crops. As in Mexico, the tropical climate of the lower regions is tempered by the elevation of the high plateaus. There are a number of harbors on both coasts, with the principal seaports on the Caribbean Sea. Most of the rivers that flow into the Caribbean are navigable.

These agricultural nations have become increasingly important in the past few years. With the organizing of the Pan-American Union, the growth of air travel, and the fostering of a new spirit of co-operation between the republics of North and South America, Central America's future became one of promise. When global war shut off supplies of many important crops to the Western world from the East, it was found that here in the Americas could be grown many necessities that formerly had been imported from afar. Great variation in soils, rainfall, and terrain afford an enormous variety of tropical, semi-tropical and temperate crops. Experiments have successfully produced important quantities of spices, fibres, and essential oils for medicinal and industrial purposes that were introduced from the East. Among the important crops exported almost exclusively to the United States are bananas, natural rubber, coffee, rope fibres, cacao and sugar.

Although there is potential mineral wealth in most of the countries of Central America this resource, for the most part, has been unexploited. Much of the land is heavily forested and some of the world's most valuable woods such as mahogany, rosewood, teak and ebony are found here. However, only a very small part of the forests have been as yet cut for commercial purposes.

ISLANDS OF THE CARIBBEAN—The
Caribbean Sea is a vital water link between the Americas and the West Indies. With the opening of the Panama Canal it took on added importance as a trade route for the ships of the world.

The island republics and colonies lying in the Caribbean have likewise become increasingly important with the passing years, both for their economic and strategic value.

The West Indies, numbering hundreds of islands, extend in a sweeping arc beginning near southern Florida and ending off the coast of Venezuela. Columbus named the islands, in the belief that he had reached India. Most of the islands, forming two main groups, the Greater and the Lesser Antilles, are mountainous. However, there is sufficient fertile land to afford a variety of tropical products. In general the climate is hot but is tempered by the sea breezes. All the islands are subject to tropical hurricanes and in many regions there are occasional volcanic eruptions.

With the greater part of the West Indies under the control of the United States and Great Britain, the islands enjoy advantages not usually possessed by small independent

Pan-American-Grace Airways

Peru's cultural past is evident to all who visit her attractive cities.

countries. Nearness to markets and the great manufacturing centers, and cheap ocean transportation are added advantages. As with the Central American republics, the West Indies have enjoyed increased production and trade with the importation of new crops from the East that are now grown throughout Middle America.

SOUTH AMERICA—It is a common error
to think of South America as being directly south of the United States. A glance at the globe will show that this is far from the truth. Except for the bulge to the west and the southern tip, all of South America is east of the Atlantic coast boundary of the United States. This places South America much closer to Africa than North America is to Europe. A theory has been advanced, though never proved, that at one time Africa and South America were joined.

Smaller than North America by nearly two million square miles, and representing one-seventh of the world's total land area,

South America is the fourth largest continent.

With the equator crossing South America on a line with the Amazon River, two-thirds of this southern neighbor is in the tropics and the balance in the temperate zone. In common with other lands situated in the Southern Hemisphere, it has the further disadvantage of being far removed from the principal world markets. These factors, together with the history of the continent, explain why it has not developed as rapidly as the United States, although discovered at the same time. But in spite of the handicaps of climate, position and history, South America has an extensive trade with the United States and Europe. And, although for centuries the Spaniards robbed it of its buried treasures, South America still possesses great mineral wealth.

South of the Isthmus of Panama, the great line of mountains which extends the entire length of North America becomes the mighty Andes. Second only to the Himalayas, they follow the western coast to Cape Horn, rising steeply from the Pacific in long ranges of snow-capped peaks and wide plateaus. Mount Aconcagua is the highest peak in the Americas and rises to a height of twenty-three thousand feet. Several lesser peaks are active volcanos. To the south the range begins to narrow and the coast is bordered by a tattered fringe of islands clothed with pines and swept by fierce northwesterly winds.

On the east are two broad plateaus, the Guiana and Brazilian highlands, which might be compared with the Laurentian highlands and the Appalachian chain of North America. Between the eastern slope of the Andes and these plateaus lie broad lowlands. The grassy, tree dotted plains, or *llanos*, of the Orinoco Basin in Venezuela and Colombia, provide fine pasturage between the dry and rainy seasons. In the dry season they practically revert to desert. To the south are the dry plains, or *pampas*, of Northern Argentina, which is the great cattle country of the continent.

The Amazon—largest river system in the world—drains over one-third of the continent. This area is equal to two-thirds that of the United States. This mighty river is thirty-five hundred miles long and in places is over fifty miles wide. It flows through the densest tropical forest in the world and much of it is unexplored.

The La Plata River is actually the estuary for three rivers, the Parana, with a drainage area almost as large as that of the Mississippi, the Uruguay and the Paraguay. Buenos Aires, metropolis of the Southern Hemisphere is situated on the south bank of the La Plata 175 miles from the Atlantic. Buenos Aires is one of the world's most beautiful cities and important seaports. The above mentioned rivers drain Northern Argentina, Uruguay and Paraguay.

Other rivers of less importance are the São Francisco of Brazil, the Magdalena of Colombia, the Orinoco of Venezuela, and the Río Colorado of Argentina.

Lying in the Andes at an altitude of over twelve thousand feet is Lake Titicaca. With an area over half that of Lake Erie, it is the highest navigable lake in the world.

Much of Argentina and Chile are in southern latitudes that compare with the northern latitudes of the United States, but there are only sections where the climate is similar. Parts of Chile have a climate that compares with the Pacific coast states, and sections of Argentina and Uruguay are comparable to the east coast of the United States.

The heat is insufferable and the rainfall extremely heavy in the low Orinoco and Amazon Valleys. In the northern countries, while hot, the climate is tempered by the highlands. At the extreme southern tip the seasons are exactly the opposite of those in North America, but there is not the variation in temperature. This is due to the influence of oceans and mountains.

The only important indentations on the Pacific are found along the rugged coast of southern Chile and the Gulf of Guayaquil in Ecuador.

The high temperature and humidity of the tropical regions, together with many insects and diseases, discourage the activity of white people and even sap the strength of the natives. Large areas of swamp and rugged mountains have made the development of transportation difficult and expensive. Only with the growth of air travel has it been possible for the Andean countries to contact one another with relative ease.

In the main, South America is sparsely settled, with the greatest density of population along the coasts. The original inhabitants were Indians, but, due to the early colonization by the Spanish and Portuguese, many of the present inhabitants are *mestizos,* a mixture of Indian and Spanish or Portuguese blood. The remainder is largely composed of Italian and German immigrants. Except in Brazil, where the official language is Portuguese, Spanish is spoken in all the other independent countries.

The three countries of Chile, Argentina and Uruguay, where there has been the largest European immigration, are making rapid industrial progress. The rest of South America is still largely agricultural. Most of the countries produce only one or two major products and there is little diversity of crops. Practically all exports are raw materials, while imports are manufactured goods.

With the exception of the three colonies of British, French and Dutch Guiana, all of South America is composed of independent republics. In spite of a common language and form of government there is little interchange between countries. In general they are more concerned with world trade than dealing with each other.

Since the early coming of the Spaniards, South America has continued to yield great stores of precious metals. The Andes are rich in minerals, and the eastern highlands contain iron, gold, and diamonds. Some coal is found in Brazil, Chile and Colombia, but not in great quantity. Water-power and oil are being utilized to make up for this lack.

Ecuador, Peru and Chile are all west coast countries, which, until the opening of the Panama Canal, were practically isolated from the rest of the world. Bolivia, having no outlet to the sea, moves nearly all of her exports through the seaports of Chile and Peru.

CHILE—Sometimes called the "Shoestring Republic," Chile stretches along the west coast for twenty-six hundred miles, from the

Brazilian Government Trade Bureau

Although in the torrid zone, Brazil's climate is tempered by rainfall, favorable winds and altitude.

borders of Peru to Cape Horn. It has a variety of climate ranging from frigid to torrid. This long, narrow and mountainous country is one of the most progressvie in South America. It is one of the three republics where there are more white people than natives. The other two are Argentina and Uruguay.

From north to south Chile is divided into three regions: the desert, a dry sub-tropical region which includes the coast, and a section that is forested. The greatest mineral region lies between Santiago and the Peruvian border. In the northern half of this area are the nitrate fields which have produced almost the entire world's supply of this important fertilizer. The nitrate beds located in the Pacific coastal desert (Atacama) were wrested from Peru during the War of the Pacific (1879-83) from which Chile emerged victorious. Chile's fame as a nitrate region has waned with the introduction of synthetic nitrate into world industry. The country is now seeking to stimulate the

1. The Alcazar, Segovia, Spain.
2. Bridge and Cathedral, Dinant, Belgium.
3. Plaza del Congreso, Buenos Aires, Argentina.
4. Castle of Neuschwanstein, Bavaria, Germany.
5. Lindbergh Theatre from across the lagoon, Mexico City.
6. Looking into the crater of Vesuvius, Naples, Italy.
7. View of the Capitol, Havana, Cuba.
8. The Sphinx at Gizah, Egypt.
9. The famous St. Sophia Mosque, Constantinople, Turkey.
10. Scene in Devonshire, England.
11. A typical canti-lever bridge over a canal in Holland.
12. Camp at Wapta, Canadian Rockies.
13. The Harbor front at Algiers.
14. Morro Castle, Havana, Cuba.
15. A typical farm house in Czechoslovakia.

export of wine, honey and livestock. In the southern half there are deposits of copper, iron, gold and silver. Chile ranks next to the United States in the mining of copper and supplies about 20 per cent of the world's output.

PERU—This country is an extension of the narrow and arid coastal plain in northern Chile, with the Andes occupying fully half of the land. A densely wooded tropical region drops down in the east to meet the low plains of Brazil.

About a fourth of the population is white, most of whom are Spanish. The balance are *mestizos* (mixed) or Indians. Descendants of the ancient Incas, the Indians of Peru, are found principally living on the high mountain slopes of the Andes, and sailing their strange fiber craft on Lake Titicaca. These Indians have domesticated the llama and the alpaca, two animals which are native to this region, and which have never been raised successfully elsewhere. The llama is a sure-footed animal upon which the Indians depend for food, clothing and transportation. Used as a beast of burden in this lofty arid country, the llama, like the camel, can go several days without water. The alpaca is too small to carry loads and is raised for its very long wool.

ECUADOR—Peru and Ecuador have a similar climate and topography except for the northern part of the coastal plain of Ecuador. This plain is as fertile as any area in South America and is the principal agricultural section of Ecuador. The principal crops are cacao and coffee, the former heading the articles of export. Ecuador's coffee has been increasing in importance since its cacao, blighted by witches'-broom, has suffered an appreciable decrease in export. Tagua, a substitute for ivory, is produced in limited quantities. Ecuador is world-famous for its amazing variety of wild birds. The country contains one-fourth of all recorded species in South America.

BOLIVIA—Shut off from the sea by Chile and Peru, Bolivia is one of the most sparsely populated countries in the world. It consists of a high plateau in the southwest that is cold and dry, and wet tropical lowlands in the north and east. Though Bolivia's surface is three-fifths lowlands, the country includes one of the highest inhabitable regions in the world. The Andes spread out into two great chains of mountains which enclose a plateau nearly as high as the peaks themselves. Lake Titicaca, one of the highest of the larger lakes in the world, is situated on this plateau.

Bolivia ranks next to the Malay Peninsula and the Indonesian islands in its tin deposits, and is well supplied with nearly all the known metals. Strangely enough, although having local supplies of coal, necessary in smelting, it is usually cheaper to import coal.

Lack of capital, the high cost of transportation, and the scarcity of labor, have retarded mining in all the countries of the Andes. Only the natives can do manual labor in the high altitudes and the people are not inclined toward mining. However, mining is the chief industry. Aside from tin, there is abundant amounts of gold, copper, bismuth, antimony, lead, zinc, wolfram and oil. Tobacco, wine and vanilla, together with quinine and rubber, are exported.

BRAZIL—Covering nearly half the continent and with half the population, Brazil lies almost entirely in the tropics. This republic is 10 per cent larger than the United States, and has three times the area of Argentina.

The Amazon and its tributaries have a total length of over nineteen thousand miles, of which thirteen thousand are navigable. This huge system extends through more than half the country's area.

The great plateau country, known as the Brazilian Highlands, lies in the south and east. It is composed of numerous mountain ranges and river valleys. Rio de Janeiro, the second largest city on the continent, is located in this region. Hemmed in by mountains and a wide bay, it has one of the finest and most beautiful harbors in the world.

Brazil at one time was the greatest rubber-producing country. Brazil has embarked on a program of intensified manufacturing. Silk, cotton and woolen mills have sprung up all over the eastern seaboard. Shoes and hats are becoming major products. Many paper mills are being built to utilize some of the billion acres of forests that cover half the land area. Its greatest mineral wealth has yet to be exploited, though one of the largest estimated deposits of iron ore in the world is now being developed. The country produces nearly fifty percent of the world's coffee. Efforts to do away with the one-crop system are gaining success and coffee is no longer the economic tyrant that it was. A growing cacao industry now ranks second in the world, while tobacco, rice, cotton and sugar are attaining commercial significance.

URUGUAY

URUGUAY—This is the smallest republic in South America. It has a fine climate with the winds of the ocean modifying the temperature.

Since the Spanish brought sheep and cattle to the grassy plains of Uruguay in the 17th century, it has been a stock raising country. Today it is one of the leading meat producers of the world. Only a small percentage of the arable land is devoted to the raising of crops and it is limited in both minerals and manufacturing.

PARAGUAY

PARAGUAY—One of the two republics of South Amercia that is completely surrounded by other nations. Little has been done to develop its natural resources.

Most of the surface of western Paraguay is a low, swampy and unhealthy plain. The climate in the north is hot and unsuited to the white man. Most of the people live in the southern area east of the Paraguay River. It is a country of small villages, grazing, and farm lands, which depends upon the rivers for means of transportation.

Extending from Bolivia, across the western third of Paraguay, and south into Argentina, is the Gran Chaco, a great plain.

THE ARGENTINE REPUBLIC

THE ARGENTINE REPUBLIC—The early colonists' anticipation of finding silver and gold in Argentina prompted them to name the country for the Latin word meaning silver. Although the colonists' search for great mineral wealth was in vain, the fertile soil and temperate climate have fostered the country's great economic progress. The Re-

Pan-American-Grace Airways

The most cosmopolitan city of South America, Buenos Aires has been strongly influenced by Europe.

public is the second largest of the South American countries.

The Gran Chaco, in the northern part, is a land of forests, lakes and swamps, which is largely unexplored. The grassy plains of the *Pampas* occupy a large area of Argentina. This cattle country and farm land extends from the Atlantic coast to the Andes in the west, and northwest to the highlands which reach into Brazil. The rich grazing lands, which have led to Argentina becoming a large exporter of meat and wool are in the center of the *Pampas;* the largest meat refrigerating plant in the world is at Buenos Aires.

Only about 10 per cent of the land is under cultivation, although it has been said that 80 per cent is capable of producing crops, grass or forests. An idea may be gained from this of the great possibilities for future development that lie ahead.

Argentina is an agricultural and commercial, rather than an industrial country. It has been hindered in the development of manufacture by a shortage of coal, the lack of water power, and an inadequate supply of minerals.

Descendants of the Spanish settlers are

the leaders of the country, with most of the farm population consisting of Italians. Immigrants from the British Isles have taken to sheep raising, and many Germans have migrated to Argentina. Today half of the population is foreign-born or are descendants of immigrants.

NORTH COAST COUNTRIES—Colombia, Venezuela, and the British, French and Dutch Guianas, are all on the north coast.

COLOMBIA—The only South American country having a coastline along both the Atlantic and Pacific oceans. Half the country is high in the rugged Andes; the other half lies in unhealthy tropical plains. Three cordilleras of the Andes traverse in a parallel line from north and south which forms a barrier between the seacoast and the rich inland valleys. The chief source of wealth is coffee. Colombian coffee is the finest in the world and the bean is jealously guarded. Ninety percent of the exported coffee is shipped to the United States. A type from the area around Medellin commands the highest price per pound in the world. Surpassed by Brazil in quantity, Colombia's coffee yields to none in quality. Next to coffee in export value is oil. The fields are to a large extent a continuation of those in Venezuela. Production has been over twenty million barrels since World War II. Other resources include platinum, emeralds and coal.

VENEZUELA—One of the most productive oil regions in the world, is on the coast of the Caribbean. Easy access to this coast from the interior affords great possibilities for commercial and industrial development. Venezuela's land area is distinguished by its llanos or wide lowlands along the Orinoco River. The river is navigable for a course of 700 miles and is connected to the Amazon system by a canal. Coffee, chiefly from the basin of the Maracaibo, is second only to that of Colombia. A ranking producer of petroleum, Venezuela's exploitation of oil is fraught with difficulties which have never been successfully surmounted. Virgin forests cover the country and include about 600 species of wood. At Margarita is located a profitable pearl industry. Salt, asphalt, coal and gold figure as the main mineral resources.

THE GUIANAS—On the north coast of South America are the only European possessions on the continent. Their combined area is 178,000 square miles. The surface is composed of an alluvial plain at sea-level and another plain farther south which is distinguished by hills and forested mountains. The climate is tolerable except in the south where the northeast trade winds do not prevail. Though their topography is similar their economic importance varies greatly from east to west. British Guiana, about the size of Great Britain, is the most highly developed. Dutch Guiana (Surinam) has no important industries except the mining of bauxite. French Guiana, the easternmost colony, is of little importance economically. Its sparse population and the excessive emphasis placed on the mining of gold has led to the neglect of its fertile soil. Mineral resources in the form of gold and diamonds are equally divided among the Guianas.

EUROPE—Eurasia is the world's largest land mass and includes both Europe and Asia. Europe occupies about a third of the western end of Eurasia, and, with the exception of Australia, is the smallest continent. It is the most densely populated for its size and no other continent has so many separate nations. Nearly all of these countries have distinctive customs and speak different languages. This does much to explain Europe's turbulent history.

Actually Europe is a huge peninsula, subdivided into a number of lesser peninsulas, caused by the oceans and inland seas which encroach upon it. Its irregular form, together with the mountain barriers, and the presence of important islands near the continent, have contributed to the growth of individual nations. Differences in language and customs have a natural tendency to arouse a strong nationalistic spirit. This keeps people apart and makes them suspicious of those with different customs, and who speak alien tongues. Among mountain people an independent spirit and love of freedom is even more pronounced.

In the northwest, two peninsulas are

formed by the Baltic Sea. The countries of Norway and Sweden occupy the Scandinavian Peninsula. Denmark is on the Jutland Peninsula between the Baltic and North Seas. To the south, Portugal and Spain comprise the Iberian Peninsula. The peninsular boot of Italy thrusts out into the Mediterranean, and the Balkan Peninsula is surrounded by the Black Sea and the Adriatic, Ionian and Aegean Seas of the Mediterranean.

Great Britain is prevented from being a peninsula only by the narrow English Channel, and was once a part of the mainland. The entire course of history has been changed by this strip of water which made England an island. The same may be said for the Straits of Gibraltar separating Europe from Africa. But for this nine-mile passage, the Mediterranean would have had no outlet to the Atlantic.

Europe may be divided into five natural regions: (1) the Northwest Highlands, (2) the Central Plains, (3) the Central Highlands, (4) the Southern Mountains and Plateaus, and (5) the Southern Lowlands.

Most of the British Isles, a section of France, and a good part of the Scandinavian Peninsula are included in the Northwest Highlands. This is the coastal region with excellent harbors where men have made their living by the sea, and commerce has become most important. In those places where coal and iron are found it has led to an industrial life. This highland region enjoys a cool, temperate climate and people are energetic.

The great Central Plains extend from the British Isles to the Ural Mountains that separate Europe from Asia. These plains range from the tundra regions of the Far North to the Caspian Sea, the Caucasus Mountains, and the Black Sea of the Southeast. In the Southwest they reach into southern France. Within such an extensive area there are naturally great differences in climate. There is also great diversity of vegetation and the occupations of the people.

South of the Arctic tundra belt are extensive evergreen forests that reach westward to the Scandinavian Peninsula. In the grasslands to the south of the forests are large areas used for the growing of grain,

England's rolling countryside is specked with tiny cottages which augment the natural beauty of the landscape.

and stock grazing is the chief occupation in the drier southeastern sections. This is the region of the dry and treeless steppes.

The Central Highlands include the plateau in central France and take in parts of Belgium, southern Germany, Austria, and the Czecho-Slovakian area. It is the region of forest, water-power, and varied mineral resources. The industrial districts of Central Europe are the outgrowth of the great deposits of coal and iron found here.

The impressive peaks of the Alps rise south of the Central Highlands, forming one of the many ranges of Southern Europe. The Apennines extend the length of Italy, and other ranges follow the eastern coast of the Adriatic through Yugoslavia and Albania to the southern tip of Greece. Spreading out to the east they include most of the Balkan Peninsula. To the north the Carpathian Mountains swing east and north around the valley of the Danube and then run northeast to almost circle the Plain of Hungary. Farther to the east, the Caucasus Mountains reach from the Black to the Caspian Sea. Separating France and Spain are the Pyrenees, and the Sierra Nevadas are in southern Spain bordering the Mediterranean.

The Alps are particularly famous for their scenic grandeur. The Sierra Nevadas and Carpathian Mountains are rich in mineral resources, and some of the world's greatest oil fields are in the Caucasus. The mountains of Italy lack valuable ores and have been largely stripped of their forests.

The Southern Lowlands of the Danube Valley and the Plain of Hungary represent some of the finest farming and grazing land in the world.

The extreme irregularity of the European coastline has been of great importance to the life of the people. With the North and Baltic Seas, the Mediterranean and Black Seas, penetrating far into the interior, only Central Europe and Eastern Russia are very far from the coast. Although the combined areas of South America and Africa are nearly five times that of Europe, the coastline of Europe is longer.

A majority of the great seaports of the world are in Western Europe. Its people have led the world in sea-faring.

Europe has a generally mild, temperate climate, particularly in the western areas, which are warmed by ocean currents and the winds blowing over these waters. Even the British Isles have a mild climate in spite of being in the same latitude as Labrador. Greater extremes of temperature exist in eastern Europe where these winds lose their moderating effect.

Due to the Alps blocking the cold north winds, and the influence of the warm waters of the Mediterranean, the southern shores of Europe enjoy a mild year-round climate. Excepting in eastern Europe, where the rainfall is light, there is generally sufficient moisture for agriculture.

An abundance of mineral resources, fine forests, rich farmlands, water-power, and the seas plentifully supplied with fish, have encouraged Europe's growth. An invigorating climate, waterways, harbors and access to the oceans of the world, have contributed to its commercial importance.

The climate and natural resources of each country have largely determined their individual occupations and prosperity.

GREAT BRITAIN AND NORTHERN IRELAND

—The British Isles and the British Commonwealth of Nations owe much of their commercial and industrial growth to the daring and initiative of their early mariners. Although we usually think of the British Isles as comprising Great Britain and Ireland, it actually consists of nearly five thousand islands. Within the small compass of the islands there is a considerable variety of topography.

In Northern Ireland there are many lakes, including the largest one of the island, Lough Neagh, as well as a range known as the Mourne Mountains. A large portion of the country consists of the basalt plateau of Antrim.

Northern Ireland, or Ulster, as the six counties are sometimes called, is the seat of a very extensive lace and linen industry. In County Down and County Antrim there are highgrade deposits of granite and bauxite which are being exploited. Shipbuilding is a major industry centered in the capital, Belfast.

In Scotland the three well-marked divisions stand out, the highlands, the southern uplands, and between these two, the central lowlands, into which four-fifths of the population is crowded. The lowlands contain the richest agricultural land, as well as the coal fields. They are penetrated by three great estuaries, the Firths of Tay and Forth on the east, and of Clyde on the west, so that communication coastwise or overseas is everywhere easy.

Scotland has some of the largest shipbuilding yards in the world on the Firth of Clyde. Sheep and cattle are raised in large numbers since the land is not well suited to agriculture.

The Welsh cliffy upland is flanked to the north and east by small coal fields, but the greatest field lies to the south. A belt of limestone running from Bill of Portland to Tees Bay, and bearing at many points valuable iron ores, serves as a rough boundary of industrial England, for to the south and east of it, apart from the metropolis, agricultural interests predominate. Lying to the west of the limestone band is the Devon-

Cornwall peninsula, where great bosses of granite and slate form the famous moors.

Wales, after 700 years as a part of the English kingdom, retains its individuality and is nationalistic in speech, dress and customs. The Welsh language is Celtic, akin to the Gaelic of Ireland. It is the only speech of nearly one-tenth of the people.

Channel Islands, lying across the English Channel off the coast of Normandy, and Scilly Islands, lying southwest of Land's End, enjoy an almost complete freedom from frost and severe weather.

Because of the density of population Great Britain is far from self-sustaining and must depend upon the raw materials and products of other countries. This has led to the development of her world-wide commerce, a large part of which is carried on with her far-flung and numerous colonies. Agriculture is intensive with much importance placed on livestock. Many of the world's most valuable breeds of farm animals have been developed on English farms. This is exemplified by such names as Guernsey, Shropshire, Jersey, Hereford, Hampshire and Plymouth.

IRELAND—Except for coastal hills and mountains, the country is largely an ill-drained plain dotted with lakes and peat-bogs, and crossed by the sluggish Shannon. In the southwest is the beautiful Killarney Lakes region which attracts many tourists each year. Although little of the land is suitable for large scale agriculture, grass and fodder crops are abundant and provide stockraising needs which is the major industry of the country. The Shannon River, Royal Canal, and the Grand Canal provide an excellent inland waterway system of transportation. Shannon airport, near Limerick, is a major international airway terminal. Horse-breeding is the most famous of Irish farm industries. A prosperous tourist trade is developing.

NORWAY AND SWEDEN—With its saw-toothed coast, great fiords, and neighboring islands, it is natural that Norway, occupying the western part of the Scandanavian peninsula, would be a maritime country. Norway's long coast line, facing the

Belgian Government Information Center

The European peasant has long been a factor in the economic development of the Old World.

Atlantic, is edged with lofty cliffs and seamed with deep fiords. Islands, countless in number, fringe the coast. Most of the country is a rocky, rugged and barren land, about 20 per cent of which is forested. The rivers are short and torrential, but provide the finest salmon fishing in Europe. The Kjolen Mountains which form the backbone of the peninsula separate Norway from Sweden. These mountains rise in many parts to over 6,000 feet, the highest peaks being over 8,000 feet.

Norway is the land of the "midnight sun". From Trondheim northward at least a part of the disk of the sun is visible from May through July. But the winter nights are 17 hours long and midday seems like twilight during the winter months. Another striking feature is that much of the area above the Arctic Circle is warmer than some regions further south. Northeast Norway is the warmest part of the country in the summer.

Sweden consists primarily of a tableland sloping from the Kjolen Range to the Baltic. No less than 8 per cent of the surface of Sweden is water, the immense number of lakes covering almost 15,000 square miles. The two largest, Vanern and Vattern, in the southern portion of the country, are connected by a system of canals. Besides the large number of small islands which fringe

Suomen-Matkat

The snow-encrusted northlands of Scandinavia force its northernmost inhabitants to lead nomadic existences.

the coast, Sweden includes the two large Baltic islands of Gotland and Öland. Most of the people live in the southern part of their country while the Norwegians have settled chiefly near the fiords. Hydro-electric development is in an advanced stage in both countries.

In Sweden, iron deposits are among the richest in the world. Swedish steel is universally famous for its fine qualities. The making of machinery for export is a major industry. Swedish agriculture is in a very high state of development, and exports wheat, bacon and butter in large quantities. In forestry and sawmilling the nation has evolved such advanced methods that foreign technicians in the industry often go to Sweden to study logging and forestry. Nearly half of her exports are in pulp and paper products.

DENMARK—Denmark occupies a peninsula and numerous islands lying at the entrance to the Baltic. It is a lowland country characterized by many lakes, ponds and short rivers. Its sandy shores are shallow, with lagoons shut in by shifting sand bars. Most of Denmark is farm land, about half of which is used for grazing. The Faeroe Islands produce fish, mutton and wool for the homeland.

Dairy farming is the country's chief industry, the products of which comprise nearly all

her exports. Greenland, the largest island in the world, is Denmark's only possession.

ICELAND—The republic is an island in the north Atlantic consisting of a great tableland averaging 2,000 feet above sea level. Of its whole area barely a quarter is habitable. The surface is dotted by over 100 volcanic peaks. There are many boiling springs and the geysers are world-famous. It is too cold for agriculture but has rich grazing land for sheep and cattle.

FINLAND—Finland consists of a great plateau, ranging from 400 to 600 feet in elevation. The southern half of the plateau has about 25 per cent of its area occupied by thousands of shallow lakes, many of them linked by short natural or artificial channels, providing many miles of navigable waterways. Forests cover the greater part of the country which has led to lumbering, paper-making and the manufacture of woodenware. Over half the population is engaged in agricultural pursuits which are carried on under great difficulties.

THE NETHERLANDS—The tiny kingdom of the Netherlands, lacking natural resources has been largely a nation of seafarers for centuries. Along the canals, the meadows are often ten or twelve feet below the water line, and between the land and the sea at high tide there may be a difference of twenty-five feet or more. The land is protected by embankments and dikes, and it may be pictured as a great trough, the floor of which slopes down from east and southeast toward the North Sea. The rivers which flow across the country from the higher continent beyond, are at their mouths, frequently below the level of the sea, into which they have to be lifted by canals and locks across the dams or dikes. A large part of the land has been reclaimed from the sea and little by little it has become a fertile country.

BELGIUM—Smaller than Holland, Belgium is the most densely populated country in Europe. Situated between England, Holland, France and Germany, it is in the very center of industrial Europe. The country is well

watered, and has two principal rivers, the Scheldt and the Maas. Four-fifths of the land is under cultivation, and although over half the people are engaged in either farming or stock raising the country still does not raise sufficient food to feed her people. Belgium's intensive industrialization has been at the expense of its agriculture, for the valley of the Sambre-Meuse, the chief industrial center, is also the richest farming land. Metals from the Katanga region of the Belgian Congo are intensifying industrial activities, and Belgium is regaining her pre-war level of output. The textile industry is reviving also. The nation furnishes a great variety of farm products and is known for its world-famous breed of horses.

LUXEMBURG—The Grand Duchy of Luxemburg, smaller than the state of Rhode Island, is one of Europe's oldest states. An abundant store of iron ore has encouraged mining, smelting and some manufacturing. International trade of the duchy has been carried on through a customs union with Belgium.

LIECHTENSTEIN—Only 27 square miles larger than San Marino, Liechtenstein is separated from Switzerland by the Rhine river and is bounded by Austria in the east. The population is largely German but Switzerland administers its postal and telegraph facilities, and its currency is Swiss. It also belongs to the Swiss customs union. The tillable soil, a long strip along the Rhine river, yields grapes, grains and pasturage for a small cattle industry.

FRANCE—France is largely an agricultural country where the farmers, instead of living on their farms, usually live in nearby villages. Although rich in minerals, it has lagged behind both England and Germany as an industrial country. The surface is diversified, but much of it is lowland, with a few level plains. In the center is a triangular plateau called the Auvergne Mountains, with a height of something over 3,000 feet. The Cevennes form the eastern edge of this plateau, and from them to the Vosges, the tableland continues. There is a mountainous area in Brittany, but the greatest heights are on the

Austria State Tourist Dept.

Austria's small villages are nestled among the deep valleys of its mountainous countryside.

frontiers, the Jura, the Pyrenees, and the Alps separating it respectively from Switzerland, Spain and Italy. The Ardennes in the northeast are less lofty. The Seine drains the north, the Loire and the Garonne the west, and the Rhone the east and south. France enjoys a delightful climate. Only in the region of the Alps is real winter encountered. Protected by the mountains to the north, the balmy area along the Mediterranean is a magnet that has drawn countless vacationers. Many semi-tropical plants and fruits are grown in this section. Indeed, France's greatest resource is her soil. Grape culture is by far the leading agricultural pursuit, for France produces a billion gallons of wine in a vintage year. Yet, the country imports millions of gallons. Textile production, particularly the silk industry centered around Lyons, is a valuable undertaking in the country; cotton mills are the leading producers of goods.

MONACO—The Principality of Monaco is one of the smallest states in the world. It possesses the administrative organs and institutions of larger nations in miniature. It has no taxes for it is supported by the gambling casino of Monte Carlo from which its own citizens are barred. The most striking feature of this 370 acre state is the Monagasque Acropolis on a headland 200 feet above the water. The Prince's Palace, a magnificent structure, is located on it. On the Mediterranean coast, surrounded by the Riviera of France, Monaco offers to the tourist auto-racing, skiing, bathing, sailing, and of course, gambling. There is also an oceanographic museum.

SWITZERLAND—This rugged little country is a completely land-locked republic nestling among the beautiful Alps. It has succeeded in maintaining its neutrality and independence while the rest of Europe engaged in costly and devastating wars. Between Lake Constance on the Rhine and Lake Geneve on the Rhone are Lakes Neuchatel, Zurich, Lucerne, Brienz, Thun, all of which drain to the Aar. Lake Geneve and Lake Constance each exceed 200 square miles in area. Many of Switzerland's mountains are permanently covered with snow. Capitalizing upon its wonderful mountain and lake scenery, and making the most of its limited resources, Switzerland has become one of the most prosperous of the smaller nations. With its snow-capped peaks rising from ten to fifteen thousand feet, it has been the playground of Europe for many years.

GERMANY—There are two natural regions in Germany, the northern plain and southern highlands. The former is the most extensive agricultural region. The land which borders Denmark is favorable to the grazing of cattle, and, in the northeast, large numbers of sheep and goats are raised. The minerals found in the central highlands have had the greatest influence upon the development of Germany in the last fifty years.

Except for ample supplies of coal and potash, Germany is deficient in natural resources. During the glacial period, sand was deposited over the plains region and as a result the soil is not naturally fertile. Only by intensive cultivation and the heavy use of fertilizers, made from potash, is much of the soil made productive. Germany's great scientific development has been largely the result of solving agricultural problems, and

of searching for new uses to utilize the coal reserves.

Germany's only access to the ocean, and world trade, is through the Baltic and North Seas. To make the most of this she has developed a remarkable system of waterways. The Rhine rises in the Alps and flows through the fertile lowlands of western Germany to the border of Holland, and thence to the sea. The Elbe, Weser, and the Oder flow north across the low plain of Germany. The Oder empties into the Baltic. The Elbe and Weser flow into the North Sea. All three are navigable far inland for ocean-going vessels. The rivers, together with fifteen hundred miles of canals, form a network of waterways which provide cheap transportation.

AUSTRIA AND HUNGARY—Austria is characterized by its beautiful mountain scenery, over 90 percent of the land is classified as mountainous, which has contributed to development of one of its largest industries—tourist and resort trade. However, over 80 per cent of the land is productive and half of this is under cultivation. In contrast, Hungary is largely comprised of a low fertile plain. The country is primarily agricultural and is a great grain and wine producer.

CZECHOSLOVAKIA—This land-locked country contains strategic routes between north and south Europe of economic and political value. The country has two large mountain ranges, the Carpathian in the east and the Sudeten in the west. Czechoslovakia is famous for its subterranean caverns and its spas and mineral springs. The people are energetic and progressive and there are valuable forest resources, fertile soil and varied mineral deposits.

THE BALKANS—They include Rumania, Yugoslavia, Bulgaria, Albania, Greece and European Turkey. Located at the gateway to Asia, and on a natural route connecting the two continents, this region has been a battleground for centuries. Repeated invasions from various directions have resulted in a number of racial groups and religious beliefs. The rugged nature of the country has isolated the people into many rival factions with intense racial and national spirit.

YUGOSLAVIA consists essentially of a mountainous core, which stretches from the Dinaric Alps in the northwest to the Balkan Mountains on the Bulgarian frontier. The only valley which cuts the mountains and forms a passageway is that of the Marava River, which with that of the Vardar, leads from Beograd to Thessalonike. Beyond the Sava-Danube, as far as the northern boundary, the land is low and swampy near the rivers, with a few minor elevations. The chief concentrations of people are around Zagreb and Beograd. Yugoslavia has recently experienced a crisis resulting from a boycott by the Cominform countries and the Soviet Union. Forced to turn to the West, the nation has signed trade agreements with several Western European states. Its greatest problem is the lack of communications between its regions. The more highly developed coastal areas have access to outside markets, but the distribution of economic aid further inland is hampered by the mountains which impose a rugged barrier between the provinces.

RUMANIA—In western Rumania the Carpathian Mountains from the northwest and the Transylvanian Alps from the southwest meet in the center to form a crescent. To the north and west of this crescent is the Transylvanian plateau; to the south and east are the plains of Moldavia and Walachia. The principal rivers are the Danube in the south which enters the Black Sea at Sulina, and the Prut in the northeast and the Siret in the southeast—both of which connect with the Danube.

BULGARIA—The country is hilly and well watered by numerous streams, of which the Isker, Struma and Maritza are the most important. Although nearly one-third of the country's area is in forests, only a small part of the wood is used commercially since about one-fourth of the forest area is completely unproductive. Many of the forests consist of scrub timber and a sizeable portion of the good forests are inaccessible. Eighty percent of Bulgaria's population is employed in agriculture, the chief crops being tobacco and cereals. Attar of rose and silk are important products.

TWA Transworld Airline

The coastal cities of Portugal draw heavily on the sea for their principal commodity.

ALBANIA—Albania is a mountainous country on the western side of the Peninsula. In the center, part of the plateau is cultivable, and in the south there is fertile alluvial soil with grazing land on the slopes.

GREECE—With a very long coast line on the Aegean and Ionian Seas, and a large number of islands, including Crete, Mitylene, Dodecanese and Chios, the area is generally mountainous. The mountains, though not very high, divide the country into a number of small districts, between which communication is difficult. It is the sea which links the different regions of Greece.

ITALY—Once the hub of the known world, Italy's importance declined as the age of exploration and discovery opened up the ocean routes of the world. Taking no part in this period of conquest and empire building, she did not acquire colonies. Lacking unity she was in no position to demand her share of the rich prizes of newly discovered land being acquired by other European nations.

With the opening of the Suez Canal and tunnels through the Alps, her trade somewhat improved, but the absence of the necessary minerals prevented her from keeping pace with industrial development elsewhere in Europe.

The south slope of the Alps belongs to Italy. At the point where the Alps reach the Mediterranean, the Apennines begin. These mountains follow the length of Italy and form a rugged backbone which extends through the island of Sicily. The southern and western parts of the peninsula have been subjected to volcanic eruptions, and Vesuvius, Etna, and Stromboli are still active volcanoes. The chief lowlands are in the Po Valley with narrow coastal plains east and west of the Apennines. The majority of the people, and most of the agriculture and manufacturing, are located in the Po Valley. Consequently Northern Italy does not experience the poverty to be found in Southern Italy. It is from the south that most of the immigrants to the United States have come.

Italy's colorful history, scenery and balmy climate have attracted many tourists which has in some measure offset an unfavorable balance of trade.

SAN MARINO—San Marino is one of the oldest republics in the world and is the smallest. It has always been on good terms with its big neighbor, Italy, by whom it is surrounded. The state was founded in the fourth century by Marinius of Dalmatia, a stonecutter. Except for a few invasions, its liberty has been respected, even by Napoleon. During World War II it declared war against Germany and was occupied by the Germans and subsequently liberated by the British. Much of its revenue is obtained through the sale of its postage stamps issued for the benefit of collectors.

SPAIN AND PORTUGAL—About three-fourths of the Iberian Peninsula is a granite plateau with a range of mountains dividing it in the center. The rivers that flow through this region through deep gorges block transportation and are unsuited for navigation, waterpower or irrigation. The dry climate, lack of water, a rugged land formation, poor soil and an absence of transportation have been great obstacles standing in the way of the economic development of both Spain and Portugal. A portion of the land in the valleys

and plains has been made fertile through irrigation and farming is the main industry. Fishing is important along the Portugal coast, although a great part of the coast is too rugged for harbors. There are forests in most of the higher areas where half the world's supply of cork is produced.

ANDORRA—Tiny Andorra is in the Pyrenees Mountains between France and Spain. It is not a republic, as is often supposed, but a joint dependency of France and the Bishops of Urgel in Spain. Its mountains are high and arid, and its valleys contain poor soil so that the people are nearly all engaged in pastoral pursuits. The one product of the soil is tobacco. Sheep-herding is the main industry, and the need of hay for winter forage further limits the use of soil for any other crop.

POLAND—Poland was for many years a chiefly agricultural country but good supplies of coal, lead, iron and zinc have helped her industrial progress to such an extent that it is now almost equally industrial and agricultural. Most of the land is comprised of a plain, although there are low hills in the northeast in Pomerania. The lower regions of the Vistula have marshes, sand dunes and lakes. The central plain of Poland with an elevation of about 500 feet is traversed by great rivers, the most important being the Oder and the Vistula. Her strategic position near the Baltic Sea, and the lack of natural boundaries and barriers, have long made the people of this country, as well as those of the former Baltic States, the victims of stronger nations seeking an outlet to the sea.

U. S. S. R.—Almost three times the size of the United States and comprising more than one-seventh of the world's land surface, the Union of Soviet Socialist Republics sprawls across two continents. Most of Russia is a great plain reaching from the Pacific to its western boundaries. Its position in northern latitudes and the absence of protecting barriers result in an extreme climate with long, cold winters. Vladivostok, on the Pacific coast, and the ports on the Arctic Ocean and Baltic Sea are closed by ice during the long winter months. Vladivostok, however, is kept open the year round by ice-breakers. In no part of the land is the rainfall heavy, and there are frequent and widespread droughts, which bring hunger and starvation to its people.

From the Black Sea in the south to the Arctic Ocean, and from the Baltic Sea to the Ural Mountains, which divide Asiatic Russia from European Russia, is a vast lowland. To the east of the Urals is Siberia, two-thirds of which is a flat, unbroken plain. In the far north the ground has been found to be frozen to a depth of over six hundred feet. This presents peculiar problems, if the government is to succeed with plans to mine the ores found there and industrialize this Arctic region. Here in the tundra country the moss, upon which the reindeer of the nomadic tribes feed, is often five feet thick.

South of the tundra belt is a great evergreen forest covering billions of acres, where lumbering and fur-trapping are the chief occupations.

Russia's supply of minerals is so great and widely scattered that the extent of many of the deposits is still unknown. There are immense reserves of coal in both European and Asiatic Russia. Copper, platinum, iron, gold, manganese and other minerals are found in the Urals. Some of the richest petroleum deposits in the world are located in the Baku region of the Caspian Sea.

Great strides have been made in industrial development, with the manufacture of iron and steel, machinery, textiles and leather goods in the lead.

In spite of climate, high cost of manufacture and difficulties of transportation, the U. S. S. R. is a country that is largely self-sustaining, and has become increasingly important industrially.

AFRICA—The term "sleeping giant," which has often been used in referring to China, can best be applied to Africa. This second largest continent is three times the size of China, and is richer in natural resources, but it has only one-third the population. Although two of the world's oldest civilizations once flourished along its northern shores in Egypt and Carthage, the rest of Africa long

TWA—Trans World Airline

Many natural phenomena, like these hot springs, are present in Africa's terrain.

remained shrouded in mystery.

Joined to Asia by a land bridge at the Isthmus of Suez, and only separated from Europe by the narrow Strait of Gibraltar, it was not until the nineteenth century that Europe finally set about the conquest of the "Dark Continent." For centuries an unfavorable climate and natural barriers combined to guard its secrets and hold back development.

Almost midway of its length Africa is crossed by the equator. Being triangular in shape, this places most of the continent in unhealthy torrid regions. Added to this its coastline is steep and regular, and offers few places for ships to anchor. The rivers as regards navigability cannot be considered in the same light as the great rivers of Europe, Asia and the Americas. None, except the Nile and the Congo, has unimpeded entrance to the sea.

The deltas of the Niger and the Zambesi are choked by silt and, on nearly all, navigation is impeded by shoal or cataract. Nevertheless the Congo and the Nile with their tributaries have many thousands of miles of navigable waterways, as have the Niger, the Benue and the Zambesi.

To the north, the Sahara Desert proved an effective barrier of sand and intense heat, which for hundreds of years prevented any important exchange of ideas or trade between the white man of the north and the black man in the south. Extending from the Atlantic to the River Nile, and reaching from the Mediterranean to the Sudan, the dry Sahara is a region of desolation. What trade existed between Asia, Europe and Africa followed caravan routes which led from oasis to oasis. The only life to be found there is at these scattered oases.

It was only following the explorations of Livingstone, Stanley and others in the last century, that Europe became aware of the possibilities existing in Africa. Then, suddenly awakened to the great wealth that had been overlooked, the European powers rushed in to carve out vast empires. When they had finished only two sections remained which were not possessions or dependencies of the white man. Only the Republic of Liberia and the Kingdom of Ethiopia remained, where the native African had a voice in the government of his affairs. Later Egypt became independent, and the Union of South Africa acquired a dominion status in the British Commonwealth. Following the second world war, Libya, Sudan, Morocco, Tunisia and Ghana (formerly Gold Coast) became independent.

Africa is a great plateau, over four thousand miles long from north to south. The average height of the entire continent is over two thousand feet above sea level. Its loftiest peak is nearly twenty thousand feet high, while the Qattara Depression in the Libyan Desert sinks to four hundred feet below sea level.

The Atlas Mountains parallel the north coast of Africa, with their southern slopes dropping down to the Sahara. The Sudan Belt, which extends south from the Sahara to the Gold Coast and the Gulf of Guinea, is a lower region of hills, valleys and plains. To the southwest are the low Cameroon Mountains; and another chain in the eastern part follows the Red Sea.

In Eastern Africa, a ridge of highlands reaches below the equator to form a series of mountain ranges. It is here that the great lakes region is found. Only in North America are there lakes which compare to these in size. Unlike the mountain ranges of other continents, those of Africa do not follow a regular pattern. This, together with their location, provides an unusual drainage system. A mountain ridge separates the lakes that drain into the three great rivers, the Nile, the Congo and the Zambesi. This ridge dictates the direction of their courses, with the Nile flowing north toward the Mediterranean, the Congo twisting and turning to finally reach the Atlantic to the west, and the Zambesi flowing east to empty into the Indian Ocean. Each river follows a devious course through the mountains before finding a way over the edge of the plateau to reach the sea. This results in many falls and rapids which interrupt transportation. The Victoria Falls on the Zambesi, the rapids of the Congo, and the cataracts of the Nile are typical.

The Congo, winding through the gloomy depths of the fever-infested forests, is three thousand miles long. It is second only to the Amazon of South America in the volume of water it empties into the sea. The Nile travels four thousand miles before reaching the Mediterranean, and today, as in ancient times, makes Egypt a habitable country. As the Nile winds slowly through the Sahara, the evaporation is so great that the river would dry up before reaching the sea were it not fed by rivers from the high Abyssinian Mountains. It is these waters of the Blue Nile which bring the great Nile floods and supply the water for irrigation to make of Egypt a fertile strip of land hemmed in by cliffs and burning sands. Africa's fourth large river, the Niger, while rising only one hundred and fifty miles from the ocean, flows twenty-five hundred miles before reaching the Atlantic.

Africa is a land of climatic contradictions. At the equator the temperature ranges from typical jungle weather at the lower levels, to a climate similar to that found well over a thousand miles to the north. This occurs in the high altitudes of the mountains. Along the Mediterranean, the weather compares with that of southern Europe. The weather in the Congo Basin is always hot and humid, although to the east, in the mountain and lake region, it is tempered by the higher altitudes. In the far south, around Capetown, the weather is mild and sunny like the climate of southern California. The same extremes exist in rainfall. At the equator it is excessive, with periods of torrential rains. Traveling north or south from this wet center there is less and less rain, with parts of the Sahara never getting a drop.

Plant life varies with the rainfall. The dense, matted tropical jungles, which are exceeded only in size by the forests of the Amazon, give way to grassy plains and open forests. The only vegetation in the Sahara is around the springs that nourish the oases. Because the hot winds of the south are blocked by the Atlas Mountains, the entire coastal area of North Africa from the Atlantic to the Nile River is agriculturally productive.

Africa is a strange mixture of white and black races. The four original races of Hamites and Semites, Negroes and Hottentots have become so intermingled that it is no longer possible to draw clear lines between racial groups. The Hamites and Semites of North Africa are white and Mohammedans. The Negroes and Hottentots are the black people of Central and South Africa. While probably members of the Negro race, the Hottentots have distinctive characteristics which put them in a class by themselves. These native tribes have a barbaric form of worship. The Sudanese, blackest of the Negroes, were sought by the early slave traders. For over three hundred years millions of these poor blacks were seized and transported to strange lands.

The slave trade was started by the son of a man who accompanied Columbus to America. Needing labor in her New World colonies to replace the Indian slaves, who preferred death to captivity, Spain granted each Spanish colonist the right to import twelve African Negroes. A year later the king of Spain bestowed a grant upon the Dutch allowing them to take four thousand slaves a year. Soon the "black ivory trade" had grown to huge proportions, and it has been estimated that as many as two million

TWA—Trans World Airline

Africa's varied topography lends itself to all sorts of livlihoods ranging from the industrial to the pastoral.

slaves were removed from Africa in a single year.

In recent years Africa has been undergoing tremendous changes. Railroads, motor roads and airlines continue to reach out and draw distant points closer together. Modern engineering genius is overcoming the obstacles imposed by climate and land formation, and Africa is rapidly taking its place among the more fortunate continents.

TUNISIA—Battleground of World War II, is the most productive land in North Africa. Its fertile valleys produce grain and tropical fruits. Seat of ancient Carthage, it was once the wealthiest city of its time until Rome destroyed it during the Punic Wars.

LIBYA— Is relatively unprotected from the scorching desert winds and, consequently, the least valuable of North African regions. However, the coastal areas are cultivated with the aid of shade and irrigation.

EGYPT—In the heart of the Nile valley, has been one of the most productive regions in the world since recorded time. Recent dam construction regulating the flow of the Nile has increased the productivity of the soil. Agricultural methods are the same today as they were 6,000 years ago.

SUDAN (former Anglo-Egyptian)—Embracing the upper Nile basin to the borders of Uganda and Ethiopia, produces gum arabic for the entire world. Cotton is raised in the fertile areas between the Blue and the White Niles. Dates, ivory and meat are also exported.

ETHIOPIA—The first country to be liberated by the Allies in World War II, has many undeveloped resources. Gold and platinum are mined. The Djimmah Province produces a fine, robust coffee. There is, as yet, only one railroad which leads out of the country. The Italians, true to the Roman tradition, built 4,340 miles of roads while they were occupying the country.

UGANDA—The Source of the Nile River. Much of the country is situated in the lofty mountains of East Africa. The climate is usually mild because of the altitude of the land.

KENYA—Eastern gateway to Central Africa abounds in big game. The lowlands bordering the Indian Ocean are fertile, the climate bearable. Western Kenya is a high plateau with isolated towering peaks, snow-capped the year 'round.

TANGANYIKA—Within its borders is Kilimanjaro, Africa's highest known peak located a few miles north of the equator. Tanganyika is famous as the gorilla country of Africa. Its jungle brims with wildlife, thereby making it a paradise for big-game hunters.

NYASALAND—A British protectorate, lies along the west shore of Lake Nyasa. Semi-autonomous and self-supporting, it has a good system of roads and railways.

UNION OF SOUTH AFRICA comprises the Transvaal, Orange Free State, Natal and the Cape of Good Hope. Its northern areas contain many valuable minerals, chief of which is gold and diamonds. Most of the world's diamonds and half the world's gold are exported from this country.

NORTHERN RHODESIA—Crown Colony on the borders of the jungles of Central Africa and the wide plains of South Africa. Copper, lead and cattle comprise its principal forms of wealth. Victoria Falls, the world's highest, are on the Zambesi River in Northern Rhodesia.

SOUTHERN RHODESIA—Border region, is well suited to agriculture and European settlement. It possesses vast amounts of gold, asbestos and chrome.

ANGOLA or Portuguese West Africa, on Africa's west coast, is a huge treeless plain, arid in many places. Diamonds are mined, and recently coffee has been cultivated for export.

The grazing lands of Ruanda-Urundi have been added to the Belgian Congo, and a ten-year plan to develop the Congo region has been inaugurated. The Belgian Congo has the richest terrain in Africa. Metals, both common and rare, are imbedded in its soil.

The most important product of the Gold Coast is cacao. Some diamonds and gold are mined to a limited extent.

LIBERIA—Long unimportant economically, is presently producing rubber and coffee for export.

French colonies are located in most of West Africa. The areas from Dakar southward yield rubber, mahogany, ebony, cacao and coffee. The interior of West Africa merges with the Sahara Desert. A narrow savanna region stretches across the French lands to the headwaters of the Nile. This area contains some of Africa's large lakes and is the best suited for grazing. The great forests on its southern edge lead into the jungles of the Congo and Cameroons. The region is a habitat for a diversity of animal life including the leopard, lion and rhinoceros as well as some of the larger animals of the country.

MADAGASCAR—One of the world's largest islands, is located off the east coast of Africa. Graphite, copper and precious stones form a part of its mineral resources.

AUSTRALIA—This island continent of the South Seas is the smallest, and last to be discovered of all the continents.

The United States and Australia are nations of about the same age and size, and in other respects have much in common. The loss of America as a British Colony directly led to the settling of Australia. It was first claimed for the British Crown in 1788 as a settlement for British convicts who had previously been sent to America. Landing in a virgin country, the early pioneers of the two countries had to conquer the wilderness before creating a nation. In the process of so doing the people of both lands developed similar characteristics. In later years Australia even patterned its constitution after that of the United States.

But, whereas the United States became a melting pot for all the races and creeds in the world, Australia has been peopled almost entirely by British stock. Today 97 per cent of the population are descendants of British colonists, and 86 per cent are Australian born. Strict laws have confined immigration to the white race. Few of the natives who originally inhabited Australia remain. These aborigines are similar to the African Negro but not so intelligent, and are believed to be a separate race.

Almost half of Australia lies within the tropics, but being surrounded by great oceans, the continent has a mild climate throughout the year. Snow normally falls only in the high mountains in the winter. Since the seasons are the reverse of those in the United States, this occurs in their winter months of June, July, and August.

Australia is said to be most level in surface and regular in outline of all the continents. There is an entire absence of towering mountains. The highest peak is only about seventy-three hundred feet above sea level. The mountains parallel the east coast, with, by far, the greater part of the continent a vast, irregular, and undulating plateau.

Australia can be regarded as falling into four well-defined regions: (1) The Great Plateau in the west extends over about half of the continent; (2) The Eastern Highlands follow along the whole of the eastern coastline, rarely exceeding a distance of a hun-

New Zealand Consulate

Modified by ocean currents, New Zealand's climate remains moderate.

dred miles inland; (3) The Central Basin is a lowland area much of which was once a sea-bed; and (4) the Coastal Plains, which form a rim surrounding most of the continent.

Despite rich coastal lands and an immense grazing area in the interior, much of this interior is unsuited for agriculture. It is a great arid region of desert and semi-desert which is sparsely settled and will never support a dense population. The heaviest rainfall is in the tropical regions of the north, and there is adequate moisture along the south coast and southern part of the highlands. Elsewhere there is insufficient rain. But for the presence of innumerable artesian wells scattered over wide areas, much more of the country would be without water. It is these wells that make stock-raising possible, but because of its mineral content, the water is seldom used for agriculture or human use.

The major rivers of Australia are of two types—those which flow toward the coast and are similar to such rivers in other parts of the world; and the inland rivers which gradually lose their water as they flow away from the coastal regions. The headwaters of most of these inland rivers are in the Eastern Highlands.

The Murray River with its tributaries is the main river system and flows into the ocean on the south coast. The Gilbert, Norman and Flinders are the principal streams flowing into the Gulf of Carpentaria in the north. On the west the Murchison, Gascoyne, Ashburton and Fitzroy empty into the Indian Ocean.

The rivers which flow inland vary greatly in volume during the year. For long periods they are mere strings of waterholes, but during floods their waters spread out over the flat country for many miles. Most of their waters evaporate or soak into the ground before they flow very far. In the center of the continent the rivers flow into Lake Eyre when there is sufficient water in them, but generally they are merely beds of dry sand.

The lakes that appear to be scattered so liberally over the land are also a disappointment as they are little more than shallow basins that carry water only after rains.

Great Barrier Reef, the largest of all coral formations, follows the northeast coast for twelve hundred miles of Australia's twelve-thousand-mile coastline. Except in a few places this reef is impassable to ships, but it does provide an inner passage for coastal navigation. There are good harbors on the southeastern coast.

Wherever there is sufficient moisture for grass to grow, the land is especially adapted to grazing. This land has proved the most suitable in the world for raising sheep. Merino sheep, which produce a very fine quality of wool, comprise most of the flocks. The heavy fleece from these sheep exceeds that of breeds raised elsewhere, so, although Australia produces less than one-sixth of the world's sheep, the wool yield is more than a quarter of the world's requirement.

Lacking navigable rivers, most of the transportation is by railways. These have been of first importance in developing the country, but one great drawback of railroad transportation is that there are several gauges. During the last twenty-five years there has been a steady expansion of motor roads, and air routes are rapidly increasing.

In addition to the mainland and the island of Tasmania, Australia has extensive territorial interests. These comprise the Trust Territory of New Guinea, Papua, Nauru and Norfolk Island.

The Trust Territory of New Guinea includes the northeastern section of New Guinea, the Bismarck Archipelago, and the northern islands of the Solomon group. Scattered over a sea area of more than one million square miles, these islands are mountainous with limited coastal areas suitable for cultivation.

NEW ZEALAND—Two large islands and several small ones make up New Zealand. Situated about twelve hundred miles southeast of Australia, New Zealand is a lonely member of the British Commonwealth.

The two principal islands, North and South Island are separated by Cook Strait which is ninety miles wide. Close as they are to each other, these islands have little in common except that they are both mountainous. North Island is of volcanic origin and consists chiefly of forested hills and plateaus. South Island is more rugged with glaciers and snow-clad peaks that rival the Alps of Switzerland.

PACIFIC ISLANDS—The Pacific Islands fall into three major regions: Polynesia, Micronesia and Melanesia.

Polynesia, or "Many islands," consists of widely scattered groups and a few isolated islands forming a rough triangle. The Hawaiian Islands are at the northern point, twenty degrees north of the Equator. The Fiji Islands, at the western point of the triangle, are the meeting place of Polynesian and Melanesian cultures, the people being of mixed stock. The easternmost point lies in the Gambier group of the Tuamota Archipelago, although isolated Pitcairn Island, inhabited by Anglo-Tahitian descendants of the mutinous crew of the "Bounty," is generally included geographically. Within this area lies the most highly developed group of Pacific peoples, a mixture of white, black and yellow racial stocks, the Polynesians. Famous as navigators, they crossed the Pacific from Asia hundreds of years ago, and sailed their canoes eastward to their present homes. For the most part, the islands are mountainous, volcanic and covered with dense vegetation, often fringed by coral reefs. Along the equator and in the southeast, low coral atolls predominate, often only a few feet above sea level, and frequently torn by hurricanes.

The people, often easy-going to the point of idleness, are not always used in local production, some Chinese having been hired to do manual work. Famous for dancing and feasting, the generally happy Polynesians strive to maintain their early customs against the inroads of European traders, missionaries and government regulations.

In the western Pacific, for the most part north of the equator, lies Micronesia, or "little islands," confined to the Marianas, Carolines, Marshall Islands, and Gilbert and Ellice Islands. Except for the latter islands, they are mostly volcanic and coral-fringed, and are peopled by a light-skinned group—the latest arrivals in the Pacific. These inhabitants show more evidence of a recent black and yellow mixture.

The earliest inhabited area of the Pacific, New Guinea and the islands spreading to the southeast of it, is known as Melanesia, the "black islands." Of early Negroid stock, this area was generally by-passed by the later Polynesians and Micronesians, as settlement was already established. Melanesia is a rapidly developing area, rich in minerals as well as the usual coconuts. Today the people range from Europeanized workers in the plantations of New Caledonia and Fiji, and the missions of the New Guinea coast, to half-naked savages, often head-hunters and cannibals, in the higher regions of New Guinea.

ASIA—To say that this is the largest continent in the world gives no idea of its immensity. Covering one-third of the land area of the world, Asia is more than a million square miles larger than the combined areas of North and South America. It extends from the ice-bound regions of the Arctic Circle to the sun-burnt islands of the Tropics. It claims the highest and lowest elevations, as well as the wettest and driest areas in the world. Mount Everest is the highest and the Dead Sea the lowest. Assam is the wettest, and Northern Siberia the driest. Asia is the cradle

Gendreau

The vast expanse of the Pacific Ocean contains thousands of uninhabited coral isles.

of the earliest civilization and is now the home of over half the population of the world.

Man has drawn a line separating Asia from Europe but the only natural division is the low Ural Mountains and a depression extending from the mountains to the Caspian Sea. Only a man-made canal at the Isthmus of Suez separates Asia from Africa.

Washed by three oceans and a number of seas, Asia has a coast line over thirty thousand miles in length. Deep indentations along the irregular coast form seas, such as the Bay of Bengal and the Arabian Sea. Twisting and pointed peninsulas reach far out into the oceans. The shores are dotted with archipelagos and island groups. Among the island groups are Japan, the Philippines, and Indonesia, all of which have become as important as mainland countries.

The mountain ranges that sweep across Europe from west to east continue in long parallel lines through Asia. These mountain chains rise in height, first curving away from one another, and then closing in abruptly in a knot of massed mountains which has been referred to as "the roof of the world." Eastward, the awe-inspiring Himalayas reach to the plateau of Tibet, turn suddenly south through Indochina in long lines of deep, forested ravines, and disappear in a string of islands, drowned by the waters of the Indian Ocean. The Himalayas, covered with eternal snows and scored by mighty glaciers, are the highest mountains in the world. From Mount Everest, their loftiest peak, they drop steeply down to the low river plains below.

To the north of the mountains lies the great plain of Northern Asia, a continuation of the North European plain. Broken only by the Urals it sinks slowly to the frozen Arctic shore. To the south, in India and Arabia, are two low plateaus with steep sides, and the river lowlands of Mesopotamia and the Ganges plain.

This enormous continent is drained by many large rivers. Flowing toward the Arctic Ocean are the Ob, Yenisei and Lena Rivers. They are often blocked with ice for months and flood the surrounding country in thaw. In the east the silt carried down by the rivers has built the wide alluvial plains of China. The Hwang-ho, or Yellow River, flows into the Yellow Sea. Yellow is a sacred color, for this is the color of the silt deposited by the great river on the fertile plain, where crowded millions of Chinese grow their crops and find their livelihood. The Yangtse Kiang, or Blue River, rises in Tibet and passes through deep walls before winding sluggishly across the lowlands of China. These rivers often overflow in disastrous floods and have changed their courses many times.

The Ganges, Indus and Brahmaputra have built up the fertile lowlands of North India and are slowly extending it in broad, swampy deltas, out to sea.

Covering so many degrees of latitude, the climate of Asia would naturally show great variation. There are great extremes of cold and heat in the Siberian lowlands and Northern China. Great areas in the center of the continent, far from the sea, are dry; with tropical conditions prevailing in the south. The heaviest rainfall anywhere in the world is in some localities of Southeastern Asia and everywhere in the eastern region there is sufficient moisture for agriculture. In Assam, India, the rainfall averages about thirty-five feet a year.

There is every type of vegetation, ranging from tundra mosses in the extreme north to tropical plant life in the south. There are great stores of mineral wealth, but much of this is still undeveloped. Asia has been slow to awaken to the possibilities of an industrialized civilization.

Southwestern Asia is that section of the continent lying between India and the Aegean Sea. It is a rugged, mountainous country which includes the two desert plateaus of Iran and Arabia, and the rich lowlands of the Tigris and Euphrates valley.

Great nations flourished in Southwestern Asia several thousand years before the birth of Christ. Composed almost entirely of the white race, their civilizations contributed much to the early nations along the Mediterranean. Mongolian hordes invaded these lands in the thirteenth century, almost destroying the civilizations which they found. Growing in power, a mighty nation which spread into Africa and Europe came into being. The Turks are descendants of these war-like people.

TURKEY—Surrounded by mountains on three sides is a high, dry plateau which slopes to the fertile shores of the Mediterranean. Among the chief mountains are the Taurus range, stretching from the southwestern shore of the Aegean to the north of Syria, their principal peaks rising from 7,000 to 10,000 feet; the Bulgar Mountains rising over 10,000 feet; and the Ala Mountains, north of Seyhan, rising 8,000 to 10,000 feet high. The highest peak in the country is Mt. Ararat, 17,915 feet. Flowing into the Black Sea are the Coruh, the Yesil Irmak, the Kizil Irmak and the Sakariya. Into the Mediterranean flow the Seyhan and Ceyhan. In the east of Asia Minor are the headwaters of both the Euphrates and the Tigris as well as of the Araks.

ISRAEL—After 2,000 years the Jewish people realized their dream of an independent homeland with the establishment of the new state of Israel in 1948. Lying between Egypt and Jordan on the eastern shores of the Mediterranean, the country is a hot and arid land. The new nation's economy is based on the cultivation of citrus fruit for export made possible by extensive irrigation of the lands of Zionist sponsored settlements. Oil refining, chemical production and light industry are also important to the economy.

SYRIA AND LEBANON

The occupations of the people of these countries have not changed since Biblical times, and are similar to those of Turkey. Mostly agricultural, there is little mineral wealth, and manufacturing is largely for local markets. Lebanon is mainly mountainous with a fertile valley lying in the center between the Lebanon Mountains on the west coast and the Anti-Lebanon Mountains which form the eastern border between Lebanon and Syria. Syria consists largely of desert surrounded by mountains. In the northeast, the Euphrates flows across the desert and irrigates a valuable strip of agricultural land. Other fertile areas are found near Homs and Hama, both in the northwest, and Damascus and the Jebel Druze district in the southwest.

IRAQ

Once the site of the Babylonian Empire, the region of the Tigris and Euphrates is the "Fertile Crescent" of ancient times. The country is a great alluvial plain, bounded on the north by Kurdistan, on the east by Iran, on the south by the Persian Gulf, and on the west by the Syrian and Arabian Deserts. Northern Iraq has a valuable supply of oil which is piped to Haifa and Tripoli.

IRAN (Persia)

Most of the country is plateau, surrounded by mountain chains, except in the east where huge salt deserts are found. An extension of the mountain ranges, locally known as the Khorasan Mountains of the Hindu Kush, enters on the northeast from Afghanistan and merges into the Elburz Range south of the Caspian, the highest peak being Mt. Demavend. Except for narrow fertile areas along the Caspian Sea and Persian Gulf the land is too dry to sustain many people.

ARABIA

The Arabian Peninsula is a land composed almost entirely of desert, mostly

TWA—Trans World Airline

Flocks of sheep and goats are the economic mainstay of the Arab's life.

of a barren and stony type, with an abundance of sand in the southeast. Besides scattered oases there are only a few small areas in Arabia with enough rainfall to permit the growing of crops. Saudi Arabia, which occupies the central two-thirds of the peninsula, has experimented with modern, mechanized methods of irrigation to improve farming conditions, and a modern railroad now reaches the interior from the Persian Gulf. The finest Arabian horses and camels are raised in the central highlands. Discovery of valuable oil reserves in the desert near the Persian Gulf fostered new economic development, and many local sheikhs, or tribal rulers, have become suddenly rich. Pearling, once important in the Gulf, is now declining. In the mountain valleys of Yemen is the most fertile soil of the peninsula, and its Red Sea ports, such as Mocha and Hodeida handle its coffee and other exports, as well as pearls from nearby islands.

AFGHANISTAN

Barren tablelands, deep ravines and snow-covered mountains leave

TWA—Trans World Airline

Representative of the fine architecture of India is the luxurious structure of the Taj Mahal.

tries, who have successfully thrown off the yoke of oppression, India, until recently, has always been subject to foreign rule. As a result it is a confusion of races, castes, and religions, with a civilization ranging from the highest type of culture to the most primitive. In 1947 India was granted independence and now takes her place among the important powers of the globe.

Except for the rocky slopes of the mountains, the soil is fertile and supports the largest agricultural population in the world. Like the farmers of France, a large majority of these people live in small villages surrounded by tilled fields. And, while primitive methods and equipment are used, surprisingly large crops are raised. Disastrous droughts, due to the vagaries of the weather, and the famines which followed, have been partially relieved by government sponsored irrigation works and the construction of railroads and motor roads.

Afghanistan an unproductive land. Lying as a barrier between Siberia and India, it has been the scene of many invasions and conquests but the war-like Afghans have never been completely vanquished. Cereals, fruits and vegetables are grown only in small areas under irrigation, and the fat-tailed sheep—a native of the country—furnishes meat and a butter substitute.

PAKISTAN—Pakistan is divided into two widely separated sections. The larger part, West Pakistan on the Arabian Sea, consists of the fertile Indus valley, the extremely rugged Northwest frontier and arid Baluchistan. Cereal raising and cotton production are concentrated in the Indus Valley which possesses one of the oldest and most efficient canal irrigation systems in the world. East Pakistan, on the Bay of Bengal, occupies the lower Ganges-Brahmaputra delta and the Assam highland foothills. This nation, while almost wholly Mohammedan in religion, is influenced politically and culturally not only by the Islamic world to the west but also the neighboring Hindu civilization of India.

INDIA—For over four thousand years, India has been at the mercy of marauding and conquering races. Unlike many lesser coun-

SIKKIM, NEPAL AND BHUTAN—These three small independent states are shut off from the outside world by the Himalayas. Several of the world's highest mountains, including Mount Everest, are in southern Nepal. Their inhabitants are energetic people who raise cattle, wheat, rice, tobacco and spices which they export in exchange for necessary manufactured goods, sugar, oil, etc.

CEYLON—The island of Ceylon has been called the "Pearl of the Orient." Situated off the southern coast of India it is famous for its tea, precious stones and tropical beauty. The broad coastal strip which surrounds the central mountains is, for the most part, fertile and produces a luxuriant vegetation. Although the climate is tropical, sea breezes temper the heat.

INDOCHINA—Included on this southeastern peninsula of Asia are a part of Burma, Thailand, Indochina and the Malayan Federation. Most of the peninsula is characterized by heavily forested valleys and mountain ridges of the Himalayas running the length of the land. This is the great rice-producing region, and most of the world's rubber comes from this area. The rainfall is heavy in the entire area and the land is very productive. In the dense forests are valuable stands of prize woods, teak, ebony and other trees used for their wood or gum. Agriculture is the chief industry throughout the peninsula but there are many important deposits of valuable minerals. Modern methods of agriculture and mining have been introduced. Singapore, situated on an island at the extreme southern end of the peninsula, commands one of the most important sea routes in the world.

THE MALAY ARCHIPELAGO — The

world's largest group of islands extends from Sumatra to the Philippine Islands off the coast of China, and includes many thousands of islands. With the exception of the Philippines, and parts of Timor, Borneo and New Guinea, the archipelago was ruled for hundreds of years by the Netherlands.

INDONESIA—Colonization and develop-

ment begun by the Dutch in the XVIIth century has resulted in the richest and most important island group in the world.

Most of the islands are mountainous and of volcanic origin. At one time they were a part of the mainland connecting Asia with Australia. Java is the most productive and highly developed of the East Indies. It is one of the most densely populated regions in the world. Much of the land is divided into native farms and large plantations. The plantation crops are chiefly for export.

Next to Greenland, New Guinea and Borneo are the largest islands in the world. Sumatra and Celebes are next in size in the East Indies. Much of the mineral wealth of these islands is yet untouched. Borneo is crossed almost in the middle by the equator and few white people occupy the island because of the humidity and heat. Petroleum is an important resource of Borneo, Sumatra and Java, and two small islands adjoining Sumatra have valuable deposits of tin. Bali, while one of the lesser islands, has been one of the most publicized, and is favored by tourists as a tropical paradise.

PHILIPPINE ISLANDS—Numbering over

seven thousand islands, Philippines, like other

Publishers' Photo Service

Japan's development as a leading industrial nation has not effaced her customs and traditions.

islands of the Malay Archipelago, are the tops of drowned mountains protruding from the sea. There are well watered fertile plains between the mountains. Being near the equator the temperature is never very low Although the days are warm, the nights are usually cool. Some of the many volcanoes in the Philippines are still active and the islands are subject to earthquakes.

CHINA—Chinese civilization is of greater

antiquity than any other existent world culture. It has shown great powers of survival and has possessed the ability to absorb all foreign influences without losing its own identity.

The Chinese people are patient, industrious, and have great physical endurance. They are among the world's best farmers, having grown more food for longer periods on the same land, without exhausting the soil, than any other people. They take naturally to mechanics and are fine traders and business men.

With the possible exception of Africa, China has the largest undeveloped natural resources in the world. There are rich de-

Indonesia Information Office

Asian art has been stimulated by many technical and cultural institutions.

posits of coal, with China ranking second to the United States in total reserves. Iron ore reserves are large enough to meet its needs for many years to come. It is believed that China has one of the most valuable deposits of copper, and tin has been a leading mineral export.

China is a land of garden farmers and the soil is cultivated intensively. Few animals are raised, which conserves acreage for food crops. Hence the Chinese diet consists almost entirely of vegetable products. In a relatively mild climate people can subsist on less food than in a colder region. Rice is the most important crop but almost every known crop is raised.

Inner Mongolia, Tibet and Sinkiang are outer provinces of China. Until the building of railroads and motor roads they were reached entirely by caravan routes. This region has extreme temperatures and is largely desert. The Great Wall was built to keep the Mongols out of China. Tibet, until recently opened up to British trade, excluded all foreigners. Sinkiang consists almost entirely of a desert basin.

MONGOLIAN REPUBLIC—This almost entirely pastoral country consists largely of an arid plateau composed mainly of the Gobi Desert. In the northwest are high mountains whose streams flow into numerous sizable lakes. The Mongolian people are almost entirely a nomadic race who wander from place to place seeking new pastures for their herds of cattle.

JAPAN—The chief feature of the country is its mountainous character, for each island has a mountainous backbone. Fujiyama, the highest mountain, reaches 12,395 feet. One of the most notable physical features is the Inland Sea or Japanese Mediterranean. It is almost entirely landlocked and surrounded by chains of volcanoes, of which few are now active. The climate is temperate and healthful, with abundant rainfall.

Only 20 per cent of the land can be cultivated and the balance is largely mountainous, with frequent destructive earthquakes and volcanic activity. While minerals have been a major factor in her industrial growth, Japan is not well supplied with them. The only large mineral deposits are coal and copper, with some gold, silver and lead. The petroleum produced falls far short of her needs.

The low standard of living and the small amount of land suitable for cultivation have made farming highly intensive. A large percentage of the farms are only an acre or two in size and most of the farmers are forced to carry on some other occupation to exist.

Manufacturing has risen rapidly in Japan with the production of textiles leading. Because of low wages and nearness to the Oriental market, Japan has been able to compete in cheaper goods to the disadvantage of other countries.

KOREA—Korea's strategic position between the Asiatic mainland and Japan has made it an historic pathway for invasion. Coveted at different times by China, Russia and Japan, she lost her independence early in the century to the Japanese Empire. During the second World War, Korea was promised her independence, but the end of the fighting brought her only division between the great powers and later renewed military conflict.

Physically and economically Korea is divided into two contrasting natural regions. The agricultural heart of the nation is south of the thirty-eighth parallel, producing chiefly rice and barley. North of the parallel, industry and mining of coal and iron predominate.

INDEX OF PRINCIPAL CITIES OF THE WORLD

This alphabetical list of cities and towns gives statistics of population based on the latest official census reports or most recent reliable estimates. Each line begins with the name of a place, followed by the name of the country or state, the population, the index reference and plate number. This index reference gives the location of the city or town name on the accompanying map plates. The name is found within the square formed by the two lines of latitude or longitude which enclose each of the co-ordinates—i.e. the marginal letters and numbers. In the case of maps consisting entirely of insets, the name is found near the intersection point of imaginary lines connecting the co-ordinates.

Where space on the map has not permitted giving the complete form of a name, the extended form is shown in the index. Where a place may be known under different names or by various spellings of the same name, the different forms have been included, to a large extent, in the index. Where an alternative spelling in parentheses is shown on the map itself, the first name gives the local official form, the conventional form following in parentheses.

* Capitals of countries, states and provinces. † Population figure includes suburbs.

Aabenraa, Denmark, 13,017	B 3	43
Aachen (Aix-la-Chapelle), Germany, 129,967	B 3	42
Aalborg, Denmark, 79,806	B 3	43
Aalesund (Ålesund), Norway, 18,143	A 2	43
Aarau, Switzerland, 14,280	D 1	45
Aarhus, Denmark, 116,167	B 3	43
Abadan, Iran, 40,000	E 3	56
Abbeville, France, 18,932	D 2	40
Abécher, Chad, 10,000	L 9	63
Aberdare, Wales, 40,432	E 5	39
Aberdeen, Scotland, 182,729	E 2	38
Abidjan,* Ivory Coast, 48,654	E10	62
Abilene, Tex., 45,550	E 5	158
Abomey, Dahomey, 16,906	G10	62
Acámbaro, Mexico, 23,038	E 4	77
Acapulco, Mexico, 28,790	E 5	77
Accra,* Ghana, 135,926	G10	62
Acireale, Sicily, Italy, 34,330	E 6	47
Adana (Seyhan), Turkey, 117,799	C 2	56
Addis Ababa,* Ethiopia, 250,000	O10	63
Adelaide,* South Australia, †382,604	D 7	66
Adelboden, Switzerland, 2,873	C 2	45
Aden,* Aden Col. & Prot., 56,849	E 7	56
Aduwa, Ethiopia, 6,000	O 9	63
Agaña,* Guam, 1,330	E 4	68
Agen, France, 28,591	D 5	41
Agra, India, 375,665	C 2	59
Agrigento (Girgenti), Sicily, Italy, 37,506	D 6	47
Agrínion, Greece, 20,981	E 6	51
Aguascalientes, Mexico, 93,432	D 4	77
Ahlen, Germany, 30,049	B 3	42
Ahmadabad, India, 788,333	C 2	59
Ahmadnagar, India, 70,418	C 3	59
Aiún, Sp. W. Africa, 3,142	D 6	62
Aix, France, 38,985	F 6	41
Aix-les-Bains, France, 12,799	G 5	41
Ajaccio, Corsica, France, 28,732	F 7	41
Ajmer, India, 196,663	C 2	59
Akita, Japan, 126,074	N 4	60
Akola, India, 62,564	C 2	59
Akureyri, Iceland, 7,143	C 2	37
Akyab, Burma, 48,492	E 2	59
Alajuela, Costa Rica, 13,903	C 3	76
Alameda, Calif, 63,425	J 2	88
Alausí, Ecuador, 4,812	E 4	70
Albacete, Spain, †69,504	F 3	46
Albany,* N.Y., 134,995	N 5	139
Albany, Western Australia, 4,761	B 6	66
Albi, France, 27,768	E 6	41
Albuquerque, N. Mex., 96,815	C 3	136
Alcamo, Sicily, Italy, 41,471	D 6	47
Alcoy, Spain, 39,417	F 3	46
Aldershot, England, 37,646	F 5	39
Alegrete, Brazil, 20,160	J 9	73
Alençon, France, 19,427	D 3	40
Aleppo (Haleb), Syria, United Arab Rep., 324,899	C 2	56
Alès, France, 20,259	E 5	41
Alessandria, Italy, 70,238	B 2	47
Ålesund (Aalesund), Norway, 18,527	A 2	43
Alexandretta (Iskenderun), Turkey, 22,946	C 2	56
Alexandria (El Iskandariya), Egypt, Un. Arab Rep., 925,081	M 5	63
Alexandria, La., 34,913	E 4	110
Alexandria, Va., 61,787	L 3	165
Alexandroúpolis (Dedeagach), Greece, 17,081	H 5	51
Algiers (Alger),* Algeria, 266,165	G 4	62
Alhambra Calif., 51,359	C10	89
Alicante, Spain, †101,791	F 3	46
Aligarh (Koil), India, 141,618	C 2	59
Aliquippa, Pa., 26,132	B 4	150
Alkmaar, Netherlands, 37,286	E 2	44
Al Kuwait,* Kuwait, 80,000	E 4	56
Allahabad, India, 332,295	D 2	59
Allenstein (Olsztyn), Poland, 29,053	E 2	49
Allentown, Pa., 106,756	L 4	151
Alleppey, India, 116,278	C 4	59
Alma-Ata, U.S.S.R., 500,000	L 5	54
Almelo, Netherlands, 40,118	J 3	44
Almería, Spain, †75,861	E 4	46
Alost (Aalst), Belgium, 41,460	C 6	44
Altagracia, Venezuela, 3,987	F 1	70
Altamura, Italy, 38,231	F 4	47
Altenburg, Germany, 51,805	E 3	42
Alton, Ill., 32,550	A 6	101
Altona, Germany, 233,287	C 2	42
Altoona, Pa., 77,177	F 4	150
Amarillo, Tex., 74,246	C 2	158
Ambala, India, 107,383	C 2	59
Ambato, Ecuador, 33,908	E 4	70
Amboina (Ambon), Indon., 17,334	H 6	61
Ambriz, Angola, 2,196	J13	64
Amecameca, Mexico, 7,573	F 1	77
Amersfoort, Netherlands, 55,996	F 3	44
Amiens, France, 87,126	E 3	40
Amman,* Jordan, 90,000	D 4	58
Amoy, China, 138,032	P 7	55
Amraoti, India, 61,971	C 2	59
Amritsar, India, 325,747	B 1	59
Amsterdam,* Netherlands, 803,847	E 3	44
Amsterdam, N.Y., 32,240	M 5	139
Ancona, Italy, 68,501	D 3	47
Anchorage, Alaska, 11,254	D 3	74
Ancud, Chile, 4,078	F12	72
Anderlecht, Belgium, 86,412	D 6	44
Andermatt, Switzerland, 1,231	D 2	45
Anderson, Ind., 46,820	F 4	102
Andizhan, U.S.S.R., 83,691	L 5	54
Andorra la Vella,* Andorra, 1,100	G 1	46
Andria, Italy, 63,937	F 4	47
Angers, France, 93,838	C 4	40
Angmagssalik, Greenland, 129	C11	36
Angoulême, France, 38,060	D 5	41
Ankara (Angora),* Turkey, 286,781	B 1	56
Annapolis,* Md., 10,047	H 5	115
Ann Arbor, Mich., 48,251	F 6	119
Annecy, France, 30,196	G 5	41
Anniston, Ala., 31,066	G 3	82
Annonay, France, 12,537	F 5	41
Anshan, China, 165,988	K 3	60
Antâkya (Antioch), Turkey, 30,385	C 2	56
Antequera, Spain, 29,855	D 4	46
Antibes, France, 18,018	G 6	41
Antofagasta, Chile, 49,106	F 8	72
Antsirabe, Madagascar, 15,120	R16	65
Antung, China, 271,115	K 3	60
Antwerp (Antwerpen), Belgium, 263,233	D 5	44
Anzhero-Sudzhensk, U.S.S.R., 71,079	M 4	54
Anzio, Italy, 9,084	D 4	47
Aomori, Japan, 106,417	N 3	60
Apeldoorn, Netherlands, 62,876	G 3	44
Apia,* Western Samoa, 10,000	J 7	69
Apolda, Germany, 33,439	D 3	42
Appleton, Wis., 34,010	J 7	171
ʻAqaba, Jordan, 931	D 5	58
Aracaju, Brazil, 68,686	N 6	71
Araçatuba, Brazil, 27,692	K 8	71
Arad, Rumania, 87,291	E 2	50
Aragua de Barcelona, Ven., 5,128	H 2	70
Araraquara, Brazil, 34,671	L 8	71
Arbroath, Scotland, 19,511	E 2	38
Archangel (Arkhangelsk), U.S.S.R., 281,091	F 2	52
Arendal, Norway, 11,751	B 3	43
Arequipa, Peru, 60,725	F 7	70
Arezzo, Italy, 39,213	D 3	47
Argentan, France, 6,804	D 3	40
Argenteuil, France, 63,059	A 1	40
Àrgos, Greece, 13,440	F 7	51
Arica, Chile, 14,064	F 7	70
Arles, France, 23,409	F 6	41
Arlington, Va., 135,449	L 3	165
Arion (Aarlen), Belgium, 11,180	G 8	44
Armavir, U.S.S.R., 83,677	F 5	53
Armentières, France, 20,274	E 2	40
Arnhem, Netherlands, 97,350	H 4	44
Arras, France, 32,298	E 2	40
Artemovsk, U.S.S.R., 55,165	E 5	53
Artigas, Uruguay, 16,500	J10	73
Aš, Czechoslovakia, 11,378	B 1	48
Asahigawa, Japan, 123,238	O 3	60
Asansol, India, 76,277	D 2	59
Aschaffenburg, Germany, 44,919	C 4	42
Aschersleben, Germany, 42,196	D 3	42
Ascoli Piceno, Italy, 29,657	D 3	47
Asheville, N.C., 53,000	E 8	140
Ashkhabad, U.S.S.R., 167,000	J 6	54
Ashland, Ky., 31,131	M 4	109
Asmara,* Eritrea, Ethiopia, 63,900	O 9	63
Asnières, France, 77,323	A 1	40
Asti, Italy, 38,412	B 2	47
Astrakhan, U.S.S.R., 300,000	G 5	53
Asunción, Paraguay, 204,085	J 3	73
Aswân, Egypt, Un. Arab Rep., 25,397	N 7	63
Asyût, Egypt, Un. Arab Rep., 88,730	N 6	63
Atbara, Sudan, 34,700	N 8	63
Athens (Athênai),* Greece, 487,045	F 7	51
Athlone, Ireland, 9,393	C 4	39
Atlanta,* Ga., 331,314	D 3	96
Atlantic City, N. J., 61,657	E 5	135
Aubervilliers, France, 58,664	B 1	40
Auburn, N.Y., 36,667	G 5	138
Auckland, New Zealand, †328,995	L 5	67
Augsburg, Germany, 184,712	D 4	42
Augusta, Ga., 71,507	J 4	96
Augusta, Me., 20,913	D 7	113
Aurangabad, India, 66,725	C 3	59
Aurillac, France, 19,375	E 5	41
Aurora, Ill., 50,508	E 2	100
Austin,* Tex., 132,459	G 7	159
Auxerre, France, 23,100	E 4	40
Avellaneda, Argentina, 282,054	O12	73
Avellino, Italy, 28,599	E 4	47
Aversa, Italy, 33,809	E 4	47
Avignon, France, 51,865	F 6	41
Ávila, Spain, †22,577	D 2	46
Avranches, France, 7,176	C 3	40
Ayacucho, Peru, 16,642	F 6	70
Ayr, Scotland, 42,377	D 3	38
Azul, Argentina, 27,082	J11	73
Babol (Barfrush), Iran, 36,590	F 2	57
Bacău, Rumania, 34,461	H 2	50
Badajoz, Spain, †76,098	C 3	46
Badalona, Spain, 40,983	H 2	46
Baden bei Wien, Austria, 21,382	D 2	48
Baden-Baden, Germany, 37,007	C 4	42
Bad Ischl (Ischl), Austria, 13,441	B 3	48

INDEX OF PRINCIPAL CITIES OF THE WORLD—253